ML 46/23   HIS   £4.50

STONE–PAPER–SCISSORS

STONE-PAPER-
SCISSORS

Shanghai
1921–1945

An Autobiography

The Stead Sisters

OXON PUBLISHING
1991

First published in 1991 by
Oxon Publishing
Market House, Market Place,
Deddington, Oxon OX5 4SW

© Oxon Publishing 1991

ISBN 1 870677 76 5

Designed and Produced for
Oxon Publishing by
Chase Production Services
Chase House, Chalford Oaks,
Chipping Norton,.Oxon OX7 5QR

Printed and bound in the United Kingdom
by Billing and Sons Ltd, Worcester

To the memory of
our dear sister
MARY
with love and
gratitude

Contents

Illustrations are between pages 164 and 165

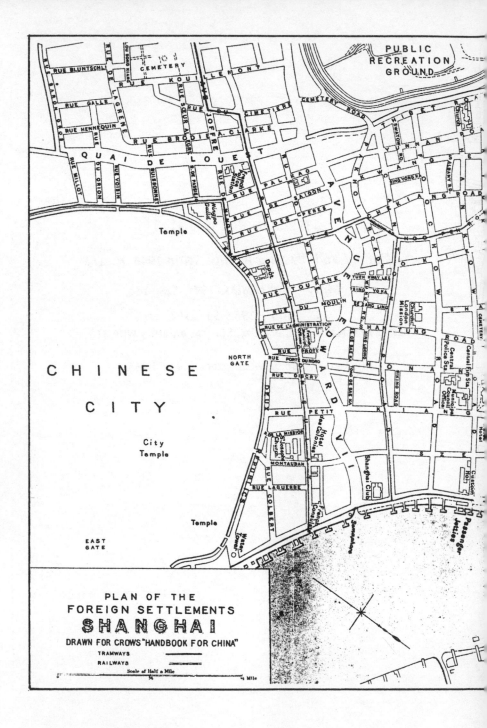

PLAN OF THE
FOREIGN SETTLEMENTS
SHANGHAI
DRAWN FOR CROWS "HANDBOOK FOR CHINA"
TRAMWAYS
RAILWAYS
Scale of Half a Mile

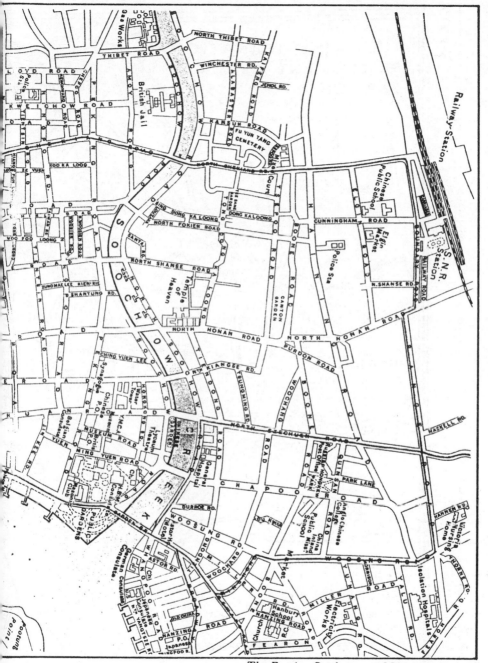

The Foreign Settlements of Shanghai, 1921

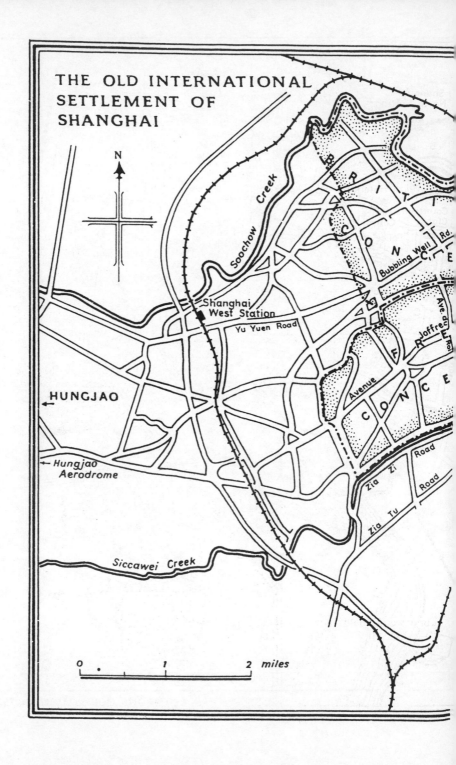

THE OLD INTERNATIONAL
SETTLEMENT OF
SHANGHAI

N

Soochow Creek

Shanghai West Station

Yu Yuen Road

Bubbling Well

Rd.

Avenue Joffre Road

HUNGJAO

Avenue

CONCE

Hungjao
Aerodrome

Zia Zi Road

Road

Zia Tu

Siccawei Creek

0   1   2 miles

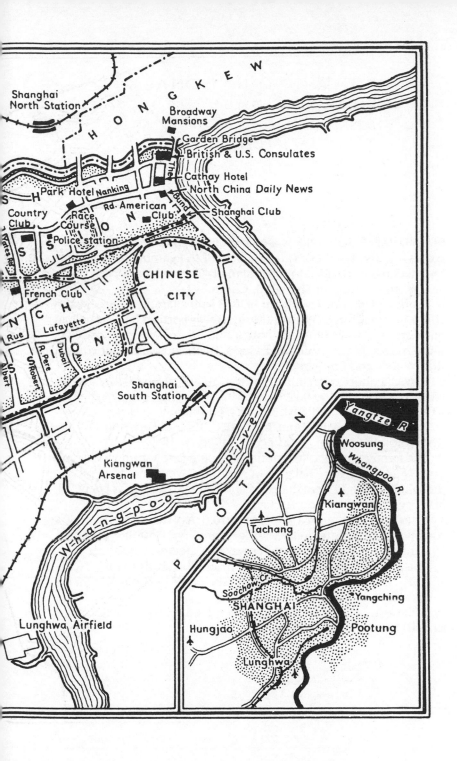

Preface

STONE-PAPER-SCISSORS is a true account told by the four Stead sisters – Mary, Ivy, Bessie and Nellie – of the gamble their parents took when they decided to travel abroad – first to Mexico, then Peru, and finally settling in Shanghai, China.

Walter Stead (Dad) was born in 1888 into a family of three sisters and a brother. Emily Wilson (Mother) was born in 1894 – she had one sister and three brothers. Both families were musically talented, some members at a professional level. It was at an amateur concert that Walter and Emily met.

It was a short courtship. Walter was full of plans to leave for Mexico and wished to take Emily with him. They were married on 23 March 1912, at the Parish Church, Oldham.

In 1913 they travelled out to Mexico, their destination Orizaba where Rosemary (Mary) was born in 1914.

The family were booked on the *SS Lusitania* to return to England in 1915. As they were delayed in getting to New York they missed the sailing date and were shattered to hear that the ship, as predicted, had been torpedoed and sunk.

After their leave Dad was appointed Assistant Manager of a cotton mill in Vitarte on the outskirts of Lima, Peru. It was here in 1916 that Ivy was born. In 1919 Bessie appeared on the scene.

The family returned to England in 1921. In April twins – Nellie and Lily – were born. Shortly before she was a year old Lily died a cot death.

Once again Dad was getting restless. He applied for and secured a position in Shanghai, China.

CHAPTER ONE

Yangtzepoo Road

1921–1925

Dad bade us farewell with sadness as he left for Shanghai, China, in 1921. He was pleasantly surprised on arrival to find it was a very modern city rather than a collection of mud huts. It was made up of three Concessions granted to Britain, America and France during the nineteenth century. The French Concession remained independent with its own administration, law court, fire brigade and police force. The British and American Concessions merged and became known as the International Settlement under the administration of the Shanghai Municipal Council (SMC) – also with its own law court, fire brigade and police force. For protection the city was visited regularly by British and American gunboats and later British and American troops were to be stationed there.

Dad lost no time in sending for Mother and their four children. Rosemary born in Mexico in 1914, is fondly called Mary by all – Ivy was born in 1916, Bessie in 1919, both in Peru – Nellie was born in England in 1921.

We sailed from England on the Blue Funnel Line, *SS Teiresias* in the autumn of 1922. There was great excitement and much planning for the voyage out. We had to be vaccinated. The doctor who performed this task must have been quite an artist – considering Nellie was still in nappies. If you look at our right arms you will see we have been branded with the same pattern of spots – not one, or two, but four. The spots are equal in size and set in a perfect square.

This new adventure to China intrigued us and the more excited we became the more envious were our playmates. On looking back, Mother must have had quite a dreadful trip. Nellie was at the

1

crawling stage, very inquisitive and into everything. Bessie was the opposite, quiet and serious.

While playing on a covered 'hold' – a wonderful play area for children and much safer than the deck areas with railings, so easy to climb – Bessie over-balanced and fell onto the deck, some three feet below. It was a nasty fall and knocked her unconscious. Mary, by now aged seven, was possibly a great help to Mother but, Ivy, in her tomboy way was more of a handful. The cabin stewards did all they could to help Mother – caring for four young children on board ship was not easy – and she could not have managed without their help.

Mary, as far as Ivy was concerned, was a seasoned traveller and took great delight in pointing out interesting things. Bessie was too young to pay much attention. However, coming through the Suez Canal we saw something that even Mary could not identify. She had to ask one of the crew and then tried to make us believe she had known all along – it was a camel, that beast of burden of the desert. She excelled herself again once we were out in the ocean, pointing out schools of porpoises swimming and frolicking in a row. Nearer to the ship were flying fish. The ship disturbed them as it cut through the water – they would skim along for a few feet then, exhausted, flop into the water again. Occasionally one would land on one of the lower decks. These kept us on the look-out for days.

As our journey was coming to an end the ship ran into a typhoon which was most frightening. It was a relief when we approached the estuary of the Yangtze river from where we would sail up the Whangpoo, not only because we would be more sheltered from the bad weather but because we would soon be at the end of our long journey, to join Dad.

As the *Teiresias* sailed up the Whangpoo, which snaked its way to the port of Shanghai, it was difficult to say whether we were travelling north, south, east or west. A pilot boarded the ship at Woosung and we slowly made our way to our destination. A new world was unfolding itself. The most exciting part of this journey was that Dad surprised us by coming on board with the pilot at Woosung. 'Welcome to China!' What a thrill. It was wonderful to see him again – he had so much to tell us and, of course, there was a great deal of kissing and hugging. Lots of jabbering all at once – no one listening – but all very happy to be together again. Dad carefully explained and pointed out things of interest as we travelled along.

On the right-hand side we crept past Yangtzepoo (said with a sneeze) and the industrial sites – paper mill, cotton mills, flour mill, soap manufacturing company – the waterworks were there somewhere, but not visible. The busy dockyard area. We continued to creep past Broadway, on past Garden Bridge which spans the Soochow Creek. On the left-hand side of the river was Pootung, with all its own industrial area as well – printing works, textile printing factory, oil companies etc. The Whangpoo is an extremely busy river – sampans busily criss-crossing the bows of ships, majestic junks in full sail, with painted eyes to see where they were going, as well as tugs, cargo ships, gunboats, passenger liners – seagoing craft of almost every description. So much activity, so much traffic. We slowed down as we approached the Bund with its magnificent buildings, hotels, banks, and commercial houses, some of which started trading as far back as 1867! Shanghai was an important import/export city.

Finally, we were ready to disembark. Once we had proceeded through customs, which all passengers had to do, we were soon driving along the Bund, over Garden Bridge – by now, we almost knew the way as it was a return journey but on land – to our future home, in the Yangtzepoo district.

* * *

When Dad first arrived in Shanghai he was allocated a terrace house – it was 33 Yangtzepoo Road – the middle house in the first row, of a two-row housing complex owned by the cotton mill for which he, a textile engineer, worked as Assistant Manager. The house was fully furnished by the company and Dad was relieved to see the rooms were painted and not panelled as had been the case in Peru. Mother had such a bad accident there while she was carrying Bessie. Though she was supposed to be taking things easy, she couldn't wait for Dad to come home to get her something from the top shelf. She got the steps out and reached for the item. She slipped – to support herself she grabbed the cabinet which came away with her. Apparently termites had destroyed the wood and the cabinet fell on top of her. It was fortunate that no harm was done to the baby she was carrying.

The next item on the list for settling in, was the engagement of servants, the customary thing to do in the eastern world. This custom was not to encourage laziness in the foreigner – which, unfortunately, was thought by many – but to create employment for the natives of the country in a return for the privilege of being permitted to work out east. A welcome and most sensible employment exchange: 'We give you a job in our country, you give a job to our people'.

Cookboy and his wife, Amah, became our staff and members of the family. Cookboy did all the marketing (shopping), cooking, saw to the fires (there was no central heating) and generally kept the brasses polished. He was a very good economical cook and was quick to pick up special favourite 'English' recipes. He was a pleasant smiling man, with a good sense of humour – and later, we discovered, he was also a disciplinarian! Amah looked after the clothes, bedrooms, washing and ironing and, no doubt, endless tidying up. An affectionate bond grew between us.

The Chinese are fond of laughter and never miss a chance of a joke. They consider a wise man should always remain calm and that learning is a good thing in itself. Their philosophy on life is something special from which we benefitted. Our Cookboy and Amah were happy people and they made us very happy too.

We had friendly neighbours like ourselves from Lancashire, England. We laughed a lot, cried a little, and were up to all the tricks, some quite unbelievable, that a family group could get up to. While the grown-ups were very young at heart, the young were desperately trying to be grown-ups, and the 'little ones', Bessie and Nellie, were just bundles of fun, with chubby cheeks – spotless, tidy and good when visitors came, grubby and very mischievous, when left to themselves. They played a lot together and never lacked company as they lived in a world of their own. A special world called 'Let's Pretend'.

The Elliotts lived next door. Mrs Elliott, a short stocky lady with a heart of gold was a wonderful friend. Mr Elliott was Dad's buddy – they worked together and had a high regard for each other. Their children were Eva and Frank who was a few years older. Eva, Mary's age, was an up-to-all-tricks leader!

Our Mother and Dad

Mother was beautiful. Her crowning glory was her 18-carat golden hair which she used to brush regularly with a bristle hairbrush – 100 strokes a day. It gleamed – there was no need for fancy creams and lotions. Her large eyes were bright blue and she had dark eyebrows

and eyelashes. Dad was so proud of his beauty and encouraged her
to keep a good wardrobe of not only sensible clothes but fashionable
ones as well. For years we kept her green and cream parasol, with
a fringe, which she daintily held to protect her face from the glaring
sunlight of the tropics. We were fascinated by her white kid boots
with the masses of buttons and would take turns at using the
buttonhook to do them up. Mary still has the silver handled
buttonhook which she treasures as a keepsake.

Mother was cheerful and like Dad enjoyed life to the full. They
both had a great sense of humour and could tell a good story. Dad
really excelled himself – he was a natural mimic. Mother's nature
was caring, gentle and anger-free. Sometimes, Dad would have a silly
half-hour teasing us unmercifully, and Ivy can remember Mother
warning him that '... there'll be tears yet'!

Dad was generous to an extreme and one of his greatest pleasures
was giving. He enjoyed showering gifts – for no other reason but
for the joy of giving. He didn't need a special occasion such as
Christmas or a birthday – just the thought 'she'll like that'. Dad gave
Mother some magnificent jewellery – real diamonds and things. Only
the best would do for his Emily.

Dad enjoyed the simple everyday things and best of all – just
living. However, he was possessive – for want of a better word – when
it came to his favourite Smiles & Chuckles chocolates and marzipan
pigs. A little bit every day. One day, a leg, the next ... he'd carve up
his marzipan pig and give us a bit too, then carefully save the rest
for 'tomorrow'. It was quite a ceremony. We were a very happy
family and the credit for this goes entirely to Mother and Dad.

They made a handsome couple. On reflection we can now
recognise that we have each inherited a bit of Mother and Dad. We
are proud of this. Whether Mother's eyebrows, Dad's musical
talents, an artistic flare or painting abilities – whatever – its a bit of
Stead that remains in us.

Nellie remembers being placed in a high chair and told to 'wait'
whilst thumping the protection tray of the chair – starving! She was
always ready for a meal and is still teased that perhaps her fear in
life is that she may suffer from malnutrition.

One day, because Mother had a septic finger she was sporting a
bandage. Nellie thought this was fun and she should have a sore
finger as well. Mother prepared a little bowl of warm water for her

to soak her 'sore' finger in – she felt so important when it was later dressed in a bandage, like Mother's – she loved the attention.

Shanghai was different from Mexico, Peru and England. During the warmer weather we had to sleep under mosquito nets which was suffocating but had to be endured as protection against those pesky insects which gave such a nasty sting. Being newcomers to the country, we were told, our blood was fresh and inviting. The sting would itch and if scratched would become septic. Out would come the bandages again. It was strange settling in to new customs but we soon became acclimatized and enjoyed the mosquito nets – day and night – as we would pretend we were playing Red Indians in their tepees.

We all like being fussed. While we were living in Peru Mary was stung by a wasp on the roof of her mouth. Being a warm day we were having tea on the verandah – boiled eggs and bread and butter. Poor Mary was in agony and the doctor had to be called. When Mother was busy comforting Mary, Ivy thought she should also have a little attention and stuck a bead up her nose. Now there were two patients – Ivy's crying didn't help, she was second in line for attention.

Bessie remembers one of the times when she was ill she heard Mother saying to Dad that it was her turn to have 'the doll'. This was a special cuddly washable doll which was used only if we were not well. It seemed to work as a tonic! Presumably when it had done the rounds of all the sick beds, it was destroyed.

Mary's special 'doll' was a piece of driftwood found on a camping weekend with Mother and Dad and friends. It was while they were living in Peru and the weekend was being spent at La Punta where there was a beautiful beach. It was during Mary's pretend stage – she had found this doll and she would play with it all weekend. Before leaving for home she used to put the doll to sleep carefully among the rocks so no one would find it and it would still be there on their next visit to the beach. On one occasion the doll was missing. Mary was heartbroken until one of the party noticed it floating on the water. The tide had been higher that day and it had been swept away. From then on Mary was allowed to take her doll home – it had a lovely seaweedy smell that brought back happy memories.

Ivy remembers a Christmas present received while travelling from Peru to England on the *SS Ordunia*. It was unusual to be at sea at this time of year and Dad and Mother were very generous. Bessie, who had just started to walk, received a soft toy but Mary and Ivy each received beautiful dolls with porcelain faces and blue eyes that closed when the doll was put to sleep. Great excitement. Ivy just had to rush up on deck to see if her 'baby' could walk which, of course, it couldn't. It ended up with a broken face which made it all the more precious and it was showered with love.

We were taught our first prayer by Mother. It was 'Gentle Jesus, meek and mild ... ' and from then on we knew that at the end of the day it was prayer time. In our short prayers we learnt to pray for others and later when Mother was ill, we used to pray that she would get better. Praying came naturally.

Mother assembled us all on the steps outside the house for a special photograph she wanted to take of Dad and his girls. We were told to sit and wait for the birdie. This was too much for Nellie, who never was, and is still not, a sitting person. She naturally toddled over to Dad and, to this day, she can hear his mutter 'you would do that'.

Mother was a wonderful seamstress and made most of our clothes – sewn and knitted. Also there was evidence of crochet and needlework everywhere. Bed linen had beautifully crocheted borders, some six inches deep.

* * *

Mother and Dad had enroled Mary and Ivy as day-girls at St Joseph's Convent, Zikawei. This was a school run by French nuns and situated on the border of the French Concession at the southern end of the Bund. They had a long journey to make from Yangtzepoo to Zikawei and the only form of public transport in Shanghai at that time was either trolley-bus or tramcar. Dad didn't have a car and there was no way he would let them use public transport at their young age so they travelled by private rickshaw – a two-wheeled, hooded vehicle pulled by a man.

Mary and Ivy were in their element – everything was new to them. There was so much to see, each ride was an adventure in itself. Sometimes they would count the foreigners they passed en route – there were very few in that area at that time. Sometimes they would count the signs on buildings, like 'Post no bills' and would make up stories as to what that meant. Who would post Bill – he was too big for the mail box! They took sandwiches for their tiffen break and a flask of something hot to drink in the winter, lemonade in the summer. The lemonade was the best as this was freshly made by Cookboy each day. This he did by slicing up a lemon and pouring boiling water over it and letting it infuse until cold, having added a good few spoons of sugar to sweeten. It was delicious. For their playtime break Mother gave them each a small packet of Sunmaid raisins.

Our Lives Changed

About a year and a half later Mother developed cancer. It was a shock to Dad. He was so very much in love with her. She had been a great friend and companion – always going along with his ambitions. She adapted to going abroad with all the hardships this brought and now he was to lose her.

When Mother became ill, Amah took over the responsibility of being in complete charge of us, and she did this on top of her normal duties – efficiently and, without much ado. We grew very dependent on her. As most children do, we used to tease her unmercifully but, truth to tell, we loved her dearly.

Mother was in and out of hospital for a long while and our last memory of her was when we were taken quietly to her bedside one evening. She had come home from hospital and we were assembled around her bed – we got as close as we could to her. We did not know she was dying. As Dad had asked us to be very quiet, none of us had a word to say. It was very sad. Poor Mother, it must have been a dreadful ordeal for her. The next day she was not there – she had been taken back to the hospital. Mother died – she was only 30 – so very young. We were told that she had gone away. We were sad – we did not want her to leave us.

It was teaming down with rain on the day of Mother's funeral. She was buried at the Bubbling Well Cemetery (now turned into a park). Mary and Ivy accompanied Dad but Bessie and Nellie being so young remained at home in Mrs Elliott's care. Bessie remembers playing on the verandah when Mrs Elliott suddenly looked up and said 'It looks as though it is going to stop raining, there is a break in the cloud'. Bessie looked up as well to see the 'hole' and was most disappointed when she could not see it. She remembers this incident, not because of the weather, but even at that tender age, she realised it was a solemn occasion.

The Elliotts were kindness in itself and did everything they possibly could to alleviate the deep sadness Dad suffered after Mother died. Mr Elliott had a car and on a Sunday, for a long while, he would take us the long distance to Bubbling Well Cemetery so that we could each place a little bunch of flowers on Mother's grave. They were sad times but Mr Elliott and Dad tried to keep us happy. On the way home we usually stopped for a little treat to ease the tension – we all needed the relief.

As time went on with Dad carefully watching Mr Elliott on these drives, he made the decision to buy a car. It was a Citroen. We don't know who taught him to drive but Mr Elliott was his navigator. We recollect it being a three-passenger car because Bessie and Nellie had the one back seat, Mary the front seat next to Dad – Ivy's special area was sitting on the tool-box, behind him.

It was fun watching Dad learning to drive in the compound. One day as he was crawling slowly around manoeuvring the car every which-way learning to reverse, Amah must have got in the way somehow – she was scooped up on the front fender calling out frantically 'Ai-yah, Ai-yah'. We thought it was hilarious. No harm done, except a little lost dignity and she soon joined us, laughing. They were great days, picnic days with memorable outings. We loved the togetherness which the outings in the car brought.

After Mother died Amah kept her promise to her that she would care for us and she did it lovingly. Amah was a kindly soul, although severe – she had to be – as we were always up to some form of mischief and she felt responsible for our welfare. Bessie and Nellie seemed to escape her wrath, if any! But, Mary and Ivy were always being checked and re-checked. Eva, next door, did not help. We were a little afraid of Amah particularly when she threatened us that she would 'tell our dad-dee' when we were naughty! This made us unite and, more than once we were a little untruthful if one of us was in trouble. Sometimes we would tease Amah, like the time when she served us prunes. Having counted them out as she served them, she was upset to find she did not get the same amount of 'stones' back again on the plates. We let her think we had swallowed them – but she called our bluff and produced the bottle of castor oil. We soon owned up and showed her the missing stones in our pockets.

Amah cunningly learnt the 'castor oil' trick from Dad. He was kept on his toes being Mother, Dad and best friend rolled into one, and grew very concerned about our health. We did, of course, pick up all the childhood diseases in spite of his 'Illness Protection Scheme'. He had many old fashioned remedies to keep us healthy. We had a Beecham's pill every Friday night, were de-wormed with Santonine once a year, followed with a large dose of castor oil! Each Spring Dad would make up a concoction of sulphur and treacle to clear our blood of impurities. He would dole out a large tablespoonful to each of us once a day until the mixture was finished. Later, when Dad was away, Mary kept up this practice but she never really got it as tasty as Dad's recipe. Dad had liquid quinine ready for a suspected cold, to be taken with Owbridge's Cough Mixture. All very well, until he decided to flavour his fudge speciality with 'Owbridges'. We also remember the camphorated oil which was kept handy for earache.

You will recall reading about our vaccination spots when we left England, and of how the scars were the envy of our peers. We're afraid we ruined any reputation for bravery we may have acquired when the time came for us to be inoculated for cholera during an epidemic. We had to cross Yangtzepoo Road to Dad's office which was in the building opposite. The medics were assembled in a large room with a pot-bellied stove in the centre. For some reason the sight of an injection needle made us turn to jelly and Dad's 'strapping youngsters' let the side down badly that day when we had to be piggy-backed faint across the road home – much to Dad's disgust and our chagrin ... out came the Keppler's Malt, but it made no difference to our wobbly knees!

Cookboy was strict and he took over when Dad was out. Nellie spent the best part of an afternoon toying with vegetables given to her at lunch-time which Cookboy said she had to eat – 'No clean plate, no pudding' he warned. Nellie hated vegetables. After gulps and yukkie sounds, Nellie managed to swallow the ghastly 'vegs' to be rewarded with a delicious custard pudding. Well worth the struggle and everyone was happy.

Living within walking distance of Wayside Park this became a favourite picnic spot as we were now old enough to go there on our own. Amah, in her inimitable fashion had dressed us up in our Sunday best, including new white lacy socks. Eva joined us this day and also wore white socks. We thought it would be great to paddle in the lily pond with the fountain in the middle. Off came our socks and shoes and we had a lovely time, until Ivy discovered she had lost her socks! What to do? We knew Ivy would be in deep trouble if she returned without them. We decided the easiest way out of the situation was to say that none of us had worn socks. Amah was bewildered when we returned home. She knew we had gone out wearing socks, but we stuck together and denied it, and adamantly proved it by showing Amah that even Eva did not have any socks.

Our terrace houses had one peculiar feature. The Elliott's bathroom window opened on to our verandah. It couldn't have been more convenient and, although the grown-ups must have known, not a word was said. Our get-togethers with Eva were great fun – very secretive – and as soon as the coast was clear after bed-time, Eva would climb out of their bathroom window onto our verandah and into our house.

* * *

Our attention next turned to swimming. Dad and his friends hired the 'open-air' Hongkew swimming pool each Saturday afternoon during the hot summer months. This was something entirely new to us, and likewise so was the district of Hongkew to the north west of Yangtzepoo. As we enjoyed the swimming so much we decided we would build Dad a swimming pool right in the middle of the tennis court, in front of the house – of all places! After all, although we didn't play tennis we could swim as Dad could, albeit with one foot on the bottom of the pool. We made a start on the pool, with allocated jobs. One was to take the entrance money, one the exit money and one had the important job of keeping the frogs out! Dad came home for lunch and soon put a stop to our fun – we were in trouble. Dad was really cross. The tennis court, his pride and joy, was now ruined.

However, we were soon forgiven and Dad engaged a team of workers to fill in the swimming pool area and prepare the court for the coming tennis season. Besides being a keen tennis player, Dad was a keen gardener. The team of workers known as 'the weeders' consisted of about twenty Chinese women who sat on minute stools, four inches high, all in a row, and worked their way from one end of the tennis court to the other – they never missed an inch. They thoroughly enjoyed themselves chattering and laughing and considered the event like a day out, rather than a job of work.

The second row of terrace houses behind ours was similar in construction, with a raised verandah and a tennis court in front. On the far side of the garden grew a magnificent beebo tree, the fruit of which is not unlike an apricot in appearance, though much sweeter, and has three large brown shiny pips. Seeing the tree was laden with fruit was Ivy's downfall. Our friends, the Chaddertons, living in the middle house, were at lunch in a room facing the verandah but, this did not deter Ivy. The verandah would hide her (she thought). She crawled the length of the tennis court to the far end of the garden on her tummy – in full view – and it was not until she reached her destination that there was tremendous applause. The game was up! However, we all enjoyed the beebos.

* * *

The owners of the cotton mills had a subsidiary company which planned to start a bus service – something new to Shanghai. The buses were to be built in a godown (warehouse) behind our terrace houses. Our horizons widened. No longer were we interested in dolls and all that baby-stuff. We were going to be bus conductors or drivers or, better still, passengers on a tour of discovery. We had to watch our timing before entering the godown. Not to be found out was part of the fun so we would creep in after working hours to play 'Buses'. Unfortunately we – Eva was also in the group – grew too bold. We thought we would be mechanics. We poured oil, followed by anything else that was handy, down the radiators – BIG trouble. The buses were now out of bounds. So, it was back to dolls and things.

Eva and Ivy were great pals and were always up to something. One day they decided we should have a club room. Eva's father had given up keeping chickens so they spent days cleaning out the pen – their plans were coming to fruition. Before they had a chance to enrol members Mr Elliott discovered the clean pen and, much to their disappointment, decided to get more chickens. End of club.

Mary was always the adventurous Stead – she didn't need a gang to back her up, she was quite capable of getting into mischief on her own. Maybe this is what comes from being the eldest – they have a head start. When in Peru, Mother and Dad were very upset, when sitting down for the midday meal, to find Mary had loops of silk dangling from her ear lobes. She had realised her ambition to be able to wear ear-rings like all her little Peruvian friends. She managed to coax the ninera (nanny) next door to pierce her ears. First she rubbed the ear lobe and then pierced it with a needle and left the silken thread to keep the hole open. It hurt a lot and when the ninera turned her head over to do the second ear, Mary nearly said 'No'

but, being vain and dearly wanting ear-rings, she let the second lobe
be pierced. Mother was sick to her stomach and furious. However,
a family friend saved the day – he was very impressed with Mary's
courage and presented her with a beautiful pair of pearl and coral
drop ear-rings. She was, of course, too young to wear them, but when
she did it was her turn to make others envious.

Around the same time Mary locked Mother and Dad out on the
verandah. She had a bunch of bananas under the table and together
with Ivy enjoyed eating one after the other until they were finished.
Dad soon spotted them but they would not let them in until they
had eaten their fill. Both had tummy aches and were dosed with
Beechams. Incidentally, they lost interest in bananas.

*   *   *

Cookboy and Amah soon realised that we were growing up fast and
were becoming a real handful. The last straw came when Amah
discovered Mary, Ivy and Eva waddling down the lane from the
corner shoe shop. They had had blocks of wood nailed to their shoes
to make 'high-heels'. They felt very grown up wearing Mrs Elliott's
old dresses tightly wrapped around their waists – waddling was
putting it mildly. By the time they reached home, the blocks had
fallen off and, back they would go to worry the cobbler for yet
another pair of high-heels.

The shoe shop at the end of the lane made shoes to order.
Nothing fancy. In fact, whenever we needed shoes made for us, the
cobbler used to come to the house to measure our feet. He would
do this with a thin strip of paper, on which he made a mark for the
length, then he wrapped the paper around the instep to make
another mark. To complete the measuring he placed the foot on a
sheet of paper on which he traced the outline. He was very serious
and couldn't understand all the giggles – it was indeed a ticklish
procedure. The shoes were a beautiful fit – though sometimes a trifle
short – and like our clothes were passed down from one to the other.
They just wouldn't wear out and certainly lasted longer than our
first effort at high heels, which had no staying power at all.

Mary and Ivy first became interested in cosmetics whilst we were
living in Yangtzepoo. There was a shop on the way to the tram stop
which sold a little of just about everything including powder papers
which the orientals used on ceremonial occasions. These were little
pages of paper impregnated with face powder made up into booklets

similar to the cigarette papers available today. There was one draw-back – they only sold white powder papers. This resulted in Mary and Ivy looking like ghosts or, as Dad would say, 'proper poorly'.

Years later in 1990 – Nellie's granddaughter, Joanna, returning from a trip, presented Nellie with a booklet of similar powder papers. Joanna is also interested in cosmetics and thought she had found something new. She said a similar booklet, impregnated with soap, is also on the market. Strange world. Her bubble burst when she found she was fifty years behind the times!

To be fair, there was a difference – Joanna's papers were a natural tint.

* * *

The responsibility of looking after us – completely – proved too much for Cookboy and Amah so Amah approached Dad and explained the situation to him. He decided to employ a governess.

Auntie Cameron to Dad's Rescue

She was not a relative – 'auntie' was the usual term adopted by children at that time – ladies were called auntie, and men were uncle. She came to meet us and her decision to join our family was made as she was leaving after supper when she decided to go upstairs to say goodnight to the little ones – Bessie and Nellie. They looked so lovely and peaceful sleeping in their cots. Auntie always said it was Nellie's golden ringlets that decided her. Auntie showed her love for us from the beginning and this was very much reciprocated by us all.

She had had a very interesting life having travelled out to the Far East as a young bride-to-be, on a train that travelled over the iced-up Lake Baikal in Siberia – The Trans-Siberian railway. She travelled out to marry Bill Brown, who captained one of the river boats on the Yangtze river run. These boats were flat-bottomed so that they could manoeuvre the ever changing mud banks caused by the fast flowing Yangtze created by the gorges between Hankow and Ichang. Bill died soon after they were married. Eventually Auntie married Jock Cameron, who was in the mining industry in Korea. He was away for months at a time and unfortunately the marriage failed. Auntie arrived in Shanghai where she had to make a living and did so by teaching the Yang children English before coming to look after us.

Auntie was a lovely lady – lovely by nature as well as being beautiful and cuddly. She had a soft peaches-and-cream complexion with rich dark brown hair, her pride and joy. She also had a tremendous sense of humour, necessary to cope with the four little sisters.

When Mary and Ivy were at school, Auntie, who could not manage to take both Bessie and Nellie with her when she went shopping would take them, one at a time, to accompany her. Auntie always brought something back for the one left behind. When she used to ask Nellie what she would like her to bring back, Nellie's choice was always 'a red balloon please'. On her return there it was – a little red balloon in Auntie's basket. Nellie would then spend the afternoon running up and down the lawn in front of the house with her balloon floating behind her on a string, like a kite – until it went 'pop'.

Forty five years on, after Nellie and Michael had retired to the Seychelles, Nellie sent Auntie Cameron, who was by then living in a home, a Christmas card, enclosing a linen handkerchief on which she had dabbed her favourite perfume. Something Auntie could feel, and smell. Dear Auntie, by this time was totally deaf and almost totally blind. Auntie replied by sending Nellie a card on which she had written, with the greatest difficulty and obviously assisted by a nurse 'to my darling baby Nellie – a little red balloon' and enclosed was a red balloon which she had saved from the home's Christmas party.

* * *

Now it was Bessie's turn to start school. She joined Mary and Ivy at St Joseph's Convent and will always remember that first day – it was terrifying. Halfway through the morning she wanted to 'spend a penny' – she forgot to do so, during the mid-morning play break being too busy making new friends. When she returned to her class and asked permission to leave the room, permission was refused and it was explained to her that she should have gone during the break. She was mortified – nature took its course and there was a nasty puddle under a bench.

There was one frightening occasion when Bessie was left behind at school. Mary and Ivy were not used to having her with them and went home without her. The Convent also took in boarders. When a couple of hours had gone by and no one had collected her, she had many offers of a bed to share for the night. One of the girls said she would have to have a bath with her vest on! This she did not relish and was glad when the forgetful culprits eventually realised she was missing and enlisted Dad's help to fetch her. He was concerned but his concern turned to anger at our forgetfulness when he returned to his parked car and found his travelling rug had been stolen. Auntie soon soothed the ruffled feathers.

At this time new transport arrangements had to be made as the private rickshaw could not possibly take three passengers, the now bulging school bags of Mary and Ivy, plus a 'tiffen basket'. So on the tram they went. Now older, between them Mary and Ivy took on the responsibility of travelling the long distance to school on their own as well as caring for Bessie. Fortunately the trams ran the full distance from Yangtzepoo to Zikawei without any changes. The journey necessitated a walk of two blocks to the main road.

In summer, because the climate was hot and humid, the tram windows were open. It was nothing to see, as the tram started off, a hand snake through a window to grab a hat. The victim was unable to do anything as the thief disappeared in the crowded street before the tram could be stopped. Also, one had to be careful where one sat as food purchased at the local market would be carried strung on a piece of bamboo – fish, or pork, or even live crabs. Sometimes, live chickens with their feet tied together. A crab scratch on your shin – or a peck from a chicken on your calf seemed to be the order of the day. We enjoyed these strange rides on the trams because we met and saw a different type of person. There would be the well-dressed man in a cheong sam. Some would hold two walnuts in a hand and constantly rub them together until smooth and highly polished. It was supposed to be a type of therapy. It would amuse us to see friends offering cigarettes – never from the packet – just one each at a time. If there were two friends three cigarettes would be selected, one each for the friends and one retained by the host.

On the way home from school, the girls would hurriedly pass an open-fronted Chinese dentist shop by the tram stop. It was an old-fashioned method – to say the least. To advertise his business, the dentist placed an enormous enamel basin full of extracted teeth in the shop window – even newly extracted teeth, with the blood still on them. This basin haunted the girls. But to the dentist the more teeth he could collect from his patients to display in the enamel basin, the better, as he hoped this would prove he was 'No. 1

Dentist' in the street. Competition was high. Not many, if any, fillings were done in those days. The dentist's chair could be detected through a flimsy curtain and it was very alarming watching his patients undergoing treatment – in fact, it was mind boggling. It was enough to put a child off for life – and it certainly affected Mary's confidence in dentists.

Visiting the dentist was quite an undertaking for Auntie, particularly when it was Mary's turn for a check up. Our dentist was a Mr Klatchiko – a kindly man who later on in our lives looked after our teeth. Mary was terrified. She clenched her teeth and refused to open her mouth even though it was suggested that if she would only just let Mr Klatchiko have a peep at her teeth we would call on the way home for a lovely cream cake from Cafe Federal, a German restaurant and cake shop on Broadway. Nothing would induce Mary to open her mouth – there was no co-operation from her whatsoever – needless to say, it was a wasted journey. In spite of Mary's stubbornness, however, Auntie still called in at Cafe Federal for a cream cake explaining that it was a pity to do Ivy, Bessie and Nellie out of a treat – adding, only as Auntie could, that because Mary was such an unhappy frightened little girl the cake would make her feel better. This made Mary feel badly and the next trip to Mr Klatchiko went off without trauma.

Auntie had not been with us long before she became very ill. Dad came home one day to find her huddled up in great pain – she said 'Daddy Stead,' (she always called him that) 'please help me'. She was rushed to hospital where she had to undergo major surgery. She was an extremely ill person and after the operation a long convalescence followed. Sadly for all of us, she had to give up being our governess. We visited her often because we loved her so much. Later, when she was well recovered and settled into a home of her own we would have tea with her once a week. No doubt she was keeping a watch on us for Dad and making sure we were having tea-time treats. Auntie had a great influence on our lives and we remained life-long friends.

1925 Shanghai Incident

... on the outskirts of Shanghai. The year Sun Yat-sen died with his dream of a united, peaceful Chinese Republic still far off.

*   *   *

The Holy Family Convent had to evacuate their premises and joined the St Joseph's Convent and Orphanage. As a consequence we were transferred to the Holy Family Convent and St Joseph's became the Orphanage.

We seemed to be more active in this new venue and now played team sports – basketball and rounders being the favourites. When making up teams the captains, unknown to the nuns, would play 'stone-paper-scissors'. For this you used your hand hiding what you were going to do until the signal – 'stone, paper, SCISSORS!':

STONE – (closed fist) – breaks scissors (2 fingers)
PAPER – (open hand) – wraps stone (closed fist)
SCISSORS – (2 fingers) – cuts paper (open hand)

The winner, usually the best of three tries, would choose first. Second winner had second choice and so on down the line.

*   *   *

Dad tried to engage another governess, but it just did not work out at all and as by this time Nellie would soon be the age to start school there was no option for Dad other than to leave us in Amah's care. Mrs Elliott kindly offered to keep an eye on us and helped Amah in every way she could. We were lucky – the compound family rallied around in their usual way.

There was Mr Robinson who kept us mesmerized. He was a bachelor who lived in the first house. He was magic and he had all the children in the compound spellbound. We saw him almost every day. He used to offer us an 'English' banana. He would tell us that all his food came from England every day – we believed him. Even the birds seemed to be spellbound by him as well. We would sit on his verandah steps on summer evenings and marvel how the birds would swoop down to him as he whistled for them. They all had names. George – Bert – Gert. As he named each one, or two, down they would swoop in ones or twos. His timing was perfect. We loved his story about the horse that had two left feet through eating curly grass.

We were surrounded with love – Amah and Cookboy looked after our every need. Wonderfully there was always someone there when needed. However, as the years passed by we became more independent. We learnt new games and Amah's family of nieces and nephews taught us Chinese games. As we grew older so the games changed. A great favourite was Chien-Tzu – kick feather. One had to be very agile. The toe, heel and instep were used to keep a brightly feathered shuttlecock in the air. If it fell to the ground you were ... out.

Another favourite game was what is now called jack stones – we called it bean bags. This comprised five small bags filled with beans which we would scatter on the ground or table – wherever we were playing. One bag would be picked up and thrown in the air at the same time picking up another before catching the first bag. This would be repeated until all the bean bags were picked up. For the second round we had to pick up two bags at a time, and so on until all were picked up at one go. There were several variations to this game.

Simple things, they say, please simple minds. We don't think we were simple – quite the opposite. However, we would spend hours playing 'cat's cradle'. This was played using a piece of string tied at the end to form a circle which would be wrapped around the fingers of both hands to form different patterns. Two or more people would have to participate in order to change the pattern – by taking the cradle from one pair of hands to the other and how they handled the cradle would determine the next step. There was no competition with this game but it was fun.

* * *

Besides the Elliotts and Mr Robinson, Mr and Mrs Walton lived near us. They were next door to the Chaddertons in the row of houses behind ours. They had no children – so we were not too popular with them. We tried to keep away because if we got too near, or were noisy, Mrs Walton would threaten us by saying 'I'll throw a bucket of water over you' ... oooh!

The attraction of going near the Waltons was the Chaddertons had a son. Jackie was his name. He was the only boy in the group.

He was very popular and both Eva and Mary had a crush on him – that was until the three of them were invited to a fancy dress party. Dad tried so hard to make Mary look great. But she was fed-up. He dressed her as George Formby with a silly hat, red nose, very heavy black eyebrows, complete with baggy black and white trousers, short tight jacket, and wobbly umbrella. Mary was so embarrassed. Eva went as Spring in a dainty yellow frock on which tiny leaves had been stitched and with which she wore dainty ballet pumps. How could one blame Jackie for his obvious attraction to Spring.

Before Jackie appeared on the scene Mary, Ivy and Eva used to play Dentists with moistened toothpicks rolled in salt. Or Opticians, making eyeglasses out of shells which had to be rubbed on the cement path until holes were worn through – nowadays the girls all wear glasses and wonder why.

Bessie and Nellie spent a good deal of time following Mary, Ivy, Eva and their heart-throb, Jackie, who was into science experiments. He had been given a chemistry set for Christmas. He had us gather around the table and demonstrated his skill in making gunpowder. As Dad tells the story, suddenly there was a bang and we all had black faces, no eyebrows and singed hair.

We had to make our own light entertainment as there was no TV or radio. The winter time was spent playing indoor games. But we did have a gramophone, 'His Master's Voice', with a large horn. We would try to dance – the 1–2–3 (hop). Dad played the piano without looking at the keyboard. Sometimes neighbours gathered around to listen and sing. He had a lovely voice and enjoyed harmonising.

It was about this time that Ivy first saw Donald Davey. Little did she know that one day he would become her husband. He was Frank Elliott's pal and like Frank, considered we were nuisances and to be avoided. Both boys attended church and Sunday school and were always armed with books – we were rather afraid of them. Their leisure time was spent playing tennis, kicking a ball around the garden and long jumping ... over garden chairs. The latter gave us ideas – we could do that. As usual, Ivy, the accident prone one of the family, came to grief and cut her leg on a rusty nail. As Dad would say, if there is a rusty nail about Ivy would be sure to find it, by way of torn clothes or bodily harm. She hasn't improved over the years – no longer does she long jump or do any other kind of jump. Her problem lies in climbing over stiles. She usually ends up being pushed over amidst giggles.

Uncle Miller – the Fireman

There was a fire at the Mill and the Yangtzepoo Fire Station at Lay Road was called to put it out. The fire was extensive and it took several hours to extinguish. Cotton when wet generates considerable heat and therefore it was about three days before the Fire Brigade gave their OK that the fire was completely under control. Henry Miller – we loved the sound of his full name Henry Harris Miller – was on duty. He had recently arrived in Shanghai from Bootle, England to take up his duties with the brigade. He was a bachelor, about thirty years of age, with straight blond hair and a waxed moustache, the ends of which he would twiddle to a fine point. He had a slight cast in his right eye with the result he was inclined to slant his head to the left when talking to you. He was extremely handsome. He was shy, did not socialise much and enjoyed family life. He seemed lonely. Dad befriended him and invited him home to tea or for a meal a few times. We thought he was great – he knew how to talk to us. Dad and 'Dusty' Miller – now 'Uncle' Miller to us – were great friends and we were to see a lot of him. We really looked forward to his visits on his days off work.

Dad traded in the Citroen for a Morris Oxford which was more suitable for the now quickly growing girls. With his new acquisition a trip was planned to spend the day out at Woosung, twelve miles down the river where the Whangpoo flows into the mouth of the Yangtze. Uncle Miller and Dad, the driver, were in front and the back amazingly took the girls. No food was taken – that would have been impossible. Uncle Miller said he knew of a place which served treble ham and eggs. After a walk along the waterfront to stretch our cramped legs and to work up an appetite, we made our way to the restaurant. Treble ham and eggs all round for the grownups – Bessie and Nellie settling for doubles. It teamed down with rain on the return trip and Dad had difficulty seeing where he was driving – with a car so crammed full the windows misted.

* * *

Dad was promoted to Manager of the Cotton Mill in 1926 and this necessitated a move to the Manager's house – 32 Pingliang Road, still in the Yangtzepoo area. We were going to miss the security of the compound life and likewise, we were all going to miss our family of neighbours.

CHAPTER TWO

Pingliang Road

1926–1932

The house was too big for us. It had a spacious dining room, sitting room and large entrance hall on the ground floor. Two large bedrooms, each with a fire place and bathroom en suite on the first floor – and two bedrooms and a bathroom on the second floor. Verandahs ran the full width of the house on the ground and first floors facing the garden. There was a pantry and kitchen at the rear of the house and a large coal shed. Cookboy cooked on a coal/wood stove. To the left of the house was a garage with servants' quarters above.

The garden was enormous, with a tennis court, umpteen strawberry beds, pomegranate tree, as well as Ivy's favourite fruit – yes, a beebo tree! Amah showed us how to make little dolls using the flowers of the pomegranate tree, which most probably was the reason why we had no fruit. On reflection, this certainly saved Amah having to launder too many stained pinafores – for pinafores Nellie and Bessie did wear and pomegranate juice stains were almost impossible to remove.

Dad was enthusiastic about his new tennis court – a hard one this time, so no more weeding by the ladies. With the change of address Dad seemed to meet new people. Bert and Doris Brownrigg of the police and their three children – Eddie, Rita and George. The Cheethams from a competitive mill – Capt. and Mrs Rogers and Mr Drake off one of the Jardine ships. Through his friendship with Uncle Miller he met bachelors Jock Loutitt, 'Annie' Caines, Monty Vincent, Jack and Georgina Shotter – of the Fire Brigade. Dad's new friends were also keen tennis players and now Saturday changed from swimming to tennis party days. They came and with them their

22

children so we had lots of company. Occasionally in the evenings they played poker – they had quite a little club going. We had an account at Cafe Federal on Broadway so a standing order was placed for goodies to be sent each weekend.

Chinese boys enjoyed coming to act as ball boys on tennis party days, but as we only needed four it was a question of choosing them. To avoid disappointment we would suggest they play 'stone–paper–scissors' amongst themselves. Loving a gamble they would challenge each other – the four winners stayed, the rest went home. Although it was a fair challenge the losers sometimes were not sporting enough and would take out their disappointment on us when returning home from school the following day. We would be pelted with fruit skins or little stones. One day Jessie our pet Airedale dog – named after Auntie Jessie Cameron – was, as usual, waiting at the gate for our return from school and saw what was happening. She ran out after the boys and caught one by the seat of his pants and dragged him into the garden. He was terrified. Thankfully this put a stop to further attacks. Jessie was a quiet, faithful dog letting us do anything to her – we were rough, but she always responded gently.

The group also played Mah Jong. A favourite Chinese game played with bamboo-backed ivory tiles – 144 in all made up of four different suits of thirty-six tiles each. (1) Bamboo, (2) Characters, (3) Circles, and (4) a set consisting of four each North, South, East and West, four each of three Honour tiles (Green, Red and White) and eight special bonus tiles depicting Flowers. They all had a special meaning. Four people played the game on a bare wooden table and they delighted in making as much noise as possible when shuffling the tiles after a game, thus supposedly frightening off evil spirits. The players then built a two tiered wall, eighteen tiles long – thirty-six tiles in all – and these were joined to form a square also to keep out those evil spirits. When several tables were playing at the same time, often outside on a summer's evening, the noise was deafening. The rules are somewhat similar to Rummy but with a special way of counting all Honours and Flowers – Doubles, Triples and so on. It was quite a gamble as far as the adults and Chinese were concerned – to us it was a social game.

It was through Mah Jong that Dad became very close friends with Jack and Georgina. Jack was an engineer and later managed the

Shanghai Bus Company – yes, THE buses that we, as kids, had messed up!

Uncle Miller gave Mary an Alsation pup which she named Dusty – after him. Dusty guarded us too well. He should never have been given to Mary as he was very difficult to train. He was a roamer and fighter and not knowing what he got up to made it more difficult for us to look after him. There were strict kennel rules in Shanghai because of rabies. If a dog bit anyone it had to go into quarantine and be tested. Alas, Dusty was taken away quite a few times and it was decided he would have to be put down. He was dangerous. Dad had to approach the Wayside Police Station to do this. They considered Dusty too valuable a dog to put down suggesting they keep him and train him for the Force. Mary who was extremely reluctant to let him go felt a lot happier at this arrangement.

Strawberries were served in season, topped with dollops of home-made ice-cream which had been churned in a good old-fashioned ice-cream mixer. This was a very essential piece of kitchen equipment, as far as we were concerned. Cookboy would make up a delicious concoction of custard which he put into the central chamber of the mixer. After fitting the lid tightly he would surround the chamber with lots of crushed ice and coarse salt. Then he energetically turned the handle which motivated a sort of paddle in the chamber until scrumptious ice-cream emerged. Needless to say, it had to be a very large churn to supply the demands of all the tennis parties – our reward for watching and helping Cookboy turn the handle was being given the paddle to lick!

Because of the local practice of using human manure as a fertiliser, we were not brought up on salads. Home-grown vegetables and strawberries were safe to eat and our friends were kept well supplied. Fruit and vegetables from the market, eaten raw, had to be soaked in permanganate and then rinsed in cold filtered water. As for fresh milk, there wasn't any. In fact, there was no dairy when we first went out to Shanghai. We were brought up on Carnation milk and tinned butter. The Culty Dairy was established in the 1930s. Our first drink of cold fresh milk didn't go down well – it had a completely different taste and we thought it was off! Drinking water was boiled, filtered and then cooled in the ice-box.

The ice-box was made of wood – about 4 feet (1.25 metres) tall – lined with zinc. It had two sections – the ice and food were put in the top half and the bottom half contained a well, into which the melted ice ran. This would have to be cleaned each day and refilled with large blocks of ice.

Though we were deprived of fresh milk and dairy products we enjoyed many dishes that are considered luxuries today. Occasionally Dad would give a dinner party and serve whitebait threaded heads and tails on toothpicks forming rafts. These were dipped in egg and bread-crumbs and fried. This was followed by roast pheasant, duchess potatoes, bread sauce and red currant jelly. With the exception of ice-cream, in any shape or form, Dad was not very fussy about desserts – instead he enjoyed his Stilton and biscuits.

Periodically there were 'paltas' – mouth watering avocados served with vinegar, salt and pepper. These were not a regular treat. Dad met a member of the crew off one of the Dollar Line ships and got chatting about Mexico and one of the things he missed – paltas. He was given one which he shared with us – that is the kind of man he was. He even kept the stone which eventually grew into a handsome indoor pot plant – the weather being too cold to grow it outdoors. Normally he was a plain eater. He would rave over toasted Bermaline bread oozing with butter and sprinkled with salt.

Developing New Interests

Uncle Miller helped us a lot and took a great interest in what we were doing and taught us new things to do as well. He introduced us to simple things children did in England, he told us stories and joked with us. He also introduced us to reading good books. He started Mary on lace making and then oil painting – her life-long favourite hobby. Mary had great artistic potential which he recognised. Her first attempt was pen painting on velvet which Dad proudly had made into cushions. Only guests had the privilege of leaning against them as they adorned our rose and white coloured sitting room.

Ivy was encouraged to draw in pen and ink. Although she said she only copied, the results were good, and she won second prize in one of the *North China Daily News* art competitions. He also encouraged Ivy to play the piano.

Bessie and Nellie were taught many games, one of which was played with a two-headed top – shaped something like an hour glass. This would be rolled along a string attached to two sticks – one held in each hand. The game was to roll the top from one side to the other, sometimes – if they dared – throwing it in the air and catching it on the string. Whilst in play the top would emit a humming sound. A fun game to watch and one requiring a lot of practice. It is believed this Chinese toy may well have started the craze Diabolo now popular in the west. Bessie and Nellie found this a most difficult game but they persevered.

During the school holidays, Uncle Miller spent most of his days off with us. Walking was his hobby and he was always accompanied by his Alsation, Nelson. He had been named Pluto but because he had lost an eye in a dog fight, his name was appropriately changed. Nelson even sported an axe and miniature fireman's helmet which he wore on parade. He became a mascot. Uncle would take us, and Nelson, out to the countryside and together we discovered many interesting things. The wheelbarrow was one – nothing like the western variety. It consisted of a large (approximately 4 feet (1.25m) diameter) wheel, with a platform on either side, to sit on, and was pushed along by a man at the back. It was quite a sight to see one of these being pushed, with four adult passengers on either side, along a narrow path between flooded rice paddies. The man in control moved only from the waist down, his arms steadied the wheel barrow. Although this looked like a difficult balancing act, he made it easier by humming his own special tune.

The walks were all very interesting but on one occasion, disastrous. Nelson was bounding ahead, chasing rabbits, when he suddenly disappeared. If a dog can call for help, he certainly did – he had disappeared into a cesspit and needed help to get out. The girls stood clear – no way were they going to help – poor Uncle Miller was on his own. As you can imagine it was the end of that walk – we couldn't get home quick enough for showers and to hose Nelson down.

Another memorable walk was through a village and seeing a very complicated plumbing system using bamboo which had been split and then the connecting notches hollowed out. It was fascinating to watch the water trickling down from the stream, via the bamboo channel to the next village.

This sparked our interest in bamboo – a kind of tropical giant grass which is used in so many different ways. In fact, this became a game – spot the bamboo – and we soon realised what an important part this evergreen played in the lives of the oriental. Some species have tender and succulent shoots – and most of you have had them in 'take-aways' – it is also the staple food of the Panda. Chopsticks made from bamboo are the most versatile item in a Chinese kitchen. They beat an egg – drain when cooking in deep fat – and are used instead of a knife and fork. Chairs, screens and other furniture are made from bamboo – we have a photo of Nellie in her bamboo 'buggie'. Bamboo is also used in floral arrangements, made into vases, whistles, ladders, kites, walking sticks as well as items of torture. The most fascinating use we could find was the scaffolding erected when working on buildings. The height didn't seem to matter as one piece was lashed to another with strips of pliable bamboo.

The walks we particularly enjoyed with Uncle Miller were in the autumn during the season for kite flying. Although we were growing up, and kites seemed to be for the young, we were fascinated. Some resembled birds, insects, a spectacular dragon or even a centipede. It was quite an art and the kite makers put a lot of detail into their work. The kites looked magnificent winging their way in the sky and needless to say, their operators were well exercised keeping them up there.

* * *

Amah had a nasty accident with the iron. We were playing in the yard at the back of the house. Amah was ironing – suddenly she was frantically trying to throw off the iron which had stuck to her hand. Fortunately Dad was nearby and able to help her by switching off the current. She was in severe shock. It took her some time to recover and thereafter she would only use a charcoal iron. This had a deep chamber, the handle forming part of a hinged lid. The chamber would be filled with live charcoal and occasionally topped up to keep the heat constant. It would take her forever to get through the laundry basket. It was fascinating to watch her ironing. When clothes were too dry she would fill her mouth with water, then puff up her cheeks and 'hiss' the water out through her front teeth to release a fine spray – thus the clothes were dampened most effectively.

It was Nellie's turn to start school at The Holy Family Convent. Nellie found it easy to make friends, much to Bessie's envy. She used to toddle up to children in the playground, or park, whom she had not met before and say, 'What's your name?' and would be off playing with them in a tick whilst Bessie would shyly be a bystander.

We all loved going to school. The Nuns were so kind to us possibly because they knew the family situation that Mother had tragically died and Dad had four little girls to bring up on his own. The peaceful, disciplined environment at the Convent made it so much easier for Dad and, later for Mary, when she took full responsibility of looking after us. Dad's four daughters were all at school – growing fast in every direction.

We set off each day with two enormous school bags, two little ones, plus the famous 'tiffen basket' to travel the long distance to school. When we got off the tram there was a sweet shop near the entrance to the Convent. We called it the 'One-Copper–Two-Copper Shop'. Here we were able to spend our few coppers spending money. At this shop we had the choice of purchasing either one sweet, wrapped in paper, for two coppers (expensive) or, purchase two sweets, unwrapped for one copper – which we preferred, because that was a bargain. It was a funny little shop or stall – it operated from an open window. Some of the children gambled for their sweets. This was a different method. There was a wheel and a stick in the centre from which was attached a string and a tiny weight. For one-copper they would spin the stick and if the weight landed on a space with one, two or more sweets – that was their prize. If it landed on an empty space, they lost. We were not prepared to lose.

Around this time Bessie became known as 'old moaner'. Dad was very concerned – she was not well and he could not understand why. She had trouble with her right eye – developing a squint. It was decided by Dr Cameron that she should have her tonsils and adenoids removed and her eyes tested. After the operation, a pair of glasses, and a daily fistful of Horlicks tablets to fatten her up, she was the envy of the rest of the family. Later, when Nellie's turn came, the adenoid and tonsil operation did not bother her – all she was concerned about were the perks – Horlicks in particular.

Sometimes Dad affectionately referred to us as his 'four holding down bolts' but he was quite proud of us. He always attended Speech Days and Prize Givings. On one such occasion the Nuns had gone to town arranging a magnificent tableau depicting the Virgin Mary and Child – the effect was like a beautiful painting. The backdrop was of dark blue velvet with little ledges behind clouds spaced out at intervals on which stood angels in white robes wearing enormous wings. In the middle of the tableau was the Virgin Mary and baby Jesus. Nellie, who was about six at the time, was one of the angels – looking very much the part until she spotted Dad in the audience, whereupon she waved to him frantically. Dad tried to deter her by mouthing 'No' and shaking his fist – Nellie took this as acknowledgement and waved even harder, much to the dismay of the Nuns. She was thereafter known to them as 'le petite diable'.

When Mary was happily lace-making, or painting – her first love – Ivy was having piano lessons. She was very keen and practiced a lot, so much so that her school work suffered and her efforts had to be curtailed. However, not before one of the Nuns in the Chinese school next door to our house had heard Ivy trying to play Colonel Bogey. They had a Prize Giving coming up, and enlisted Ivy's efforts to play for the festivities. When she got there, it was to find the only instrument was a very old organ which had to be pedalled for air! The result was a discordant mess – out of time, and out of tune.

It then became Bessie's turn to be encouraged to play the piano. She was eight at the time and did very well until she found she was missing out on playtime. She and her school friend, Delia Colombo, had to play a duet at the school Prize Giving. Always seeing the funny side of things Dad could hardly contain his laughter. Before starting Bessie very seriously adjusted her piano stool, polished her new glasses and when ready with Delia commenced the duet. Delia was a much better player than Bessie and had learnt the whole piece off by heart. Bessie couldn't memorise and had to follow the music implicitly. All went well for the first two bars and then Delia missed a beat and couldn't find the spot on the music sheet. Bessie couldn't stop to help her. They carried on playing right to the end then had the audacity to bow to the audience before walking off to a tremendous ovation.

Bessie didn't enjoy practising whilst others were having fun out in the garden. She made the excuse that her hands were too small to reach an octave and Dad got the message. Too bad really as Dad would have dearly loved one of us to show some musical talent. This was the end of piano lessons for all, and resulted in Nellie, the only one who can pick up a tune by ear, missing out.

1927

The arrival of British and American troops to protect Shanghai
and its inhabitants while Chiang K'ai-shek was trying to liquidate
the communists created a great feeling of safety ...

* * *

With the arrival of the troops there was a celebration at the Race
Course on Empire Day and Auntie Cameron saw to it that we all
enjoyed the many rides and games as well as cakes and ice-cream.
It was an event that only the forces could in their inimitable way
arrange. 'Billy Boy' – Auntie's special nickname for tomboy Ivy –
came to grief on the aerial flight. She should have been hanging on
to two handles attached to a wheel which slid down a stout wire
until hopefully she was stopped at the bottom of the run. Luckily
there was a safety net underneath the run because ... Billy Boy fell
off. Dad and Auntie were sitting in the stands watching the
proceedings and once they knew she was all right couldn't stop
giggling as they watched the spectacular trampoline act! When
Ivy at last managed to work her way to the edge of the net and alight
she got a well deserved applause from those near at hand. Mary was
also in trouble. A canvas shoot had been rigged up from the top of
the spectator stands to ground level and Mary just had to have a ride.
She sat on a mat and was given a shove to start her on her way –
unfortunately she lost her balance on the way down scraping her
elbow and arm along the side of the canvas causing friction burns.
These were most painful and took a long time to heal.

* * *

The first crush Ivy had was on Tommy Buchanan and Mary thought
Malcolm, his brother, was pretty nice too. They were very young
at the time. They met at one of the Saturday swimming parties at
the Hongkew Baths. After having settled into 32 Pingliang Road,
Mary and Ivy joined the Junior Tennis Club at Wayside Park. As
Tommy and Malcolm were not members their affections turned to
Charlie and Jimmy Taylor, (another set of brothers), both good tennis
players but, more interestingly, they played the pipes in the Shanghai
Volunteer Band and, wore KILTS! Also, they attended the same
Union Church and when we got out of Sunday School Mary and

Ivy would wait around until they saw them again. They never plucked up courage to talk to them.

Nellie was seven when she contacted typhoid fever and was in hospital a long time. Whilst recovering the nurse would ask her at elevenses what she would like (a milk drink or, perhaps fruit juice). She used to say, 'red jelly please'. It was such a treat, she loved to watch the jelly wobble. She missed her balloons.

Dad was very concerned. He remembered helping to nurse Mother when she was so desperately ill with typhoid while in Peru. Her temperature was so high that the only way to get it down was by placing her in a bath of ice. Dad stayed in the hospital with her – down in Lima – and left Mary and Ivy and their ninera in the care of his manager.

While Mary was visiting Nellie in hospital, Ivy, Eva and Bessie attended the annual Sunday school picnic. We would gather outside the Union Church, on the south side of the Soochow Creek, and travel in open trucks out to Jessfield Park – singing all the way. Lots of fun. By the time we arrived at Jessfield, games would be organised and a fabulous spread laid out by the ladies of the Church. We hopped off the trucks ready to enjoy ourselves – we had a sack race, three-legged, egg and spoon and obstacle races.

The weather was usually ideal but the day eventually arrived when the heavens opened and there was a steady downpour all day long. This did not stop us arriving at the Church on time – masses of kids all wanting a repeat of the previous year's fun. What to do? – the ladies were in a dilemma – but not for long. It was soon arranged for us to pile into the trucks (by now covered) and we were taken to an enormous sports hut right in the middle of town. It was obvious the games crew were with us because games commenced immediately we got there – slightly cramped – but still fun. Unfortunately the food had gone straight to Jessfield. We were all getting a bit peckish when Ivy and Eva had the bright idea of going across the road to the Anglo Chinese Dispensary to get some sweets. Ivy knew Dad had an account there – only to be used for medicines and emergencies. Well, this was an emergency! All they could get in the form of sweets was chewing gum – Feenamint. They went back to the hut with the gum, making shapes out of the large quantity they had knit together (2 or 3 tablets each). Bessie was given one tablet much to her disgust – as it turned out all to her good. The picnic came to an end with a shortened sing song back to the Church and home. Eva spent the night with us and a very uncomfortable night it was. There were two bathrooms on the first floor and they were occupied throughout the night by Eva and Ivy – Bessie had to go downstairs to the cloakroom off the gloomily lit hall – full of spooks. Wherever Eva is today no doubt she, like us, associates Feenamint with one very wet Sunday school picnic.

We attended the Union Church Sunday School where we first met Grace and Joy Lavington. Their father was one of our teachers as was a Mr Harmon. The latter played a large part in the lives of Ivy and Donald during their war years.

Only once did Mary and Ivy feel extremely guilty. They set off in the morning, with Eva, presumably with the intention of going to Sunday school but played truant instead and visited the conservatory, part of the Bund Gardens. Dad decided he would collect them from school and waited and waited at the door of the Church for them to appear – they didn't. The girls saw the car and knew that Dad would be furious with them so remained hidden wondering what to do next. As it happened they had found a silver and sapphire bracelet which had been dropped under one of the seats in the conservatory. It had to be advertised and the rightful owner found. With so much excitement the episode was forgotten but Dad made a point of picking us up thereafter. We had to toe the line – we thought he was a spoil-sport.

*   *   *

It was a relief to Dad to know that Mrs Shotter would look after Nellie when she left hospital – Mary, Ivy and Bessie being at school. Mrs Shotter had to teach her to walk again – being weak Nellie had to be carried around. Her hair fell out – it was cut short and massaged every day with Glover's Mange Cure. When her hair grew in again it was thick, curly and auburn in colour. She loved being with the Shotters. When she was stronger Graham (later on, one of our brothers-in-law) looked after Nellie at times when his mother went out. He was a Boy Scout – about fourteen. He was so tall, Nellie still weak and nervous. She was terrified, particularly when he and his friends played 'Bobbies and Thieves' or whatever game they made up – which involved chasing around, hiding behind pillars, the Bobbies shooting the Thieves. Nellie had to run with Graham and hide with him otherwise she would give the show away and he would be caught. She took it all for real ... and was scared like crazy.

However, she soon got used to the tough-boy company and as a result gradually became quite a dare-devil.

Because Nellie was staying with the Shotters – there were many visits between the two homes and of course Mary and Ivy got to know Jack and Graham (more brothers) better – and you guessed it, Mary and Ivy fell for them. Jack, the eldest, was very debonair and had a sidecar attached to his motorbike and when he gave Mary a ride in this, she thought she was in heaven. He had a nice voice and strummed a ukulele and when he played the ever popular 'Five Feet Two, Eyes Of Blue', blue-eyed Mary was sent into raptures. Graham, the youngest, was a whiz on his bicycle and he was never without it, busily showing off his prowess. He was quite a lady killer. In later years Jack married Grace Lavington, of whom you will hear more and Mary married Graham in 1940.

Dad Commutes to Hankow

Dad was highly respected by his employers and became the firm's trouble-shooter, which now entailed him visiting Hankow two or three times a year, for one or two weeks at a time. It was a relief to him that we were well taken care of by Amah and Cookboy. As we were no longer living in a compound, and '32' was fairly isolated, it was arranged by Dad's office during the 1927 unrest that we would be assigned a guard whenever Dad was away. He was Russian and he lived in a room above the garage. He reported for duty each night – it was his responsibility to make sure we were safe. Other than that we managed on our own while Dad was away – Mary looked after us, with Amah's help of course. We were on our honour and it worked. Mary was 14.

As a help to Mary and Ivy who were, at that time, struggling with oral French, Dad decided that they should speak French only every Saturday. This new resolution lasted a few weeks after which it gradually faded out. His multiplication tables exercise lasted much longer, perhaps because he took part. He would suddenly point a finger at one and say, for instance, 4 times 4. If the answer was correct there would be a reward. We enjoyed that. Bessie and Nellie were rather young to participate in these lessons but each had in turn been through his methods of learning the alphabet and how to count etc.

The story goes that while he was teaching Mary her ABCs she would repeat each letter after him until she came to 'W', 'Double-me' she would say. 'No dear, double-you'. Mary – 'double-me'. 'No dear' – pointing to himself 'double-me'. Mary, excitedly getting the picture. 'Double da-da'. Dad had a lot of patience but regrettably the only language, other than our own, that we became adept at was Pidgin English.

Saturdays was letter writing day. Poor Dad never got much news from Nellie – her letters usually started with 'Dear Daddy, I hope you are in the best of health as we are here' … (Fullstop) – all inspiration gone.

Cookboy's brother, who lived on the premises, was our gardener. He was a problem, particularly when Dad was away, as he was partial to a drink or two. Sometimes he returned home very much the worse for wear. Admittedly, he did not do this too often but when he did, he would get fighting drunk and there would be a great commotion (or, as Amah would say 'walla-walla') from the servants quarters until Amah and Cookboy could settle him down. On one particular night when Dad was up in Hankow, the 'walla-walla' was worse than ever and we were really frightened. It was quite late at night. We were safely tucked up in bed and the noise woke us up – we were startled. We thought he was trying to get into the house so armed ourselves with the best weapons we could find around us upstairs – pokers, fire tongs, a walking stick from Dad's room, anything we could lay our hands on – and waited! Eventually Amah and Cookboy quietened him down but it was a long time before we went off to sleep again. He was becoming a heavy drinker, and obviously getting short of money. It was at this time things began to disappear from the house. Our possessions were being pawned and the pawnshop tickets left on the back doorstep for the goods to be retrieved. No doubt in his way of thinking he was not stealing because he 'returned the goods' by way of the pawn tickets. We had to buy them back from the pawnshop. Perhaps there was method in this madness – but he was honest enough to give us the opportunity to reclaim our possessions – logic! When things got out of hand on one occasion after a particularly large haul, the Police were called in. He was dismissed and we had no further trouble.

*   *   *

Dad was one of those lucky people who are able to relax completely. Everyday after lunch he would settle back in his chair, fold his hands over his generous tum, close his eyes and have his 'forty-winks' as he called it. After a short time he would waken and feel as fresh as a daisy. Of course, we respected this short siesta of his, and made not a sound. But that did not stop us from communicating. We worked out a sign language of our own and chatted away happily.

After his forty-winks Dad always had two (no more) very special soft-centred 'Smiles & Chuckles' – imported chocolates which he kept locked up in the safe in his bedroom away from people like us. He knew we girls were envious so he took advantage of the weekly sale at the Chocolate Shop on Fridays when their local chocolates were sold for half price. We could pick our own flavours and enjoyed the different varieties they had to offer.

Another special treat was 'Twigg's Tip Top Toffees' made and sold by the Chemist on Broadway. There was a special flavour to them – looking back, coming from a Chemist could it have been Owbridges ... ?

It was said that Mary resembled Dad. She had his colouring and hair so dark it was almost blue-black. It was thick and glossy and very straight and she wore it bobbed with a fringe. With her big porcelain blue eyes surrounded by dark lashes and heavy dark brows she had the look of an Irish colleen. She was beautiful.

Ivy and Nellie inherited Mother's looks. Both were fair skinned with blue eyes and each sported a handsome crop of freckles. Ivy had golden brown hair and like Mary, wore it in a bob. Nellie had long auburn ringlets, a round chubby face with a ready smile but like the little girl, with the curl, she was sometimes 'orrid. Other than that she was a friendly little soul.

Bessie had fine straight hair which started out very blond. Later it darkened until is was a golden brown like Ivy's – unfortunately her hair style was limited by a cowlick. She was a very serious little girl but when she smiled she had an attractive feature – a Shirley Temple dimple on her right cheek. She had Dad's hazel eyes.

Besides the cobbler calling to measure our fast growing feet for shoes, we had a tailor who used to come for a week at a time and work in the house. He hailed from Kumping Road. It was a long while before we got used to him. He had a nervous disorder and when he approached with a pin his hand shook so much we were convinced he was going to stab us. Most of his time was taken up by altering, letting down or letting out. The usual story of 'Father's pants will soon fit Willy' – except in this case it was Nellie. She was very proud of her new knickers made from Dad's old shirts – which prompted the remark 'Have you got them on ?' a favourite saying of his. Dad's trousers were also put to good use. First they were unpicked, washed, turned and pressed then they were made into skirts. Nellie remembers being awestruck when one day she heard Dad say to the tailor, on choosing a 2 x 4 inch piece of sample material 'You make a four piece raincoat from this one' – to her, the tailor was now a wonderman and it bothered Nellie for ages how he could possibly make four raincoats out of 'nothing'.

* * *

It was through Graham we became interested in bicycling. In addition to our Yangtzepoo friends we now added some new ones. This included not only the Cormack girls, Edith, Irene and Lyall, who went to the same school as we did but also the younger Gilmour girls, Helen and Edna, from the next street. Since leaving Shanghai our lives have crossed on more than one occasion over the years. We enjoyed many a bicycle ride together and would take a picnic tea with us, just in case we became hungry. Ivy, the tomboy, of the group caused us many an anxious moment. She excelled herself on one of the rides by actually pedalling head-first into a filthy green creek. She still insists her foot came off the pedal and she was trying to get it back on – but that's no excuse. She was a mess, and we were a long way from home. Eventually a Japanese gentleman, the manager of a mill nearby, saved the day by offering her facilities for a wash.

Helen Gilmour, although not an 'Eva' insomuch as being an up-to-tricks leader, never missed an opportunity of playing some prank. The telephone rang while we were in the middle of lunch – Auntie Cameron and Uncle Miller were with us that day. Ivy answered the call and looked very upset when she returned to the table. When Dad asked her who rang, Ivy said 'no one'. To get the record straight, Dad asked again who called and enquired if there was any message. Poor Ivy, was so embarrassed when she had to admit that the person on the line told her they were the telephone company and were testing the line and would she please whistle. Ivy obliged – and the reply came ... 'you need a packet of birdseed ... !' (Helen).

It was while living at Pingliang Road that Ivy developed rheumatic fever and was confined to bed. Her recuperation period lasted several weeks and being alone all day it was a very frustrated and depressed Ivy that we had to cope with. This was shortly before

Christmas and Dad had sent a suitcase of presents down on Capt Rogers' ship – ahead of his arrival for safe keeping. The suitcase presided in the bedroom and curious Ivy let temptation get the better of her. It became a daily ritual for her to open the suitcase, take the adhesive-tape off one of four tins of Nestles Milk Chocolates, have two or three chocolates and replace the tape. Needless to say, when the tins were opened on Christmas morning, they were almost empty.

The fever left Ivy subject to cramp in both calves. One night during a particularly painful attack Mary decided enough was enough and rubbed Ivy's legs with Sloan's Liniment. This disastrous treatment ended the cramp though Ivy spent the night on the bathroom floor trying to cool her legs!

Christmas and Festivals

Dad returned to Shanghai in time for Christmas. It was exciting. Santa – played by Uncle Miller – landed on the lawn with much accompanying of bells from his reindeer and appeared, sack full, at the French windows. We never did see the reindeer but there was always lots of noise to indicate they were there and, of course, it was too cold for us to go out and inspect. Christmases were wonderful. Lots of presents and parties. We hung bolster covers for stockings – they were always full. Bessie's usually had a packet of dried figs at the very bottom – her favourites then, and now. A few years later Ivy let the cat out of the bag. She took Bessie and Nellie on a pre-Christmas viewing of presents on the top of Dad's wardrobe – in that forbidden room wherein lay the safe and 'Smiles & Chuckles'. It was their first indication that Santa did not bring the presents down the chimney and they were shattered.

Bessie met Uncle Miller years later when visiting Australia – he was still playing 'Santa' but now to his grandchildren.

Soon after Christmas it was time to celebrate Chinese New Year, also known as the Spring festival. This was celebrated on the day of the first new moon after the 21st January and lasted four days. It was an important festival and comparable to our Christmas. The home was cleaned from top to bottom, it being unlucky to enter the new year with any dust of the past clinging to you. Food was prepared ahead – working in the first few days was also unlucky. No knives were used at this celebration in case they cut through good fortune. Families would gather on New Year's eve when presents would be exchanged, all debts settled and a feast enjoyed. Homes would be decorated with lanterns and paper dragons and everyone would wear their new clothes in red, bright pink or green – specially bought for the occasion. The children delighted in making-up, using rouge and lipstick. There was much to celebrate – a new year, and a new beginning. Joss sticks were lit and placed in the temples, cymbals clanging to create a deafening noise to frighten off evil spirits. Strings of fire-crackers were set off spluttering for good luck. It was a holiday period with lots of merriment usually ending with marathon Mah Jong sessions. Gambling. 'Kun-she-faz-zay' Happy New Year wishes seemed to fill the air.

During the Dragon Boat Festival boats are decorated to look like Dragons and are raced against each other. The celebration we were more familiar with credited the control of clouds and rain to the river dragons. The festival takes place during the summer and farmers make offerings to the Dragon King hoping for rain and a good harvest.

The Moon Festival is very much a women's occasion. It is a time to sit outside and admire the beauty of a full harvest moon and make offerings of pomegranates (the seeds symbolise money), spirit money and moon cakes – round pie-like cakes with sticky sweet fillings which we also enjoyed.

The festivals are usually linked to farming seasons. The dates on which they fall change according to the phases of the moon. The Chinese calendar has a repeating twelve year cycle, each linked to an animal which supposedly affects the personality of those born during that year. In our case they seem very apt:

Mary	–	*Tiger*	Bessie	–	*Horse*
Ivy	–	*Dragon*	Nellie	–	*Rooster*

The most exciting celebration we can remember took place in Lima, Peru. This was a 'Water Festival'. The fun was being able to help Mother and Dad fill tiny balloons with water which were then aimed at neighbours across the street or anyone else who happened to show themselves. When a balloon burst or hit a person – it was a score. When aiming at a lady it was customary to fill the balloon with cologne. The day ended with a street party – everyone was friends again.

*   *   *

There were so many different scenes and customs that were uniquely Chinese. They are a very industrious nation, everything is put to good use and the simple things seem to be the ones they like best. Nothing is wasted – in fact they are very ecology minded.

They loved noise as that meant company and company was security. Crowds were special – they could get lost in an anonymous throng. Singing birds were an interesting hobby as well as being musically noisy and good company. A familiar sight was the birds in their bamboo cages, specially designed to fit one on top of the other, being taken for a breath of fresh air on a balmy summer evening. The gentlemen would meet their friends in the park or sit on the side of a pavement and listen, proudly praising the melodious noise of their own song-birds. The sound was reminiscent of a choir.

The children had their special toys and pets. Where today we might have a dog or cat, their pet would be a goldfish or a simple cricket caught with a pole, the tip having first been dipped in syrup. The cricket had its own song and delighted the children. The pets would be kept in small boxes with holes in the top or in tiny bamboo baskets and it was not unusual to see the children copying their parents on their evening walk. The little boxes or bamboo baskets have now been superseded by round brass boxes, highly decorated and with a brass carrying handle on the top. They even appear in gift shops in the UK.

Bessie and Nellie had their pets too – they were frogs! They had a little family of frog-children when they played 'Let's Pretend' – to be mummy, this time. They would collect the frogs from the garden and keep them in the bedroom and spend hours trying to dress them. They struggled, wardrobe mistresses and frogs. Then, when their frog-children seemed to have won the battle of nudity, the girls became more motherly and decided it was bath time before putting them into nighties ready for bed. The frogs' beds were cardboard Easter Egg boxes because they could be rocked and cotton-waste from Dad's garage was used for the mattresses, a piece of material for the sheets. If they tried to jump out of bed and not 'go-to-sleep' as they were told to do, they were spanked on their bottom. The frogs obviously liked the bath time best. Bessie and Nellie would fill the bath with a little water and pop them all in. Great fun and games – for the frogs as they tried to make their escape. One day Dad came home early to find two panicky children rushing down the stairs past him and out through the front door – at great speed – to retrieve a frog which had gone down the outlet when they had pulled the plug out. No escape! Dad was not, repeat not, amused. The frogs had to go back to the garden and the children, to their bedroom.

* * *

Dad decided it was time to change his car again and bought a four-door Talbot. It was chocolate in colour and had ample room in the back – it even had his initials painted by the handle of the two front doors. He took every opportunity to discover new areas with us on our Sunday drives to the cemetery – afterwards we would enjoy tea together out in the country.

We were spoilt for choice. Closer to home, on Broadway, on the border of the International Settlement, was the now familiar German Cafe Federal – they specialised in pastries which really were Dad's favourite. We would order a take-away from there, when we went visiting either Auntie Cameron or Uncle Miller. Marcel's, a French tearoom, was pish-posh – with its cool decor of lilac and pale grey. They offered a delectable selection of dainty cakes. On occasions we would drive over to Didi's on Avenue Foch, in the French Concession. Didi's was an Italian nightclub but on Sundays they served special teas. It had a rather gloomy atmosphere of black and silver furnishings and neon lights – their ice-cream cakes compensated for the gloom. Occasionally we would drive out to Jessfield, in the Bubbling Well area, where there was a country tea-shack run by Scots. We would sit in the garden and enjoy home baked scones and goats-milk cream cheese and other delicious goodies. On longer drives we would go round the rubicon and stop for tea at a tearoom where there was a fortune-teller. That was exciting though we never had our fortune told. We imagined the proprietress to be a real-live 'gypsy'.

On one of our outings to call on Auntie we were dressed up in our best white silk dresses and as a treat on the way Dad bought us each an ice-cream cone. He warned us to be careful and not let any drop on to our dresses. After a little while, we couldn't help giggling as Dad noticed a large blob of ice-cream on his tie! (We agreed with Bessie when she moaned … 'if that had been me'!)

Movies and Things ...

Around this time we were introduced to the movies – in particular the Eastern Cinema in Seward Road, Yangtzepoo. It was a very small theatre and usually showed Chinese films. However, they did show the odd Charlie Chaplin or Harold Lloyd movie and Our Gang shorts – all of them silent. When Dad was home, and transportation available, Bessie would be detailed to phone and ask 'what you got'? These were fun times except for the Chaplin films – Dad could never understand how Ivy could find something to cry about while the rest were laughing.

Ivy was not the only one crying when Dad and his buddies formed a party to see the much advertised 'talkie' – 'The Singing Fool'. The theatre was packed and we were spread out in the front row – we had to be as near as possible just in case we couldn't hear! As you can imagine, Al Jolson's 'Mammy' brought the house and the tears down and we all left with red eyes, the snivels and, in our case, stiff necks. We had had a wonderful time – sniff, sniff. What a memorable outing that was – a talking movie – unbelievable.

Bessie and Nellie were reaching their ambition of being 'big girls' and becoming more independent. They had a long way to go though – they couldn't understand why they never caught up with Mary and Ivy – to them, there was no age-gap and it frustrated them to always be those few years behind. 'Maskee' they thought – it's bound to even out one day. It did.

Again they were playing 'Let's Pretend' – this time actresses. High heels, hats, fur stoles, dresses. They rummaged around for props and acted and danced for hours on end. They had their fans and were definitely sent – their destination, of course, Hollywood.

We now met Mrs Jarvis of the tennis club who had a daughter Mavis, Bessie's age, and they, with Nellie made a lovely trio. It was Mrs Jarvis who enlightened Mary and Ivy on the problems of growing up. They were becoming selective in their wardrobe, sketching dress styles for the Kumping Road tailor to copy. Instead of coming for a week at a time to make the many alterations that needed to be done, the tailor would take the sketches home to work out. There were no patterns to be bought. Chinese tailors are very clever and can copy sketched dresses exceedingly well. Materials were purchased the tailor called in and at the end of the month in came the bill. Our vocabulary was increasing as the bill read along these lines ... 'one clipsation Missie Mary, one clipsation Missie Ivy'. Mary's downfall came when she gave the tailor a Kestos bra to copy. He did, too, and made a beautiful job of it – but, the bill? It read 'Six pairs of "bell pockets"' Wow!

At the last Prize Giving which Ivy attended before leaving school the priest who was presenting the prizes handed her a bundle of six books – each a prize – and as she curtsied, as was the custom, he placed a crown of laurel leaves on her head. Unfortunately for her he didn't fit the crown square-on so she had great difficulty with her arms full of books and certificates balancing the crown whilst getting back to her seat – the crown slipping over one eye. Her friends, of course, thought this a huge joke.

*   *   *

Uncle Miller was looking forward to his first home leave and decided that instead of going by ship he would go via the Trans-Siberian Railway – across Siberia and Russia. He was heading for Bootle, Lancashire, where he would marry his fiancee, Emily. We missed him so much and were overjoyed when they returned and set up house in a large apartment in the Hongkew Fire Station. We often went for tea on Fridays – such a lovely way to start the weekend but missed the country walks we had enjoyed so much in the past. Things change and we now were beginning to be interested in mixed company house parties. We were growing up.

Dad Transferred to Hankow – Permanently ...

The Mill changed hands in 1930 – Dad was transferred to Hankow on a permanent basis – his Talbot sold. Mr Elliott left for India – Mrs Elliott, Eva and Frank moved into the attic flat. It was a lovely arrangement. Dad was happy that we were not entirely alone and Mrs Elliott was still as wonderful to us as ever. Also we had Eva, our pal, back with us again. Frank was busy working and he still thought we were a nuisance.

It was a big break and Dad must have done a lot of soul-searching before agreeing to this transfer. We had Dad's closest friends, Auntie Cameron, the Shotters, the Millers and the Brownriggs eager to help Mrs Elliott to keep an eye on us. They were so different in personality but wonderful people. Dad was extremely popular and they did as much as they could to make him feel comfortable in taking up this new post. It was a promotion. The Elliotts stayed with us until Mr Elliott could make arrangements for their transfer to India.

Before Dad was transferred, he gave Mary a crash course on bookkeeping and arranged for her to sign cheques and so keep the house accounts in order. Mary was 16. She sent Dad an account each month. One effort was a perfect example of innocently 'cooking-the-books'.

> *Cash:*
> 1 purse bought for Ivy $1.00
> 1 purse bought from Ivy $1.00
> Unaccountable $<u>12.00</u>
>   Total: $<u>14.00</u>

Apparently when Mary wanted to borrow the purse Ivy said 'No, I'll sell it to you'. Dad paid twice for the same purse! Mary's accounts were a source of enjoyment when summed up for light entertainment in Hankow.

Frank was a quiet person and had a lovely broad smile but one evening he wasn't smiling so broadly when he tried to explain to Cookboy that he was fed-up (pun!) of eating the same sort of meals. He said, 'What I would really like to have are some peas for a change ...' change he got, though he was possibly a bit short-changed. The next night, even Frank had to laugh when all he got for dinner was one large overflowing plate of peas! 'I makee spech for you' said Cookboy. 'You likee?' he continued. Cookboy was always so ready to please.

It was whilst Eva was staying with us that we decided to go swimming at the Hongkew Baths. Nellie had no idea how to swim. As we were changing into bathing costumes, Mary asked Nellie to wait until she was ready. Nellie was too excited and didn't listen. She followed Eva out of the changing rooms. Poor Mary, she was horror-stricken when she saw Nellie sitting on Eva's lap going down the shute. Swish-and-away they went and down, down, down and under – it seemed to go on forever. They were nearly drowned as Nellie, struggling for air, dragged Eva down. They were saved by a life-guard and severely told off. Quite rightly. Mary was shattered. Nellie in tears.

Dad was only able to visit us for short periods of time each year – instead of growing apart, absence certainly made the heart grow fonder and, with the trust and faith that Dad had in us, and we had in him too, a relationship developed between us all and, the 'four Stead sisters', as we were referred to, grew closer. The loyal bond which encircled us has survived nearly three-score years and ten. We must have been a handful for Dad, all growing up so fast, with our education to take care of – we living in Shanghai and he, in Hankow, he could not allow himself to show an outward appearance of worry, he dare not, it would have ruined not only his life, but, ours as well. He had to look forward and that taught us to look forward too. We learnt most of our important lessons through his exemplary ways. Sometimes he would tease us and say we were 'worse than a barrel load of monkeys' – he was fun and sometimes just a big kid himself.

We were thrilled when Jock Loutitt asked us to be bridesmaids at his wedding when his bride-to-be May arrived from Scotland. It was decided we could design our own dresses. We felt so grand and pretty on the big day. Mary and Ivy wore pale blue georgette ballerina length gowns and large brimmed blue light-weight transparent straw floppy hats. Bessie and Nellie, being younger, were decked out in white satin empire-style long dresses and wore flowers and silver braid head-dresses. It was a happy day for us all and we believed we carried out our duties well. The bride, a very sweet person soon settled down to a happy life out east. Jock and May made a delightful couple.

[A personal note from the chief bridesmaid: 'I've romanticised our dresses, but why should I admit I was a two-ton Tess in those days, and that my dress had a little long sleeved jacket to match – how matronly can you get. Apologies also to Bessie and Nellie, their white satin empires looked more like nighties by the time George Brownrigg saw them at Seymour Road.']

Mary and Eva being the same age, not only left school at the same time, they both took up secretarial courses and were now working and very grown-up, and out with the boys.

Mary wasn't keen on her first job particularly as the man she had to take dictation from had a peculiar accent which caused her a lot of difficulty. Her first letter addressed to a 'Mr Macdonough' she was told was wrong so when she asked how it was spelt and told, she said 'Oh, you mean Mr MacDonald'. A few days later she was trying to reach for a file, but being short couldn't quite reach it so she was helped, for which he received her thanks. It happened again a few days later, this time he came up very close behind her. When this happened several times Mary started to wonder why he always wanted 'that' file and then, he came far too close for her liking. Mary went home for her lunch and didn't go back again, so she never did receive her first week's pay packet. Mary was too shy to tell anyone about this experience at the time. She then got another job with the uncle of a world famous actor, who traded in wool. He also employed a young Chinese accountant. Mary had to help the young accountant deal with all the business matters whilst the boss spent his time at the Palace Hotel enjoying a leisurely lunch. Floundering around and not knowing what on earth she was doing she decided to try a third place to work. What a happy change – Mary worked in her new office for about six very pleasant years. In fact, until she was married – yes, to one of the boss's sons.

* * *

Occasionally our hot water system would break down. We would then avail ourselves of the services of the hot water shop just down the road. Like most shops in Shanghai, this was open-fronted – we knew they sold hot water because of the steam which enveloped the whole shop. The inhabitants were invisible. The tubs of steaming water were surrounded by a counter top. In fact their only evidence of service was vocal and an arm reaching out from the steam for your money or container. For ten cents they would deliver two large wooden buckets of hot water – one on each end of a bamboo pole carried over a shoulder. By the time the water arrived and was carried upstairs half of it had slopped out but it was still a lovely warm bath – except on one occasion when the plug hadn't been used and it all went down the drain. The shop would be boarded up at night with planks of wood and battened down for safety.

* * *

A garden party was held in the lovely home of our Russian neighbours in the house across the road to us. Mary was most impressed with the beautiful furniture they had, finely carved, gilded and upholstered in delicate silk brocade but, she was not one bit impressed with the refreshments. When asked what she would like to drink, Mary asked for a lemonade but got tonic water! On taking what she thought was an open-faced apricot jam sandwich, she found to her embarrassment it was caviar. Finally she thought she would have a black grape – on trying it she discovered that it was a black olive. It was just too much for Mary and inwardly she thought everything had gone off and was bad. She went hungry.

During the Easter holidays of 1931 Bessie and Nellie visited Dad in Hankow. Mary was working. Ivy having just left the Convent had started her secretarial course. The Elliotts had sailed for India. Bessie and Nellie travelled on Captain Rogers' flat-bottomed ship owned by Jardines – one of the big import/export companies. The journey took four days. On the way up the Yangtze river they stopped at several ports – Bessie and Nellie remember Nanking most vividly. They were taken by Captain Rogers and his Chief Officer Mr Drake to Sun Yat-sen's mausoleum. He had been the leader and inspiration of the republican revolution in China.

The mausoleum was built on the hillside out of the city. There were over 360 steps to climb which proved difficult for their escorts. However they made it with rests every twenty steps or so. It was the first time Bessie and Nellie had seen anything quite like this.

On the trip they were introduced to deck tennis. Playing the game posed no problem for Nellie – serving was something else and Bessie kept a deckhand pretty busy making new quoits to replace those propelled overboard.

Dad was so pleased to see them and took great delight in introducing them to his friends – he was like the cat who had eaten the canary – he was so proud. He had arranged for them to stay with the Eisenhowers, a German couple – friends of his – as he did not have his own accommodation in Hankow and lived with the Trends.

Bessie and Nellie played Mah Jong with the Eisenhowers and because of the rains at that time they also learnt to play a few more indoor games. They were introduced to Dad's quartet – Captain Rogers, Mr Drake, who had a way-down-there voice, Mr Trend and Dad, of course, at the piano – harmonising. Beautiful.

As the weather cleared Dad took them sight-seeing and to visit other friends. There was a magnificent race course – Dad had loved horses ever since his stay in Mexico. There he had had to learn to ride to be able to go on inspection trips – the alternative being a bicycle which was rather difficult on the hilly terrain. Although his riding days were over he enjoyed a 'flutter' – occasionally with a little success. There was a lot to do and their holiday just slipped by too quickly.

Hankow has quite a history – it was one of the original Treaty Ports. When Dad was there it was an important cotton manufacturing town, the climate being ideal for the manufacture of cotton cloth. Today there is a bridge – the only one across the Yangtze river – which amalgamates Wuchang, Hanyang and Hankow. Together they are known as Wuhan – the capital of Hupei Province – chosen as one of the major cities for industrial development under the First Five-Year Plan (under Communist rule). The annual rainfall is 50 inches (125cm), ten of which fall in June, when it becomes China's furnace.

Bessie and Nellie had lots to tell on their return to Shanghai – they were full of excitement.

Whilst up in Hankow the girls took the opportunity to ask Dad if they could take dancing lessons. As they were so enthusiastic Dad promised that he would write to Auntie to see if she could come up with some idea of where they could go.

Auntie, now living in a little terraced cottage in Avenue du Roi Albert had become friends with her American neighbours, the Greenbergs. Their daughter, Evelyn, was having dancing lessons at the Ann Summers School of Dancing. 'Yes' she wrote to Dad 'I know someone who knows someone ...' and soon Bessie and Nellie were looking forward to their first official lessons in the new year – after Ann resumed her classes following the Christmas break. Each year Ann Summers put on a revue called 'The Shanghai Follies of 193_?' in which all her pupils took part. She was rehearsing for one at the time, so put the girls on a waiting list, but meanwhile encouraged them to join in on the classes before the actual rehearsal started to see how they enjoyed them. They were going to be taught acrobatic and tap dancing.

Ann Summers – an American lady married to a Chinese gentleman – had two dance studios. One in Seymour Road and the second studio in her home in the country on the outskirts of the French Concession. During the warmer months lessons were held in the garden on an outdoor stage – it was a health studio. We were going to start our lessons at her Seymour Studio. This would be more convenient as Avenue du Roi Albert was the extension of Seymour Road into the French Concession thereby making it easy to see more of Auntie after lessons and somewhere to meet up with Mary and Ivy before going home together.

As soon as the Christmas holidays were over, Bessie and Nellie were ready – new pale blue dance tunics with bloomers to match had been made by the Kumping Road tailor (of course) and their patent-leather tap shoes with brightly shining toe-tips, and little jingles embedded in the heels, were tried on umpteen times with excitement and apprehension. Would they ever become dancers? They were set to change their home-made efforts of tap-tap-crash (bang!)-tap steps into rat-a-tat-tat machine gun staccato action. They were going to be Ruby Keelers – 'Yes' – and Eleanor Powells of the 20th Century!

They were keen pupils and it was an experience learning to dance properly and something they found came easily. They seemed to have a natural aptitude for tap and rhythm. As for acrobatics, with a lot of stretching exercises they became supple and able to do a cartwheel and the splits as well as the next pupil. (Secretly, Nellie fancied herself as a contortionist – she was alone on that thought!)

More wonderful news. Uncle Miller and Emily were expecting a baby in the Spring. So much excitement – out came the knitting needles and a terrific effort was made to knit something for the expected arrival. We weren't very successful but dear Amah struggled to put us right – we didn't do as much as we planned but were very proud of our accomplishments. Bessie showed her prowess with a crochet hook, a skill she inherited from Mother. She had a doll dressed in a crocheted jacket which she very successfully copied on a larger scale. This sort of work was beyond Amah who then took lessons from Bessie. Nellie unpicked as much as she knitted.

Early in 1932 Joan, their only child, was born and Dad was asked to be godfather – such an honour and taken very seriously by Dad. Joan was a beautiful baby and developed into a very intelligent child. Her only fault was being too precocious. She had marvellous reports from school – the ideal pupil – but she was a horror at home. When asked why this was so, her reply was that she 'couldn't be good all the time'. Fair enough.

'Annie' Caines of Dad's tennis parties had just returned from home leave and surprised us all by announcing he had become engaged just prior to his departure from England. His fiancee was Gwen, one of Monty Vincent's nieces, and she was due to arrive towards the end of August. They talked over wedding plans before

'Annie' left England and Gwen had agreed to his suggestion that he ask Rita Brownrigg to be the bridesmaid and Bessie and Nellie the flower girls – they didn't need a second invitation – they were thrilled to bits. Rita's mother, Doris, provided such particulars as size, colouring etc, which he was to pass on to Gwen so that she could decide on her colour scheme and the style of dresses. These would have to be made in Shanghai to ensure a perfect fit.

There was no air mail in those days so the girls had no option but to be patient.

*   *   *

Meanwhile the political situation in Shanghai was worsening with Japan again on the attack and rumours of serious trouble were rife. We began to worry about the wedding and Gwen's safe arrival but 'Annie' was full of optimism and told us not to worry as everything would work out as planned.

CHAPTER THREE

Seymour Road,
Bubbling Well

1932

Living with the Brownriggs

Japan launched an attack on the Chinese sectors of Shanghai which was repulsed after bitter fighting.

There were aeroplanes droning overhead and they woke us up. What was happening? Something was wrong – were we frightened? Or, were we excited at something new.

* * *

Dad was in Hankow – the telephone rang – it was Mr Brownrigg suggesting that we should spend a few days with him and his family in Seymour Road. It was difficult for him to go into detail over the telephone but he said he would feel much happier if we could pack a few clothes, and stay with them so that we could all be together. He would arrange everything. Telegrams were sent to and fro and Dad realised that obviously it was no longer safe for us to live in the Yangtzepoo area, for the present anyway. He was so grateful to the Brownriggs for their offer and for caring so much for his girls. Mary was advised to pack a box with the family silver, or whatever she thought Dad would want to keep safe, as well as a suitcase of clothes. History was in the making – a completely new life-style for us.

Bubbling Well was in the international settlement, west of the French Concession. Not only was it a new area to us, it was considered the 'West End' of Shanghai with fashionable shops, good roads, modern buildings, avenues of trees – it was regarded as one of the safest areas of Shanghai.

Mary and Ivy duly filled a box with Dad's favourite bits and pieces but before we were ready to leave the house Cookboy and Amah said they would only be able to stay and look after the house if it showed a British flag. Capt Basham had previously given Dad an old ship's flag and no doubt Cookboy knew about this. It was found and the Union Jack, a very large one, was draped from the upstairs verandah. It almost reached ground level.

As promised Mr Brownrigg arranged everything. Transport arrived and with Dad's box and our suitcase of clothes for a few days, we motored past Wayside along Broadway towards Bubbling Well. It was a slow nerve-racking journey as thousands of people had the same idea – to reach the safety of the settlement over Garden Bridge, as soon as possible. The planes still droned overhead.

Leaving the Union Jack flying over '32' was a good move, as it was later learned that several friends' houses had been broken into and vandalised by Japanese soldiers – photograph albums torn to shreds, golden syrup strewn over carpets, then covered with flour, the same treatment used for the inside of pianos.

The Brownriggs were made up of Mr and Mrs Brownrigg (Bert and Doris), Eddie, Rita and George and their ages matched ours beautifully. Mary and Ivy got on well with Rita – Eddie was big brother and George was Bessie's heart-throb.

We stayed with the Brownriggs for the duration of hostilities which lasted for approximately two months. We had moved from the 'one-copper–two-copper' sweet shop to the more sophisticated cafes – from our old cobbler and tailor to the beautiful clothes, lingerie and dress shops of Yates Road – better known as Petticoat Lane. However, we did later get in touch with the Kumping Road tailor – he was part of our family.

The Brownriggs lived in a tall house with two staircases; one in the front section, and one at the rear. The girls shared one bedroom, the boys another. They had overhead fans in all the rooms and at night Mrs Brownrigg pinned little blankets around our waists to keep our tummies warm. There was no need for a covering sheet as it was so hot whilst we were with them.

Mary and Rita were well established in their jobs – Ivy had just completed her secretarial course and had secured a job with *The China Press*, a daily newspaper. She was a raw beginner so the experience she gained there gave her a lot of confidence. At the weekends Rita would take Mary and Ivy shopping and show them her favourite haunts, including a theatre just around the corner. There they enjoyed a three dimension film first having donned eye-glasses with one red lens and one green lens. It was an action packed film with the audience dodging articles seemingly being thrown directly at them. There were shrieks, giggles and outright laughter. Unfortunately the glasses had to be returned on leaving the theatre.

Rita was fond of sketching so, as you can imagine, Mary was delighted to have a sparring partner. Not to be outdone Ivy also got involved – though while Mary and Rita were sketching live, she was still copying. Rita was also very self-confident which the girls found rather overwhelming. She was most attractive with a sort of Scandinavian complexion – outdoor girl type – a second Doris Day. She had beautiful skin and big blue eyes, she exuded health – in fact, she later went to America and easily obtained a position with Coca Cola because of her healthy looks.

George was a terrible tease and he enjoyed nothing more than taking the micky out of Bessie and Nellie. He teased them about their dresses. They only had two. The white satin empire clipsation which started life at the Loutitt's wedding – now shortened. The other was a dyed dress which was supposed to be a soft buttercup yellow but turned out to be jaundice-yellow – ghastly. They hated wearing them – the styles were dreadful but Mary said, 'you must' and that was IT. Other than their school uniforms, that was all they had during this period of evacuation and George never let them forget it. They dressed alike, usually the white on Saturday and yellow on Sunday – occasionally, to ring the changes, they would wear the yellow on Saturday and, the white on Sunday. Whatever they wore, it had to be the same otherwise that dreadful George would tease them that they were wearing each other's dress and that would have reduced their skimpy wardrobe to one dress each – shared!

We did not have too much to do with Eddie. He was out working most of the time, and when in, he kept to himself – too many girls around for his liking.

Although we did not know the Brownrigg children too well, perhaps because we attended different schools, and had different friends and interests, we got on extremely well together. The household at Seymour was a lively one. We entertained ourselves. The manually operated wind-up cabinet gramophone was the mainstay with a not-too-large collection of '78' records. If we wound the machine up tightly, it managed to play two records. We took turns in choosing our favourite tunes but somehow or other – we never did find out how – Bessie and Nellie were either (*a*) the record changer, or (*b*) the flip-side changer. We would cunningly manipulate to play the (*b*) flip-side – no winding up! We taught ourselves real ballroom dancing and this was done by waltzing around the room hugging a cushion – good idea! No toes to crunch. We put on mini shows. George was usually the star. He was a natural. Comic or imitator, he was excellent and his interpretation of 'The Dying Swan' has yet to be bettered. Bert and Doris were truly special. They must have been. They were very young at heart and joined in the fun and games as well. To cope with seven children – ages ranging from 11 to 18, always ready for a meal – more dancing, enthusiastically rehearsing new mini shows, playing games as well as the 78s, not forgetting George's practical jokes, must have taken some beating.

Fortunately Ann Summers' studio was in Seymour Road which made it so much easier for Bessie and Nellie to keep up their dancing lessons which they increasingly enjoyed.

Auntie was a favourite with everyone and although she was most concerned about the unrest prevailing, she was delighted that we were 'evacuees' and living with the Brownriggs – just down the road from her. She would invite us to tea – Rita as well. Auntie did not mind how many children turned up. She just loved us all. Even little Evelyn Greenberg would join in, so we got to know her quite well. We would show off our new dance routines to Auntie, much to her joy.

These tea times turned out to be special party occasions with rich home-made ice-cream – hot toasted currant buns oozing with butter and IXL strawberry jam (you got whole strawberries in this brand) and delicious cakes and whatever. No wonder we were 'sturdy' girls.

Being the youngest Bessie and Nellie were continually doing favours – such as fetching and carrying – they didn't mind except they were scared if they had to go upstairs at night to fetch this or that. George knew this. The second staircase at the rear of the house seemed to be made for George who was very quick to play a trick. On one particular night it was Nellie's turn to fetch something or other from upstairs and after all her efforts at trying to dodge out of this request there was no way other than to go up and get it and be done with it. George dashed out of the room, up the back stairs and hid just in the doorway of the room Nellie was to go into – he was going to frighten the wits out of her, he thought. She reluctantly crept up the front stairs in the dark, whistling to frighten away any intruder, and as she reached out to turn the light switch on in the bedroom where 'it' was, her hand ran down George's face. Not expecting this they simultaneously shrieked and George was down the front staircase like a streak of lightening – scared out of his wits.

*　*　*

Meanwhile the Japanese were really giving the Chinese a dreadful time on the outskirts and treating them ruthlessly. We were having a comparatively peaceful time in the settlement with our troops to protect us should that be necessary. We were unaware of the atrocities taking place and as far as the Brownrigg/Stead 'ménage' went – it was great.

War and Peace reigning at the same time, only a few miles apart, could and did exist.

*　*　*

When shopping in the street, George would stop to look up, knowing full well someone else would do the same – his practical joke was to see how many followers he had and then he would stroll away contentedly, leaving them to find out what they were supposed to be looking at, or 'wha-for you see', as the Chinese would ask.

George went through a phase of skiving school, his excuse being he was not feeling well. There was really nothing wrong with him and Mr Brownrigg knew this. On one particular morning when George came down to breakfast and said he could not go to school because he was not well, his father sent him upstairs to bed saying '… if you are feeling that ill you had better spend the day in bed'. George dutifully went up to bed, anything rather than go to school. Mr Brownrigg gave him a few minutes to settle and then asked Bessie and Nellie to go up with him carrying a tape measure. There was George in his pyjamas ready to spend a lazy morning reading in bed. Mr Brownrigg asked the girls to help him measure George, and got him to lay out full length on the bed whilst he did so. George was a bit bewildered and asked what the measurements were for. Mr Brownrigg quietly told him he needed them to give to the funeral directors when he died as a result of his illness. George was dressed in a flash and off to school.

* * *

Radio was taking off in a big way. The first station to get established was called RUOK, run by Americans. To fill airspace they ran request programmes and one could phone in and request any tune one wanted. The Brownriggs had a radio and so did Auntie. Once Bessie and Nellie returned home from school they were detailed to book 'radio time' until the bigger girls returned from work. This became a nightly occurrence when Rita would organise the phone-ins – requesting favourite tunes to be played for each of us. Even Auntie became intrigued with this 'radio time'. We would request special surprise tunes for her as well. Happy hours. There were six of us, including Auntie. One evening, after the fifth request, Rita coyly said she would leave it to the DJ to chose a record for her. He got his own back by announcing 'For Rita: "You! You're Driving Me Crazy"'.

In the evenings after supper we had family gatherings – when we would chat about the day's events and interesting things we had seen or done – it was a lovely way of rounding off a day. Much time was taken up excitedly talking about 'Annie' Caines's forthcoming wedding to Gwen who was expected to arrive mid August.

One evening 'Annie' phoned and said he had heard from Gwen. Because of the trouble the mail had been delayed – her letter arrived after she had set sail. She would, she hoped, arrive soon after the end of August, slightly later than planned. He would be visiting us to tell us more of the details. Gwen realised that time was getting short – she had sent full instructions and hoped Doris would not mind getting the dresses made. She would have asked her aunt Helen, Monty's wife, but as they lived rather a distance from the shops and she hadn't been too well, it would be a great help if Doris could help.

'Annie' arrived with copious notes. Rita was to wear a soft green organdie dress with a full skirt, a fitted bodice and short puffed sleeves. She would wear a posy of flowers in her hair. Bessie and Nellie – the flower girls – were to wear Edwardian crinoline dresses. The high bodice was plain, with short sleeves, and the skirt made up of row upon row of tiny frills worn over a stiffened petticoat. Organdie was also chosen as not only would it match the bridesmaid's dress but it would have enough body to stick out rather than to flop. Bessie's dress was to be pink and Nellie's blue. The dresses would be calf-length and, to look authentic, worn with white pantaloons which would have rows of frills from the knee down. To complete the picture they would wear bonnets to match and carry baskets of flowers to tone with the dresses.

There were all sorts of other instructions but the girls weren't listening – they were trying to visualise the total picture and letting their imaginations run riot. Doris had a great time collecting samples of colours etc, for the dresses. Once Saturday arrived they were off to Yates Road to Doris's favourite tailor, measured up, and then marched off to the shoe shop where Rita ordered shoes to match her dress and Bessie and Nellie were fitted out with black patent flat-heeled pumps.

Gwen arrived as things were getting back to normal. She stayed with her aunt and uncle until the great day and was very pleased to meet everyone, not forgetting her attendants – the outfits were ready to be worn and looked a dream.

Things were beginning to settle down and get back to normal; 'Business as usual' sort of thing. Dad was much relieved that we had been safely ensconced with Bert and Doris and more than grateful for their tremendous hospitality and the responsibility they took upon themselves to look after us – not knowing how long the unsettled situation would last.

Dad was becoming increasingly concerned about our welfare. He realised that Yangtzepoo was no longer the right area for us and wanted us to be nearer town. He would return as soon as possible, find us alternative accommodation and close up '32'. He felt that a flat with neighbours around would be more ideal.

CHAPTER FOUR

Embankment Building

1932–1937

The furnace-like heat of the summer continued but the heat of the hostilities was in the process of being quashed. Soon law and order would be restored. Dad had been in touch with E.D. Sassoon & Co. Ltd in Shanghai – associates of Arnhold & Co. Ltd for whom he worked in Hankow – and it was through them that he learnt of a new apartment building in town – the Embankment – which was nearing completion. Dad was well up-dated on the situation. At this time Ivy had left *The China Press* and joined the property department of Sassoons. What could be better – a member of the family on the spot, so to speak. As delightful as it was staying with the Brownriggs, we knew that our stay with them couldn't go on forever. Living in town would be so much more convenient for us. The new apartment building was near to Ivy's office and as Mary was working for The Bus Company which had its offices out of town, in the opposite direction to Yangtzepoo, her journey would be halved.

The Embankment was a new construction, very modern, with all the latest conveniences, including central heating – we had only been used to fires – and there was also a swimming pool. There were four entrances, each with a large foyer and lifts. The building was situated on the north side of the Soochow creek bordering the settlement fairly near North Railway Station in Chapei – not that it mattered an iota to us at that time as we never had occasion to travel by train.

Yes, the Embankment was a good choice. Dad agreed, and finalised his plans to visit us to get us settled in. After much deliberation we settled on apartment 305 on the third floor, facing the creek. It was nice and airy. The flat consisted of a lounge/dining room, bedrooms, kitchen and bathroom. Servants' quarters were on another floor.

Dad was relieved that we would be nearer town and now decided it was time Bessie and Nellie changed school from The Holy Family Convent to The Public School for Girls on Yu Yuen Road, Bubbling Well. There was an excellent bus service available, and a canteen at school which made life easier. Our circle of friends widened and no longer were the little ones living sheltered lives hiding behind the nuns' habits.

*   *   *

The front of the building facing the Soochow creek was designed rather like a ship, insomuch as the verandahs had a concrete base a foot high followed by horizontal railings up to a safe height. Sitting on the verandah with one's feet resting on a railing one could imagine you were actually travelling up the creek to Soochow 'more far' – a local Chinese expression which means a long way away. Enormous barges plied up and down the creek in what seemed to us an endless journey conveying cargo to and from Shanghai. We loved watching all the activity. The barges were fascinating but it was the sampans that charmed us. Whole families lived on the boats. We never ceased to be amazed that the little children on them did not topple into the water. Grandmothers, grandfathers, aunts, uncles, mums and dads, brothers, sisters and cousins lived *en famile*. They all had their role to play. Women cooked, mended, and looked after the children who also had their specific duties. The babies were more often than not looked after by grandmother. Their everyday needs were purchased from sampan vendors. They had their entire possessions with them – chickens, dogs, cats, and their much loved birds in tiny individual cages. They worked hard but were happy and content.

The barges and sampans were propelled by a pole one end of which was shaped like a blade – resembling an oar. This rested on a pin and was steadied by a rope attached to the side of the barge. The oar slanted from one side to the middle back of the barge and propelled the boat by leverage. The sampans could be manipulated by a single person – man or woman. On the other hand, the barges – depending on the weight of the cargo – needed a team of two, three or more men all working on the one oar. This backbreaking job was accompanied by their own special boat song which provided the rhythm to help them along. It was freezing cold in the winter and exhaustingly hot in the summer – no shelter from the elements. Today, the barges are linked together and towed by a launch forming a barge-train.

Opposite us on the other side of the creek was a house which only came to life at night. In the summer Nellie used to watch the ladies, all beautifully dressed, cool themselves sitting on the riverside – or rather creekside – wall. Nellie loved day-dreaming that she would one day grow up to be like them – glamourous! She loved the pretty long dresses they wore and, being really imaginative, went so far as to imagine she could 'smell' the perfume they were using. It was years later that Nellie was educated to the fact that the house on the opposite side of the creek was a brothel.

* * *

'Annie' and Gwen's wedding having been delayed worked out very well for us. Dad had come down to Shanghai to help us move to the Embankment and so was able to attend the wedding. The bride was beautiful in her ivory satin and lace frock and carried a bouquet of arum lilies. The bridal party looked gorgeous. Gwen was a lovely girl full of *je ne sais quoi* and a great asset to the community. Everyone had a terrific time. The bride had a lovely surprise for her attendants – the gift of an engraved gold lucky bean and gold chain as a memento. They were overwhelmed.

We were soon settled into our new home and it was great having Dad with us – if for only a few days. But, there was one thing missing. Jessie. We had to find a nice home for her as she would have hated to live in the confines of a flat – she had always lived in a house with a garden and wandered around freely. Fortunately our Russian neighbours – the caviar and black olive (apricot jam and black grape) lady knew Jessie well and offered to take care of her for us. Jessie was ageing a bit and no doubt a more restful life would suit her better as we were a bit boisterous for her. So all ended well and we were relieved – she did not have to move out of her beloved area.

By living with the Brownriggs we had caught radio mania. Most of our friends had a radio, the big question was how to persuade Dad that we just couldn't live without one. Mary had a brainwave. She hired a radio and arranged to have it installed on one of the days Dad was to be out with friends. She also arranged for a request to be played for him. When Dad got home and saw the radio his sixth sense told him that we were going to pressure him to let us have one. He made it quite clear the answer was 'No'. Mary's timing was perfect. Suddenly it was announced 'specially for Walter Stead "Moonlight and Roses"' his favourite song. He was sold. The fact this could all take place with just a coil of wire beneath the table – the radio was only on hire – amazed him and we got our radio.

Ivy was intrigued by her job and enjoyed meeting prospective tenants and getting to know them on a more personal basis while coming and going in the new building. It had the usual teething problems. One of the letting points was that the building was served by an artesian well which produced pure icy cold drinking water – something very new to Shanghai. Unfortunately the same water was used for the swimming pool. It was freezing and not until many of the tenants had complained was it decided the water had to be heated. From then on you couldn't keep us out of it; it was such a delightful and economical way of entertaining friends.

Rita was a constant visitor and we enjoyed her company. Mary and Rita's art work continued but Ivy was getting bored with her copy work. Mary and Ivy were aware of her good looks but had not yet figured out a way of competing – it must have seemed impossible at that time.

Captain Basham and Dad originally met on one of the Jardine river boats on the Shanghai/Hankow run. It was he who had provided the Union Jack which graced 32 Pingliang Road during the recent troubles and saved it from being ransacked. He and his wife also moved into the Embankment soon after we did, and we spent many an enjoyable evening with Mrs Basham. She was another Mah Jong fan and, as the story goes, once held a session in company with our friends Mrs Shotter, Mrs Cheetham and a Mrs Strike. Who won remains a mystery but it sounded like a bang-up party!

As we mentioned earlier, the Chinese are great gamblers and at long last they had established a State Lottery. Tickets cost Chinese $10 but were divided into ten equal parts and sold for $1 each. Monty Vincent's wife, Helen, whom he married on his first UK leave, had tried so hard to get him to buy her a ticket for $10 but he argued that the deal was crooked! Her last try was before he went to work on the day of the draw. He gave in and said 'yes' he would buy her a ticket but, he only purchased a $1 chance. The ticket won first prize! The money received was one tenth of $400,000, or $40,000. Poor Monty – did he ever get a tongue-lashing from Helen. Even so, with

With Compliments

of

THE STEAD SISTERS

their winnings he was able to take early retirement. How he was envied.

Dad's Dancing Girls

Ann Summers was very ambitious and had great ideas. She had just returned from a holiday/refresher course in the USA and was armed with material from Broadway shows. She was planning her next revue when she saw a photograph in the newspaper of Bessie and Nellie in their gorgeous Victorian flower girl dresses with bonnets to match. Ann asked Gwen Caines for permission to make up a dance routine using the Victorian ladies in her forthcoming show. Gwen readily agreed – in fact, she was most complimented.

The 'Follies' was to become a popular slot on the calendar and ran for three days each year to packed houses at the Lyceum Theatre on Rue Cardinal Mercier, French Concession. Bessie and Nellie's 'Let's Pretend' days were over ... this was for REAL!

As this revue – called 'The Shanghai Follies of 1933' was going to be something more spectacular than her usual ones, Ann decided to advertise it by having a movie made of some of the dance routines. The movie was to be shown at the cinema a couple of weeks before the opening night. Bessie and Nellie were very enthusiastic and did a lot of practicing so it did not take them too long to become a 'pair' – synchronising their tap dancing steps came easily to them. They looked like twins at that time – the same height, sisterly resemblance – although Bessie was more tubby than Nellie. They were delighted to be chosen for quite a few 'numbers'.

To encourage her pupils to do their best Ann ran a competition. Each member in the audience could nominate their favourite dancer – the dancer with the most votes won a years' free tuition. We worked hard and did our best and had our fans. Someone voted 'Nearly Stead' as a favourite. That was a tremendous morale booster and to this day Nellie wonders who her fan was and why she was singled out as his/her favourite.

When the show did open, Bessie and Nellie's first duet was an acrobatic/tap dance wearing black velvet tunic shorts with white satin blouses with voluminous sleeves and a big black bow at the neck. The first number involved the whole school. Bessie and Nellie were to come on again for the second number whilst a change of scenery was taking place. They danced in front of the curtains – with a black backdrop and a spotlight following them around the stage. It was very effective. As they had only just come off stage, they had a very quick change to make and the assistance of a rather excitable lady by name of Mrs Jackson got Nellie's small costume mixed up with Bessie's rather larger one – which didn't help – no time to change. They looked Little & Large – but the show had to go on.

Their second dance was a waltz tap, dressed in the early Victorian bridesmaids dresses worn at the Caines' wedding. Quite a number of the audience had seen the movie at the cinema and, as Nellie and Bessie appeared on stage, they were given an ovation – something that had never happened before. This rather threw them and for one moment Bessie thought Nellie would take stage-fright – she recovered with a bit of a push from Bessie who was second on.

Some of Dad's friends who had seen the movie advertising the Follies managed to borrow a copy of the film and Capt Rogers – of the Yangtze run – offered to take it up to Hankow for Dad to see, as a surprise. The Trends, who Dad lived with, arranged a special supper party – with a difference – to which Capt Rogers and Mr Drake were also invited. The invitation included a movie first, to be followed by supper. The guests met at the cinema and thoroughly enjoyed the movie. When the audience left the cinema at the end of the movie the Trends had arranged for their party to remain in their seats as there was, they said 'more to come'. The auditorium was now reserved for a private viewing of the well advertised 'Shanghai Follies of 1933'. Dad was so surprised and thrilled and needless to say emotional when he saw his little ones on the movies.

Dad, always pleased with the girls' progress, encouraged them further in their activities. This time he had a special tap dancing sheet made at the mill. It was made out of highly polished strips of wood held together underneath with a strip of leather – to prevent it from slipping. It resounded sharp and clear when tapped on – a wonderful sound. Dad was delighted that at long last some theatrical talent was beginning to show through as he himself liked nothing more than taking part in a show. It brought back happy memories of when he and Mother performed in the Minstrel Shows to raise money for the war effort whilst in Peru in 1916.

Bessie and Nellie were exhilarated and thoroughly enjoyed their dancing days, more so, the spotlight shining on them. The exciting hustle and bustle of having costumes made, rehearsing for the big night never tired them.

Teenagers – Bessie and Nellie

Like Nellie, Bessie felt liberated on changing to the Public School for Girls – not that the nuns kept them down, they just had a more sobering effect on them. Their uniforms were now gym slips instead of sailor suits – that was an innovation. There were more sports in the curriculum and generally a sense of freedom – the fact that they were now old enough to travel without an escort of big sisters may have contributed to this.

The teachers were less reserved – they seemed to come down to their level. The one in charge of Bessie's form would invite five or six different pupils at a time to a super tea. Miss Munday, the French mistress, was rather eccentric which fascinated all the girls and unwittingly aided them with their lessons.

Bessie was a little more conscientious than Nellie in her lessons – her favourite being maths in any form. She loved solving problems, so she took in her stride the rapidity of the emptying tanks of various capacities but don't ask her about them today. She was not a good speller. She realised her inadequacy when she started work in an office – turned to crossword puzzles for help as well as a much used dictionary. Somehow she got by.

There were more singing lessons with end-of-term shows. Bessie was involved in the production of *A Midsummer Night's Dream*, being given the part of Mustard Seed. All she had to say was 'I do' or, 'Me too' – or, something along these lines. She was chosen because she could dance – however, she was very unfairly partnered with Vera Patershinski – a very petit fairy. There was only one bit of drama as far as Bessie was concerned – she lost her costume (left it on the bus) the night of the dress rehearsal. What to do! She went off to the market and bought some yellow silk lining material and set to at home to make another. The costume was simple enough to make as it was a cape of petals sewn together rather like a gored skirt with slits each side for the arms to come through. Fortunately she still had her cap.

*   *   *

Nellie became friends with Peggy Brewer of the Embankment Building, Joan, Nina Hodges, Valia Vachinsky and Geegee Wootton. They all went to the same Public School although they were in different classes – it was the bus that brought them together. They were very compatible and give or take a couple of years, they were of the same age – five healthy fun-loving girls. They did everything together. They went on picnics, walks, to the parks, ballroom danced together, went to the movies and – in between times – studied. Homework was more often than not done on the lid of a suitcase on the bus going to school – or, depending on the subject, they did each other's work – not very responsible young people. They thought nothing of disturbing the peace of the tenants of the building by roller-skating, all starting together, at the same time on different floors of the six-storey building, madly roller-skating the full length of the corridor, dashing up the stairwell to another floor and continuing to race. This manoeuvre was planned to almost clockwork precision – the object was not to be caught by angry tenants, or, better still, not to be found out – they never were. The din was deafening. It was most important that Nellie was never caught because Ivy worked for the Property Department! Although it was thrilling the thought of the consequences if found out was scary.

On quieter days – usually on a Saturday morning – with no gardens to play in, no parents around as they all seemed to be out working, they would meet and swop clothes. The tall girls wearing the short girls clothes, and, likewise, the plump girls wearing the thin girls clothes. They looked a dreadful sight but giggled on. Then they would proceed to 'visit'. Doors were opened by houseboys and to get an 'in' to the apartment they would pretend they had been invited to a cuppa by 'Phsycee Gardener' – obviously a made-up name. Then they would ask the 'boy' if they could go into the apartment and wait for her. Perhaps the houseboy recognized them, who knows, but he politely let them in and did his bit of entertaining for his lady of the house (whilst she was out) and offer them food and beverages ... this was great fun.

Melody in the park. Nellie and her pals decided their annual picnic would be held at Jessfield Park. It was Easter. They dressed in their most fashionable clothes and, believe it or not, for a picnic – sported hats! Being the time of year for Easter bonnets, they decided they should really look 'pish-posh'. It was a lovely day, they looked and felt great and were quite sure other people thought they looked great too – they were as elegant as they could make themselves. (There was definite potential in their appearance!) As they sauntered around the park they could hear people singing but the never-to-be-forgotten melody Nellie remembers was from an open window of an apartment overlooking the park. It came from an unseen Chinese boy, strumming his banjo, singing with all his heart – 'The Object Of My Affections' ... sadly the melody faded into the distance as they passed by.

Though like her friends Nellie was harum-scarum when out with the group, she did know how to behave and was a good stick really. No one girl could be blamed for the things they got up to – they were equally of the same mind – hell-bent on enjoying themselves with no destructive thought towards mankind. Bessie envied Nellie and her pals.

Bessie and Nellie's Holiday at Wei-Hai-Wei

They were invited to accompany Auntie Cameron, and her now constant companion Mr Chandler, on holiday. They were going to Wei-hai-wei famous for its sulphur springs. It meant a sea voyage which excited the girls – this one would take three days and having a cabin to themselves they felt very grown up. Bessie was about eleven at the time and was so eager to get going that she packed her suitcase months ahead of time, then kept delving into it. As was inevitable, she left without her bathing suit. At that age she was very conscious of having to keep her top half covered but the water being tempting she went in with only knickers on. The next day a very old-fashioned suit was purchased for her in the market – it came down to her knees but that was the least of her worries. She got the message.

Madge Paterson, a friend of Auntie's, ran the hotel in which they stayed. She was kindness itself and took them on several tours. One was to a convent where they watched little girls, younger than themselves, embroidering table cloths in coloured cross-stitch. We still have some of this work – which must be every bit of 65 years young – tucked away is our linen cupboards.

They also had a day over on the island of Wei-hai-wei, which was then a British naval base, and were shown around one of the ships. Most of the shops on the island catered for the navy and one outfitters with a branch on Broadway, Shanghai, was called 'Sin-Jelly-Belly & Co.' – the name no doubt coming from a sailor-comedian!

On the return journey they ran into a typhoon for which the China Seas are well-known. Nellie, not being a good sailor at that time, was very ill. Auntie just could not make her comfy – she tried her in two different bunks, one running fore and aft, and the other port and starboard. She was well wedged in with pillows and although she couldn't move her tummy seemed to follow the ship as it rolled, lurched, pitched and shuddered, with sickening effects. It was with relief that they came ashore in Shanghai – Nellie a pale, pathetic figure with a wan smile when she greeted Mary and Ivy.

Ivy's Holiday

Madge and her husband, Willy, moved into the Embankment and after hearing about the super holiday the girls had enjoyed in Wei-hai-wei, Ivy decided that this was where she would go for her holiday. Though the island was restored to China, it was still a very popular spot. To increase accommodation the hotel had a row of rooms, each with private bath, built of bamboo and situated at the end of the garden. Ivy was delighted to have one of these rooms until it came to bath night. The tub, standard size, was portable and made of tin. It was filled with hot water from the springs and all went well until Ivy wanted to get out. From a prone position this is an almost impossible feat – the weight having to be evenly distributed otherwise one ended up like a beached whale.

After supper, a group of us would congregate on the beach and chatter while dangling our feet in the water. If it was a moonlit night you could see the light reflected in drops of water – we later learnt that this was phosphorescence. It was very pretty to watch and fun to try and make new patterns. All in all a most enjoyable holiday.

* * *

On Madge's return to Shanghai she became quite a buddy. She saw how Mary and Ivy were struggling with a weight problem and helped to work out a diet for them. With perseverance they both lost weight – not overnight – but enough to make a difference in their lives.

Amongst other things, Madge was very active in the Mission to Seamen and would hostess dances for the navy lads. As expected we were roped in and spent many an enjoyable evening dancing. Carrie and Jean Todd also attended – we hadn't seen them since our young days at St Joseph's Convent – and it was good to renew our friendship.

With all the encouragement and activity Mary and Ivy now paid more attention to their looks and Mary went so far as to have her hair permed. A most uncomfortable experience in those days. After the curlers were in, clamps were attached and connected to the electrical current then used. The whole affair was like a ton weight on the head and lasted about half an hour. However, it was worth it – the transformation was fantastic and it wasn't long before Ivy followed suit.

Mary also invested in curling tongs which Bessie used to try and get a curl in her dreadfully straight hair. It wasn't very successful and she was glad when she found a Chinese hairdresser nearby who excelled in Marcel waving (also using tongs) for a small fee. Bessie had a daily appointment when appearing in an Ann Summer revue which was rather hard on her hair but pride will out.

Ivy decided to dye her eyelashes with a kit she found on sale at a Japanese shop just down the road. Her friends were using mascara but, not being waterproof in those days, more often than not Ivy had dark circles under her eyes. The dye job was the answer and saved a lot of embarrassment.

* * *

Bessie and Nellie had appendix operations at the Great Western Hospital, Bubbling Well, whilst living in the Embankment – not at the same time of course. It was in the days before intensive care units were used for the recovery patients. Mary spent most of the day at the hospital when Nellie was operated on and kept an eye on her until she had completely come round and all was well.

There was a patriotic film – 'Cavalcade' – being shown at this time: it was a tremendous movie and took Shanghai by storm. Bessie was the last of the girls to see it – it was a Saturday – and she promised to visit Nellie at the hospital after the matinée performance. The film overwhelmed her by the wonderful story and acting – ending with the entire audience standing to the British National Anthem – an almost unheard of thing in Shanghai – especially for a film. It was getting late and to save time Bessie took a rickshaw to the hospital from the bus terminus. She met Mary and Ivy half way and had a chat. Ivy asked Bessie how she had enjoyed the film at which Bessie promptly burst out crying saying it was 'wonderful'.

Although the visit to Nellie was short that day she was full of chat, as usual, and gave full gory details of how she was allowed to see the appendix they had taken from her – comparing hers with another patient's – some competition!

When Bessie had her operation it was Ivy's turn to watch over the patient. She kept coming round and trying to fight her way clear of the bedding and then go off again. This happened several times until she was finally awake, when we found that her bandage had been pinned to her!

*   *   *

Bessie met Donald Gaffney at a party given by one of her classmates. They used to go to quite a few parties, borrowing Mary's and Ivy's dresses to do so. She thought she was now grown up, but how can one be grown up when stink-bombs were being let off. Donald caused Bessie to think spooks inhabited the corridor between the lounge and the bedrooms. The corridor was rather a long one, dimly lit, and the telephone hung on the wall outside the bedrooms. They had been to see 'Frankenstein' at the Capitol Theatre. That particular evening Bessie happened to be the first home. She had not thought much of the film until Donald phoned about half a hour after getting home. He asked her if she could still see the face of Frankenstein. That did it. She was so terrified she refused to let him off the phone until someone came home – two and a half hours later – thus creating a record in the Stead family for the longest telephone call. From then on she never walked with confidence along that corridor. Not long after that Donald was sent 'home' to school and she lost contact with him – the last she heard he had sent a cable to his father for money, having successfully got through Dunkirk.

Ivy's Holiday with the Sands

Jean and Carrie's parents had a holiday home in Pei-tai-ho where they spent a few months each summer. To cut a long story short Ivy was delighted to be invited to spend a holiday with them – thrilling. She travelled by ship to Chinwangtao and then by train to her destination. The girls shared a large bedroom; spent hours on the beach and going for fairly long walks. It was a great way to relax and recuperate after a hectic year of hard work.

* * *

Before any of us started working we went through the stage of $1 per week pocket money. We had passes on the trams or buses so were able to spend our money on luxuries. For sixty cents we could enjoy a movie at the Grand Theatre – downstairs with the crowd. During the interval we could purchase refreshments but best of all with our ticket we could go in at any time and remain to see the movie a second time if we wanted to. This was super on a hot day when the air conditioning would be going full blast. The Grand Theatre was very modern – we have yet to see a theatre to equal it – with a fountain in the huge foyer and two wide staircases, one on each side, which curved up to the first floor. It was beautifully decorated and the carpeting was wall to wall. The seats were padded and were designed so that they moved back to let someone pass without the viewer having to stand. It cost $1 upstairs at matinée times but we only went up there when boyfriends paid.

With the balance of our forty cents we could go to the chocolate shop for a bun and a cup of tea. When we were broke we went to the depression seats at the Capitol Theatre almost opposite our apartment. This treat cost thirty cents but we could only sit in one of the first five rows. It reminded us of the first 'talkie' we saw – again we suffered stiff necks, but it was worth it.

* * *

Due to various reasons Bessie and Nellie played a low profile in 'The Shanghai Follies of 1934' – both had undergone appendix operations and were taking it easy. They were so disappointed. However, they continued to enjoy their lessons but on a less strenuous basis and on the big night they danced in group numbers only, no 'solos' – neither of them were up to it.

The following year Ann visited Broadway, USA, and on her return she was at bursting point with new ideas. Her stage designer was brilliant and the costumes were out of this world. Ann certainly had the knack of putting on a show and we were all keen to get started on the new themes.

The Follies of '35 was something quite different for Bessie and Nellie. They were more into acrobatics and were in a really beautiful dance routine – 'The Song of India' – a harem scene, as well as a very active Russian tap and acrobatic dance in which they did one of their solos as part of the Russian scene. They were both, once again, well away! Bessie and Nellie were getting to be known as 'the sisters' and headed the bill.

Ann was unable to put on a '36 Follies as she herself had not been too well and had to take it easy – so we continued with our lessons, but no show.

Enjoying the Pool

Bessie took up swimming seriously. She bought a book written by Johnny Weismuller and spent hours in the pool downstairs practicing the crawl as given in his book – the correct angle of the arms, leg kicks, breathing, turns. Now that the pool in the building was heated it was open all the year round. She would have the odd ear-ache as a result of the swimming but it did not deter her. She loved it.

Although inviting, the pool also looked forbidding to Nellie – her only swimming effort to date was paddling knee-high by the sea at Wei-hai-wei. Mary encouraged her down the steps at the shallow end of the pool. 'Push yourself off and follow me,' said Mary, as she made one big curve at the breast stroke. 'Oops' – it didn't work. After relentless tries with Mary supporting Nellie's chin above water, wearing 'wings', Nellie did manage to become a swimmer – quite a fast dog-paddler. However, she persevered jumping first off the bottom step and progressing up the steps, one at a time, until she made it from the top step on her own. From then on we couldn't keep her out of the pool.

Next lesson, learning to dive – quite another thing and Nellie was taken over by Ivy. It was a whole Saturday afternoon's persuasion – Nellie found it most difficult to put her hands above her head, bend forward, and 'LET GO - flop in the water' said Ivy. 'Nothing to it' Ivy continued.

Giving serious thought to Ivy's words 'Flop in the water? – no nose to hold – head first'... 'No way' Nellie said anxiously. After all, she thought, if she dropped or flopped in and touched the bottom of the pool – how would she ever get up if she was still pointing down? 'Thick' – Ivy gave up! They were hardly on speaking terms by this time, and all promises of a treat or a prize for effort, abandoned. Much later, when Nellie qualified by age to join the Rowing Glub and had paid her subscription of $20, she made her first dive. No way was she going to lose face (big thing out east) by

being a member of a swimming club and not be able to dive? So ...
with her hands above her head – she remembered – bend slightly
... head first she went! Easy peasy. Now, a swimmer and an off-the-
board diver – she was able to compete in races at the club's weekly
mini gala. Not a winner but an enthusiastic competitor.

Nellie's strength in swimming was the back-stroke and it still is
to this day. One day as she was practicing for the races she gave
herself a forceful push from the side of the pool and as her arm went
over her shoulder and hit the water – someone had thrown a
lifebelt in the pool to jump into. It was one of those heavy life-saving
lifebelts. Nellie caught the full force of the lifebelt between her thumb
and first finger and dislocated her thumb. She was hauled out of the
pool. Luckily Mary was swimming that day. She hurriedly got
Nellie dressed, hailed a rickshaw which took them down the road
to the General Hospital run by nuns. The doctor looked at her hand
and took hold of her thumb and gave it a hefty tug.

Still loving the attention that bandages brought she was quite
happy to go around with her hand resting in a sling for a day or two.
What was more exciting and drew sympathetic attention to herself
was when she made the effort to write yet another weekly letter to
Dad using her left hand – saying, as usual, ' ... hope you are in the
best of health as we are here ...'!

* * *

Amah befriended the sweetest little kitten up in the servants'
quarters and, well – Nellie fell for it – boy, or girl, it did not matter,
'she' was named Tilly. A most affectionate tabby who was no
trouble at all. She ate, and slept and purred most of the time. We
had to leave her in Amah's care when we were evacuated at the time
of the Sino-Japanese hostilities. When we returned to Shanghai and
had to move – once again – Amah asked if she could keep Tilly. We
were happy to leave her in Amah's good hands.

* * *

Ever since Yangtzepoo days and Dad's well kept tennis courts, Ivy
had been keen on the game. She joined the Cathedral tennis club
on the racecourse and the sister badminton club for winter activities.
Helen Gilmour was also a member. They were allowed out on a
Saturday night with 'boys' but not singly – the only way they
could accept an invitation was if it was a foursome. This led to some

peculiar evenings. They were asked to a dinner dance at the Canidrome – Shanghai's famous dog racing course. The dinner was superb, the dancing lively and they stayed away from the dogs. The highlight of the evening was going for a row across an artificial lake in the grounds. Helen and her current boyfriend in one boat and Ivy and blind date in the other. The blind date had no idea how to row and Ivy got more and more drenched as the evening went on.

Soon after that, at a formal dinner dance hosted by Mary's in-laws-to-be, Ivy met Jimmy Forbes. He was super. He had a keen sense of humour and was a beautiful dancer (two important attributes, or so she thought) and life was just a bowl of cherries. He was also a keen tennis player, representing Shanghai in many a match. Ivy was smitten. Watching Jimmy play was always a treat and with a little coaching Ivy's game began to improve. Being a Scot he then prompted Ivy to join the Reel Club and she made a valiant effort to master the eightsome reel, amongst other Scottish dances. It was a laugh a minute though Ivy must have had two left feet as the romance soon began to fade.

Ivy a keen knitter, was busily knitting a cable-stitched white sweater for Jimmy's birthday. Uncle Miller and family came for the day and Joan, possibly bored, threw Ivy's ball of wool over the verandah railings. Instant commotion. Nellie was sent flying down to the road to guard the wool while Ivy frantically wound it up. In the meantime, Joan, trying to see the result of her throw, stuck her head through the railings and got it caught. She then panicked and it was not easy to free her. The sweater ended up being various shades of white and had to be washed. Ivy laid it out on a towel on a table on the verandah and, when testing it to see if it was dry, found Tilly, Nellie's cat, had done a pee and the sweater had to be re-washed. Jimmy loved the sweater and was thrilled that Ivy had taken so much trouble. He never knew about Tilly!

Dad was very upset when he heard about Joan's head getting stuck, he had never liked the railings as they reminded him of an incident in Peru. When he went out on the verandah one morning he froze with horror when he saw Ivy sitting nonchalantly swinging her legs and singing to herself, on the other side of the railings on a very narrow ledge with a big drop beneath her. Dad thought quickly, and decided it best not to make a sound or call out, as this would have caused Ivy to turn round and she would have fallen off the ledge. Instead he crept up to her quietly, and leaning over the railings, grabbed her and pulled her up to safety. He never discovered how she got there but he made sure it never happened again.

Ivy then met Pauline and Leslie Smith – they were new tenants in the building. Ivy met them through the office. They invited her to many a party when Leslie had to entertain out-of-town clients. She got to know some lovely people but, unfortunately, they were always 'passing through'.

* * *

We enjoyed visiting the servants' quarters. They seemed to live with a tidy muddle of possessions around them. They, of course, had homes of their own in different areas of China – family homes – and when we enquired of them where they came from, the answer was usually the same, 'me stay Soochow more-far'. The tiny accommodation they had on the premises was their current home – in some cases lasting for years – and they have to be admired. How they managed to keep these little quarters – no more than say 10 Feet (3m) square – so neat, clean and welcoming. The main piece of furniture was a bed which also acted as a sitting area – a table and a chair – a shelf for their pots and pans. Masses of personal photographs – jars for joss sticks and incense. They would gently shoo us away if we became too boisterous but this did not often happen as the Chinese, as we have mentioned earlier, love people and noise. Could this be the reason why we see them smiling so easily? On reflection we rarely saw a depressed or disgruntled Chinese.

Shopping

Nanking Road was world famous. It was the main artery from the down town business area out to the West End. The shop windows bulged with goodies – many imported – though local handicrafts were much in evidence. Some of the well remembered foreign owned shops were Hall & Holtz, Lane Crawford & Co., Kelly and Walsh, Mappin & Webb, Watsons – the chemist where Dad bought the sulphur for our once a year inner beauty treatment.

Further west were shops which sold exquisite jewellery, silks, embroidery, ivories, jade and the like. These shops displayed enormous long banners with Chinese characters sewn on them advertising their name and their wares. To avoid them being blown away they had holes in them placed in an orderly fashion so that they hung resplendently. We were unable to read the characters but we soon learnt which banner belonged to which shop so knew where to go as if we could read Chinese. The banners were in various colours but the lettering was mostly in black and gave a fantastic atmosphere to the environment. They were business-like and at the same time cheerful and welcoming.

Then came three large department stores, all Chinese owned – Sinceres, Wing Ons and Sun Suns. A recent video documentary on Shanghai states one of these is now known as 'Shanghai's No.1 Store' – to us, they all were that. We could purchase almost anything – big or small, exquisite items only to be looked at (for us) and items which were super and prices which suited our pockets. The stores were brightly lit up and also had several neon signs each which gave the area a very festive air.

We then came to the racecourse after which we were into the West End and equally famous Yates – lingerie – Road.

Down our way
North Szechuen Road – an extension of Szechuen Road – runs from the north side of the Soochow creek ending outside the settlement. It is a very busy road – the 'Nanking Road' of the Chinese sector. The further north one went the more native the area became with huddles of buildings sporting open-fronted Chinese shops which, in their traditional way, were boarded up and battened down at night.

On our way home from school after we got off the bus we would walk past many a fascinating Chinese shop. The dentist shop was one – similar to the one you read about in our Yangtzepoo days.

There was one particular shop in North Szechuen Road which Dad promised to buy for Mary when she grew up – it was the dried fish shop. Mary cringed every time she had to go past this shop. She couldn't bear the smell of it, nor the sight of all the dried fish – hanging row upon row – highly salted (or, whatever they do to preserve the fish). Of course, this was a speciality and, we were told, most delicious but to a young girl who was always a bit squeamish at the sight of any raw flesh it threw her into vegetarianism in a big way.

But the one which quietened us was another open-fronted shop. It intrigued us in a different way – we were puzzled. We were not too sure that what we saw could be real. To advertise his ware, the owner of the shop – similar to the dentist, with his enamel bowl of extracted teeth – had row upon row of glass jars with things 'in' them, covered with liquid – spirit for preserving, no doubt. What made us curious was that the things were different in size and appearance. When we spotted a larger jar with something big in it, we peered at it closer; our eyes opened wide in a transfixed stare of horror when we recognised it was a baby! Nausea overcame us at this sight and we did not know what to make of it or, the type of shop we were looking into or, what was being sold! Many years later we realised that the trade was not another dentist, but that, possibly, of an abortionist.

Another shop which had a mesmerising influence on us was a pawnshop – with its beautiful jewellery on full display. Mary and Ivy were attracted by a ring having a large oval Alexander stone set in gold – on sale for $10. Ivy feeling very frustrated with no Saturday night date was thrilled when Mary compensated her with a gift of the ring. Forty years later, when Mary had lost her engagement ring, Ivy returned the ring to her hoping it would now compensate her. One good turn certainly deserves another.

Poo Kye (our own phonetic translation) is the Chinese equivalent of a duvet and was a very important part of our bedding. Very cosy and warm but became unnecessary when we moved into our steamheated apartment.

Cotton was more plentiful than wool and there was a special shop which teased the cotton to a fluffy consistency to be used for Poo Kyes or padded jackets or other garments. Incidentally the hands could be slipped into the opposite sleeve – so no gloves were needed.

* * *

If you needed any personal attention you were in the right place. It didn't cost much to have a letter written for you particularly if you knew what you wanted to say. Or, to have your hair cut, a shave and ears cleaned at a pavement barber's stall – a seat and a stand with an enamelled wash basin. Or, if in a studious mood, you could pick up a book from a portable library – two hinged slim bookcases which closed up to form one unit. If you had a laddered stocking there was an Amah with a small hooked instrument who could repair it in a few minutes. If you felt peckish there were always sticks of watermelon or in cooler weather roasted chestnuts or baked sweet potatoes. The last two were cooked in a large wok filled with anthracite dust and placed over a charcoal fire. The result was delicious. Sometimes we would buy a packet of the chestnuts to munch at the movies.

Whereas Nanking Road was famous for its banners, a unique feature in this area was the bamboo poles balanced in windows and used as clothes lines. The poles were threaded through trouser legs or the sleeves of a shirt and the clothes dried flat so no ironing was needed. Necessity being the mother of invention and living in apartments or rooms with no facilities to hang out washing, a new use was found for the bamboo. This strange custom of hanging out washing has become quite a tourist attraction and is the subject of many a photograph.

Japan – Another Holiday

Nellie and Bessie were again invited to go on holiday with Auntie Cameron to Japan for a two-week stay at the seaside resort of Shimabara. This time in Auntie's party was not only Mr Chandler, but his son and Russian wife. Shimabara is situated near Nagasaki to the east, on Kyushu Island at the foot of Unzen-dake – an active volcano. To get there they had to go by train from Nagasaki (anyone who has seen the film 'Shogun' will remember the beautiful scenery of this part of Japan).

The hotel was built in the traditional Japanese style with tatami (straw matting) on the floor and flimsy partitions separating the rooms – these would slide to and fro, whichever way you wanted to enter or leave the room. For two weeks they slept on bed rolls on tatami and wore kimonos. Shell-fish seemed to be served up at every meal, the older generation revelled in it but Bessie was not too keen. The strong smell of crabmeat on the table was enough to put her off her meals – no doubt she took off a bit of weight that holiday which she needed to do. It was through Mrs Chandler they learnt their first Russian words and phrases – 'neit' and 'dah' and also 'crasli noss' (red nose) – the latter not appreciated by Auntie.

There was excitement at the hotel during the second week of the holiday. There had been a murder in Shanghai and the body put into a trunk and shipped to Yokohama on the *Nagasaki Maru*, the ship on which they had travelled to Japan. The Japanese had strict immigration laws and thus before going ashore at Nagasaki all had to fill in vast questionnaires – Bessie and Nellie, though teenagers, were not exempt. The body was discovered at Yokohama and a police hunt set up. The official who came to the hotel told them that everyone on that ship had been traced and was being questioned.

The highlight of the holiday was an excursion to Unzen – a precarious journey up a narrow mountain road. Unzen is famous for its sulphur springs and the smell of it hits you round the last bend arriving at Unzen – a revolting smell of rotten eggs. They couldn't get out of the place quickly enough, though the plop-plop of the thick mud ponds was fascinating.

Dad's Young Ladies

Dad was always amazed to see the changes developing in his girls – they were now 20, 18, 16 and 14 – who were becoming very fashion conscious and desperately trying to keep up with styles. Dad was very fastidious when it came to appearances. To him styles didn't matter – it was more important to be well groomed. Suspenders were necessary to keep stockings wrinkle free. A suggestion of a ladder or hole was acceptable if it was neatly darned. Shoes had to be highly polished – any run-down heel should be mended – attention to detail counted far more than fashion. We had to be up and fully dressed and ready for the day before breakfast – no slippers or curlers permitted.

We all favoured different modes of dress. Mary opted for Peter Pan collars. She knew they suited her and so she kept to them even though we teased her unmercifully.

Ivy, like her artistic skills, was still copying. She and Helen decided they would dress alike and enjoyed walking the length of Yates Road for ideas and then getting the Kumping Road tailor to make up whatever they fancied.

Bessie aimed at being original and went to great trouble working out patterns, textiles and yarns.

Nellie was still at the borrowing stage and delighted to borrow anything that took her fancy – as long as it wasn't white satin or jaundice yellow!

* * *

This book would not be complete unless we mentioned some delightful people, mostly men, who worked at the Calico Printing Works, which was some distance up the Whangpoo river at Pootung, opposite Shanghai. They kindly invited us and our friends to spend the odd Sunday with them. They were great fun and had us in stitches – their sense of humour and laughter was so infectious. To get to the Calico Printers we assembled early in the morning at the pier by the Customs House and the company launch would convey us to the works. It was most interesting being taken through the printing factory and although it was not, of course, in operation on a Sunday, we soon became quite well informed in the printing of fabrics. Our hosts looked after us very well. We were even offered a refreshing swim in their 'pool' to cool off on one particularly hot day. We were gullible or naive enough to take up their offer! The pool, an enormous open water tank covering the total area of the building opposite the residents' flats. The water, we were told, was used during the week for whatever was needed in printing material but at weekends, permission was granted for it to be used as a swimming pool. To reach the opposite building we had to walk across a small platform bridge between the two buildings! The plank soaking wet from wet feet could have been dangerously slippery. Likewise, there was only a wooden plank with a protection rail around the three sides of the tank. At the fourth side of the pool, there was a platform from which one could make a shallow dive into the pool. The tank was about five feet deep. Mary, going first, dived her usual deep dive and came up 'skinned'. Her forehead and nose were badly scraped and she was in a dreadful state. We had to return to the Shanghai side as soon as possible for medical attention. The nicest part of the outings were funnily enough the return journey home. We were more often than not escorted back on the launch by the boys and this was usually highlighted with a sing-along. The outings did us a lot of good and gave us happy memories to treasure.

Dad Visits Britain

Dad's holidays were usually spent visiting us from Hankow, but after thirteen years – and knowing that his girls were more or less settled – he decided it was time to take his well deserved 'home' leave and visit Britain. He hadn't seen his family for so long that he was almost out of touch. After making several enquiries as to gifts, he took the plunge and purchased Shanghai's famous silk undies from Yates Road for all female relatives. These we wrapped up for him with the respective names attached, but on passing through Customs in England he was asked to open up all presents for inspection. Dad's first reaction was shock but then his sense of humour rose to the occasion and he made the inspector laugh when he said he would but would the inspector guarantee that 'aunt ... didn't receive cousin ... 's underwear, because it surely wouldn't fit'. He was waved on with a smile.

Dad had a lovely time visiting everyone – he stayed with his cousin Frank Stead and family and their three daughters, Myrtle, Hilda and Edna who were the same ages as Ivy, Bessie and Nellie. We were introduced by mail and have been in correspondence ever since. It was to Hilda that Nellie wrote about her experiences during 'Bloody Saturday' – coming up later – an account which found its way into the Oldham Evening Chronicle and for which Hilda was paid seven shillings and sixpence much to Nellie's amusement when she heard about it 47 years later when they finally met in England.

Dad decided to bring gifts back with him and used Myrtle and Hilda as his models. They must have had a ball judging from the many things he brought back – we each had overcoats for Sundays and overcoats for weekdays, skirts and sweaters. We had never seen so many beautiful things and enjoyed them for years. Actually Ivy's Sunday coat, with the addition of fur epaulettes, was the basis of her going away outfit following her wedding in 1940.

Edna married a Canadian after the war and went to live in Canada. She later developed a rare blood disease and passed away. Myrtle, who now lives in Oldham and Hilda, who lives near Worthing, keep in touch and visit occasionally and our visits to them are always special to us.

Dad is Transferred

Whilst Dad was visiting the Head Office in England they took the opportunity to sound him out about a transfer to India.

Dad being in Hankow was one thing – he was fairly near to us and on the same continent – but a transfer to India was a different story. Mary and Ivy were now working and happy in their jobs. Bessie and Nellie were still at school: soon Bessie would be starting her secretarial course – it would be difficult for them to pursue these activities in India. After weighing up all the consequences Dad unselfishly suggested that they stay put in Shanghai and, having little option, he agreed to the transfer.

His holiday over, Dad returned to Hankow to prepare for his departure. He was well known for his liking of ice-cream. In fact, so much so that his Chinese business friends, instead of giving a big Chinese dinner in his honour when he left Hankow, decided instead that the meal would be solely of ice-cream! To make it really exciting and special they imported ice-cream from Shanghai in every conceivable shape and size. Poor Dad, of course, tried to do this special meal justice. His ardour for ice-cream waned a little after that.

While Dad was in Hankow we moved into a smaller apartment as the bedroom reserved for him would not be needed and thus would reduce our overheads. We moved from apartment 305 to 323 which was at the rear of the building facing in the direction of North Station and which later gave us an uninterrupted view of the hostilities in 1937.

After a few weeks in Hankow and some sad farewells to his friends he travelled for the last time on Capt Rogers's ship down the Yangtsze to Shanghai – a very nostalgic journey. He naturally stayed with us in our apartment 323 – it was cramped but we squeezed in somehow – and there were many more farewells for Dad besides affairs to be settled.

Nellie treated Dad to her own farewell party. Knowing his love for ice-cream she invited him to meet her at the chocolate shop in Nanking Road and as a treat she ordered their latest concoction – a 'Snowman Sundae' – and hoped he would enjoy it as much as she knew she would. Poor Dad, it must have been the last straw for him. He had just been put through a whole dinner party with course upon course of ice-cream – some made in a fish mould for the fish course and so on. But he was a good sport and never let on to Nellie who was taking this special party seriously. When it arrived he must have felt an awful ninny for this 'thing' – all ice-cream, cones, nuts and marshmallow seemed to reach the sky. The boy, who served their table, worked for our next door neighbour at one time and, of course, to show favouritism, made the biggest snowman with the tallest cone-hat that he could find.

It had been a traumatic and difficult decision for Dad to make and we were all very upset to see him set sail on the Blue Funnel *SS Aeneas*. How we hated to see him go. We were really on our own now with no idea as to when we would see him again. As for Dad himself, he was going to fresh fields once again but unlike his journey to Mexico and Peru he was going alone with no thought of anyone joining him. He didn't know anything about India and was leaving the country that he loved and where he, in turn, was loved so much and was so popular. He was provided with accommodation in Bombay – his destination – but had no one to share it with. His family suddenly split up. How we wish now that things could have been different. However, one nice surprise for Dad on his arrival in Bombay was that one of our neighbours when we lived in Yangtzepoo, George Robinson – the 'English banana' boy – was once again a neighbour. Small world.

Auntie Leaves China

Mr Chandler and Auntie were planning a big move – to Britain to see how they could settle in a country which they both hardly knew. Mr Chandler was more ready for it than perhaps Auntie – she had been out east since she travelled out to marry Bill Brown when she was 18. A lot of water had flowed under her many bridges. We were considered her little girls still and she would feel sad to leave us. However they both realised that as they were no longer young it was a case of now or never! They had a quiet wedding and left Shanghai – in fact, they slipped out of Shanghai without farewells and a send off. We thought it was just another trip, admittedly perhaps a little further afield than their usual holidays. So we were delighted to hear from 'Mr and Mrs Chandler' telling us that they had purchased their first home and were settling down happily.

As we had no plans, or hope, of ever visiting England – we had no idea what the future held for us, or if we would meet again.

Things Chinese

With the move to 323 we missed the sampans on the creek but found other interesting things to watch. We loved our ring-side seats. We would have liked to have seen a wedding but these were very private affairs – the bride being carried in a sedan chair to the home of her husband for the ceremony. Red and green – the lucky colours – were worn on these special occasions.

At a funeral the mourners followed the coffin on foot and were hidden from public view by a three-sided screen – the back end being left open. They were dressed in rough unbleached calico long gowns, or Cheong Sam, tied with a sash. White was worn at funerals. There were several traditional rituals. One we found very interesting was the burning of paper money – brightly coloured paper shaped to form a 'tael', one of the original forms of silver currency shaped rather like a boat. This tradition was to ensure that the departed would not be in need. They hired professional musicians and sometimes mourners to accompany the coffin on its way to the grave. Burial grounds are using up farming land at an alarming rate, therefore in the cities more and more people are being cremated. When we were in Shanghai the coffins were not 'buried' but covered with earth and then grass to form miniature hillocks. These were dotted around the countryside rather than in a cemetery.

*   *   *

There was much to learn about Chinese culture. We were introduced to Chinese opera by Uncle Miller. The big bangs – deafening unless you knew the reasons why such an incredible bang-clashing of symbols had to be – indicates a 'change of scene'. Once we understood this we thoroughly enjoyed the operas and although we had no idea what the dialogue was about as the acting was such that one's imagination did not have to be stretched too far. We could grasp the story quite easily – the actors and actresses were most expressive. The lead – always a man dressed up as a woman – was great and the make-up a work of art. It was a study in itself.

The intermission was as much fun as the opera. After eating oranges and munching peanuts and chestnuts which all had to be cracked out of their shells, to clean sticky fingers and chins an usherette would come around with hot face towels which she would chuck to the audience. After freshening up we were ready for the second half of the opera. The fun was in the catching of the towel and throwing it back after use.

Another exciting entertainment was a night when the Fire Brigade engaged a Chinese troupe of acrobats and jugglers resulting in Bessie and Nellie practicing their diabolo more than ever. Ivy eventually managed to juggle three oranges at a time but was forbidden to spin our crockery on a bamboo stick! Mary was interested in juggling the Clubs until Graham intervened for safety reasons – they looked too much like a rolling pin to him!

* * *

Bessie had only one girl friend at a time. Eleanor Guillet and Bessie were very close for about three years. Eleanor was a gentle person. Her father was French and her mother Russian and they had parted. Mrs Guillet was very bitter and used to give Eleanor a bad time because she looked so like her father. Just being friendly with Bessie was all she wanted.

Like Nellie and her pals they did everything together – tried to dress alike and went to the cinema every Saturday without fail. Eleanor was petit, olive skinned with large brown eyes. Bessie was slightly taller and about twice as heavy. Dressing alike was not always the smartest thing to do.

At one stage she came to live with us at 323 until her mother had settled herself into a new abode. Eleanor and Bessie did their best to emulate the fashions of the film stars. Hampered by the cost of 'off the peg' items, they reverted to the Kumping Road tailor. He would make anything they drew and his failures were few.

Nellie's group spent a good deal of time at Nina Hodges' home – her father worked for the Prison Department and had a house on the corner of Thibet Road on the opposite side of the creek to the Embankment. The house was spacious and had a nice garden with lots of games areas – like skittles, wee golf and bowls, besides a makeshift area for badminton. Nina had two Airedales called Bessie and Nellie much to the girls horror! They couldn't believe it.

Nina also had two brothers, John and Bill and of course they had friends. Ronnie and Norman Crouch (brothers) – Charlie Knox and Henry Eardley. We had lots of fun and laughter. Eleanor, Bessie and George Brownrigg joined us for a while after the Seymour days. We had house parties – always at Nina's. The girls would spend all day getting ready for these do's – washing and setting their hair was a full time job; it took hours to dry. Borrowing each other's dresses and making adjustments, if necessary. Manicures and pedicures were a must – and at the end of the day they were too shy to talk to the boys, and worst still, to dance. The boys were only just learning to dance – in fact we were all amateurs. Bill in particular with his side, step, step, bend knee and TURN, side, step, step, bend knee turn, over and over again – we used to dread. He for sure had two left feet but unlike Mr Robinson's horses – not because he ate curly grass! Bessie fell for Ronnie Crouch. However, this romance petered out when she was asked to wait ten years for him.

* * *

The white Russian man was never more than a few yards away.Peggy Brewer who lived in apartment 525 and Nellie were being followed – daily, and it was weird. He would mysteriously appear in a seat next to one of them in the cinema after the lights dimmed. Likewise, he would mysteriously be on the footpath around Jessfield Park when they went for a Saturday morning walk. He would be at the bus stop in North Szechuen Road near the Embankment – he would be ON the bus. It was either Peggy or Nellie who intrigued him, we didn't know. They were invariably together and when they met up in the mornings to go to school – to avoid him – they would sometimes use a different entrance, dash over the bridge, hurriedly cut across the town and pick up the same school bus on the corner of Honan/Nanking Road en route to Yu Yuen Road. This was a nuisance as they had a long way to walk – he would be there. Nellie's concern grew when she realised that she was the one singled out. Peggy was not well and had been housebound for a couple of weeks. Nellie felt tormented. Not wanting to worry Mary, she gave some deep thought to her fears. The last straw came when he was actually waiting for her outside the rear entrance to the building when she was on her way to school. She decided to take no notice and continued on her journey down a rather busy side road to the usual stop in North Szechuen Road. He also waited for the bus. Nellie met up with other school pals as they boarded at various stops – he stood holding the overhead strap directly in front of her. She chatted merrily on and ignored this man and was determined to show no fear whatsoever.

On arrival at the school bus stop – he remained on the bus – but, she knew he would be there at the end of the day.

Travelling alone – Bessie travelled independently with her girl friends – with no Peggy for moral support, Nellie decided to try to put a stop to this once and for all. For help she went straight to the Headmistress's room – Miss Alexander was fantastic. She listened carefully and asked questions like, how long had they been followed? – which route they took to school? – Nellie's answer was that they varied their route depending on what they were going to do after school. Miss Alexander much appreciated the fact that Nellie approached her and that only they knew about the man – Peggy paid little attention besides, she was ill in bed. At the end of the meeting she told Nellie not to worry any more and to carry on as usual. She commended her on her calmness and for not talking about it although she felt Mary should have been advised. However she appreciated Nellie's reasons for not burdening Mary.

At the end of the day Nellie was aware of the police. They were at the school bus stop and a policeman, she noticed, was at every bus stop all the way home – from Yu Yuen Road to North Szechuen Road – a good number of miles away. Nellie also noticed that at the various stops (two) which she and Peggy occasionally alighted there were more police, every fifteen to twenty feet apart – or, as Nellie recalls, within eye distance of each other. When she alighted from the bus and reached the building the police were also manning every entrance.

Nellie was not followed home and never saw the Russian man again. It was a comforting thought to know that one could be so personally cared for in such a big city.

*   *   *

Doris Brewer, Peggy's sister, was a lovely person, with an equally lovely gentle personality – sometimes she would be on duty by the cloakroom when we were leaving school and changing into our outdoor clothes and heavy shoes. She was there to hurry us up to get our respective bus home. She was a senior prefect. The last time Nellie saw Doris was on such an afternoon. Then sadly we heard that she had been rushed into hospital – quite unexpectedly – with rabies. What a shock. It was almost unheard of – but it was always in the air – as we were constantly reminded of ' ... be careful, don't touch stray animals ... no, don't try to "kiss" it ... '. This is exactly what Doris did. Her pet dog was ill and was resting on her mother's lap when apparently Doris came in and went up to it – nosing her sort of 'hello' kiss – when, accidently it snapped at her (because it was so ill) and bit her lip. Poor Doris; we were all shattered by this terribly sad unnecessary death. A more tragic way of going is hard to describe.

* * *

Bessie left school at sixteen, following in the footsteps of Mary and Ivy by attending Mrs Corneck's Secretarial Institute to learn shorthand, typing and bookkeeping. The course lasted six months.

Eleanor left us to join her mother in her new home which was in a guest house. Eleanor's mother was the housekeeper and accommodation was provided for both of them. Eleanor was given a delightful bedsit to herself and she seemed to settle down quite happily – her relationship with her mother improved, which was a relief to us all. She started to work at Kelly & Walsh the leading bookshop in Nanking Road. She had kept up her friendship with John, Nina's brother, whom she married before they emigrated to Australia.

* * *

Whilst at Mrs Corneck's Bessie met and struck up a friendship with Ginger Lumsdaine. Ginger was a great pal. She was very tall and vivacious and lots of fun. She lived on the other side of the creek to us and almost opposite the Shanghai Rowing Club. They became members, not to row, but to swim. They were permitted to use the pool any time they wished.

Ginger had another friend who lived in the Broadway Mansions also situated on the Soochow creek. Her name was Pat. They had seen an advertisement for radio talent. They rather fancied themselves as singers, and decided to form a trio and offer their services. Ginger, Pat and Bessie practiced for weeks before the event – it did not occur to them that it was strange that they did not have to put in an appearance until the night they went out on the air. A name was necessary so they called themselves the 'Soochow Sugars' – Bessie even practiced a tap routine in case it was needed. The sort of material prepared was songs from the latest movies and jazz hits. They were asked to report at the broadcasting station one evening – and, full of nerves, were horrified to find the programme was being put on by a religious group. They had to quickly change their repertoire and the unsuitable title of 'Soochow Sugars' to 'The Willing Three'. Having got all their friends to listen in it took a long time to live that one down.

Later Bessie was to be chief bridesmaid at Ginger's wedding.

* * *

Bessie's first job was with The Bus Company under Mary's wing. It was a temporary job lasting three months. She then joined the Maintenance Department of Sassoons. Bessie worked for three men, excellent experience for one so young. She had a wonderful desk with typewriter which slipped out of sight at the flip of the wrist (this was the invention of the engineer of the department and her desk the prototype). The position was very enjoyable and all went well for three years until a new accountant was taken on. He spent a lot of time leering at her through the glass partition. She found this very disturbing. One night he called her up on the phone with a proposal of marriage and Bessie was hard put to convince him that she was not interested – he even expected her to take on the Jewish faith. Eventually he got the message. However, having eyes following her around at work was embarrassing to say the least.

Bessie delighted in designing her own clothes, not always with the approval of Mary whose taste was on the conservative side. With her first pay packet she got the Kumping Road tailor to make her a light-weight green tweed three piece suit – skirt, jacket and a sort of tabard, so that she could wear it as a suit or a skirt and top. With this she had shoes, bag and hat made to order by a shop in Yates Road and the shoemaker also made a fringed Robin Hood suede collar to match. She had a tall orange feather in her hat to pick up the fleck in the tweed and the bag was trimmed with an orange clasp. Perhaps she should have kept up this hobby of designing as she was good at it and was most artistic. Besides, she had courage to wear some of her designs – they were by no means outlandish, just too 'new' – and she always seemed to manage to keep one step ahead of fashion.

About this time Bessie met Vera Dodd at the Rowing Club. Vera and her brothers, Ray and Jackie, were good swimmers excelling in the breast stroke. During the summer months there was a gala every Saturday and at the end of the season a grand finale – an extravaganza affair with a dance to follow. Someone had the bright idea of putting on an aquacade – a first. Bessie was given the task of staging the show, becoming a bit of a bossy boots in the eyes of her friends who were not so dedicated as she would have liked them to be. However, they did not let her down on the night. Fifteen girls in all participated, including Vera, Ginger, Linda, Nellie, Peggy and Sadie Beattie swimming up and down and making formations to the tune of 'The Blue Danube'. Vera did a spectacular dive from the high board on the opening down beat of music followed by two girls either side of her one step down on the next down beat, and so on until all the girls were in the water. The Club was taken by surprise as the 'act' was only meant to entertain during the interval. They received tremendous applause.

* * *

As time went by, and always looking for something new to experience, a number of us decided to hire a launch and with some older friends spent a day picnicking on the Whangpoo river. It was glorious. Everything was going well and we were a considerable way down the river when the engine broke down. The boys tried their best to get it started again to no avail. In the end, as it was getting late and beyond our expected return home time it was decided that we should abandon ship. Fortunately we were alongside a grassy verge. We clambered ashore each having to carry some picnic paraphernalia. We had to walk, single file, through some tall grassy fields (scared of snakes and things)! George, one of the leaders, was carrying the portable gramophone so thought he'd play a record to help us on our way – to where we did not know. Soon it started to drizzle – up went an umbrella to protect the gramophone which we were enjoying. George had a great sense of humour – he decided to change the record – and out came the then favourite 'Gloomy Sunday' to cheer us up. We eventually got our bearings as we had arrived on the outskirts of Lungwha airport and after about an hour transportation was arranged and we got home safely – late, tired and hungry. No one was worried as all parents knew through the bamboo telephone system that we were OK and ashore. The only ones worrying were the owners of the launch.

* * *

As much as Nellie enjoyed being with her lively group of friends, she was lucky in that she could enjoy her own company. She never felt left out or lonely if she found herself the only one at home on a Saturday, for instance. She soon found something to do – on occasions she would get herself nicely dressed up and go to the Cathay Hotel to their Palm Court for afternoon tea (admittedly, on a shoe-string) and listen to their string quartet – that most certainly took care of her weeks' $1 pocket money – but it was well worth it. She has always enjoyed music – the atmosphere of the Palm Court had a soothing effect on her and she came away feeling really good.

* * *

In 1937 Ivy was promoted to the Private Office of E.D. Sassoon Banking Co. Ltd and again found much to interest her. The work was very demanding, her boss, the managing director of several companies, was mostly interested in finance and, of course, the political situation which could affect the stability of the companies.

She now became familiar with the compradore system – the compradore being an English speaking intermediary through whom much business was conducted. The word comes from the Portuguese.

His department was a large, busy and noisy one. The clerks each had their own abacus – a wooden frame with wooden balls sliding on horizontal wires attached to the frame at intervals. The counting was done by 5s and 10s – similar to the children's toys on the market today. They loved nothing better than having a race against an adding machine and they usually won. Pre-computer days obviously.

The compradore was a jolly friendly soul. Ivy remembers passing him on his way out of the lift while she was waiting to be taken up to the office. A few minutes later, on hearing gunfire, she rushed to the window to see the compradore had been held up and shot. Thankfully he recuperated but the incident made us all very nervous.

We had always heard Mexican silver dollars referred to as being the currency of the country. We were fascinated but it was not until we started to work that we learnt Mexican silver dollars were first imported by Spanish and Portuguese traders who brought them from the silver mines in their American colonies. All went well until the importation of opium had to be paid for in silver. This harmed the economy and was one of the causes of the opium war.

* * *

Nellie's school work! She tried hard – her fault was that she was a day-dreamer. She lived and fantasised everything she was taught – a female 'Walter Mitty'. On reflection Nellie feels that Miss Alexander (her Headmistress) seemed to create so many new classes for her and the likes of her – as the old adage goes 'birds of a feather flock together'. After joining the Public School Nellie and her pals made it quite easily from junior school to senior school – but from then on their learning period seemed to be like the broken record, in a grove! First it was 4-Lower – they thought to themselves, hopefully, that the following term it would for sure be 4-Upper. Not so. From then on the class names ran something like this. 4-Upper (B), then 4-Remove (whatever that meant) and the last term when the 4s disappeared entirely they found themselves in 'Intermediate'. Alex gave them enough rope to hang themselves but although they worked hard the 'feathers' never seemed to quite make it. The studies seemed to be the same each term – particularly geography (Africa) – and the only thing that improved enormously, as far as Nellie was concerned was her vivid imagination. Nellie 'Mitty' glamourous floated up and down the Nile in her barge as only Cleo could – dressed in her diaphanous robes bedecked with jewels galore – lolling lazily with one hand draped listlessly over the side of the boat as she drifted on. Mark Anthony ... ? 'Who was he?'

Despite her Mitty ways, Nellie managed to be elected Class Captain several times – it was either Nellie, or Ludmilla, a Russian classmate. This was a period when Nellie learnt how to delegate. Another friend in her class was Norah Hardoon, of the famous Hardoon family in Shanghai. They got on extremely well. Norah felt the cold, and in the winter months acted as Nellie's lookout. Her 'payment' for services rendered was that Norah (and only Norah) was permitted to stand by the one and only radiator by the classroom door and would give a signal when the teacher came down the corridor. Until that moment, the class was at ease. (Nellie as well.) Her teachers, school pals – and, of course, Miss Alexander – were delighted and proud when Nellie's class won the prize for being the best behaved class in the school for two consecutive years. They got a gold star. In the school magazine Nellie was able to report that there were eighteen different nationalities in her class. To name a few they were, Latvian, Portuguese, Russian, French, Austrian, Italian, German, Greek, South African, Spanish, Chinese, Indian and so it went on.

In the summer Nellie left school – she was 16. The next stage of her growing up was to attend Mrs Corneck's school. It was to be a six months' course covering shorthand, typing and bookkeeping – she was definitely following in Bessie's footsteps. Poor Nellie was nagged and nagged by Mrs Corneck as both Bessie and Ivy had done well – Ivy, in particular, had been her star pupil having completed her course in three months with flying colours. Nevertheless, Nellie tackled this stage of learning with enthusiastic gusto. She just loved living and cheerfully attacked everything that came under that heading. Unfortunately the Sino-Japanese hostilities were to disrupt her studies so it was nearly a year before she was able to become a secretary – too long. One can become sluggish on a dragged out course of any description.

Bessie in Pei-tai-ho

In early July, after various tests and X-rays, because she had been having chest pains, it was thought that Bessie may have developed a spot on her lung. Her doctor advised her to take a rest and recommended a longish holiday, if possible, by the sea. She had never been out of Shanghai on her own before and was a little apprehensive – where to have a holiday by the sea? When she got home and told her news to Mary and the family, Ivy reminded her of the lovely holiday she had had the previous year with the Sands and Jean and Carrie Todd at their holiday home in Pei-tai-ho. Ivy couldn't recommend a better place. Bessie got in touch with Mrs Sands to ask if it would be convenient for her to stay with them for a month – as the doctor ordered. Mrs Sands was delighted to have Bessie, in fact she said quite a number of Jean and Carrie's friends were also planning part of their summer holidays with them that year and it would make an enjoyable house-party for them all to be together, as they all knew each other well.

There was great excitement and planning, and borrowing of each others things – just in case they came in handy. However Bessie had recently bought herself a rather special dress which she had not had the opportunity to wear, and knowing Nellie's habit of borrowing she made her promise that in no way would she do so – no matter what. This Nellie agreed to. All the girls were in on planning the trip as though they were going too – it was going to be something special.

Mary who looked after the more serious things wrote to Dad in India to tell him about the doctor's report. Bessie returned to her office to request permission for a months leave – unheard of in those long-ago days. Her boss was most concerned for her and readily granted whatever length of time it would take to make her well again. Bessie and Ivy arranged the shipping details and whatever was needed – passport, inoculations etc. A berth was available, everything seemed to fall into place easily. Her suitcase packed – ticket in her handbag – Bessie was ready to leave on her first solo trip 'overseas' which was going to be a two nights sea voyage away. Surprisingly it did not seem to upset her now to be travelling alone – she had a lot to look forward to and no doubt would know some of her fellow passengers on the ship. This was good as it would help the recuperation period.

Bessie set sail for Chinwangtao about mid-July. We bade her farewell and reminded her to write to us and tell us '... all about it!'(mimicking the newspaper boys in movies when they were selling their wares, calling out 'latest news – read all about it').

* * *

After two nights aboard the ship to Chinwangtao, Bessie had a further short train ride to Pei-tai-ho where she was met by Jean and Carrie. She was the only passenger to alight. The station was just a platform with a small shelter. It was mid-day, the sun was beating down – everywhere was silent except for the sound of bees buzzing round the pretty flower beds at each end of the platform.

The Sands had built an extra room at one end of the bungalow above the bathroom with access by an outside staircase. Jean, Carrie and Bessie shared this room. Laurence Beattie arrived about two days later and stayed ten days and then Helen Gilmour joined the party early in August to stay for two weeks. It was a happy household – lots of swimming and sunshine. When it rained, usually in the afternoons, it would pour only for about ten minutes, so rain really never spoilt any planned outings.

Pei-tai-ho was a pretty little seaside resort situated twenty five miles south of Shan-hai-Kwan, where the Great Wall of China meets the sea. In the old days it was a quiet fishing village until it was discovered by foreigners as an ideal holiday resort. The sandy beach stretched for miles and faced south. Halfway along the beach there was a natural breakwater called Tiger Rock thus creating an ideal beach for swimming as it shelved gradually for some considerable distance. Apparently the rainy season was short but heavy enough to cause flooding. Because of this there was a network of open drains along the roads and gullys ran down the hill slopes.

The holiday homes were mostly bungalows with corrugated iron roofs – the gardens were spacious. The Sands' bungalow was well situated – not too far from the beach and it was in the centre of activity. It was a continual open-house to holiday makers and the many Shanghailanders used it as a meeting place to exchange news and tales of their adventures. Everyone looked forward to the mid-morning or early evening gatherings. The real magnet was Mrs Sands – a lovable Scottish lady, very caring, radiating happiness. She was blessed with being able to see the bright side to every situation.

There was lots to do besides swimming and sunbathing – in fact one need not sunbathe at all – a gentle warm breeze blew constantly and one became windburnt just sitting under cover. The Sands had erected a makeshift shelter on the beach – just four poles with a bit of matting stretched between them. Bessie was chocolate coloured in no time.

There were very pleasant walks along streets lined with shady trees. They also hired bicycles and donkeys – neither of which helped Bessie's image, especially when the boys were around. During one cycle ride Bessie came to grief at the bottom of a steep hill when a few people suddenly appeared at the bottom. Her reflexes were bad, she failed to locate the brakes, and had no alternative but to go into the hedge on the left, landing bottom up.

This did not seem to deter her, she was game for the next adventure on the back of a donkey. She cannot remember how the ride ended being mortified by its beginning. It was Bessie's first attempt at mounting a donkey and the result was literally like something out of a slapstick comedy. She did not seem to be able to make it up, so someone gave her a forceful lift resulting in her sailing right over the beast, landing on the other side having nearly done the splits. What added to her embarrassment was that she had had an accident at the beach the previous day – a small boat had overturned on to both of her shins. She had been given a tetanus injection and bandaged up to protect the two quite deep cuts, looking very much like the beast she was trying to mount.

*   *   *

It was a promising summer. Nellie at her secretarial school and Bessie settled at Sassoons, Mary happily working for Graham's Dad at The Bus Company and Ivy in her new position in the Private Office, also Sassoons. Dad must have sighed with relief that we had made it. On top of that, with the exception of Bessie's minor set back, we were extremely healthy and managing to care for ourselves sensibly as he used to advise us to do.

We spent our leisure time in the usual way – a cinema show on a Saturday afternoon – swimming in the Embankment pool and on occasions at the Rowing Club. As tennis was the 'in' thing during the summer months off to the racecourse we would go, meeting more friends, where various clubs had courts of their own. We did not have to play tennis to be a member – we could walk around the racecourse visiting friends at other clubs and so on. Lovely days and a super way of life. We would congregate on the roof of the Embankment and more often than not there was a ukulele among us – or, just an assortment of voices and we would sing (or try to) the latest tunes until it was time to go home for supper. We were young enough in spirit to enjoy every moment and we seemed to be able to drift along without a care in the world.

Nellie was tackling her lessons with daily confusion – why shorthand? – it had taken her most of her sixteen years to learn longhand! Nevertheless, she persevered and Peggy (who went to the Farmer's secretarial college) and Nellie were able to compare notes. Better still, compare their new wardrobes. It was great being sixteen – new business-like dresses, shoes, handbags and ... hats. Mary and Ivy were a great help and the advice on etiquette and the do's and don'ts were noted by Nellie, who realised that although life seemed to her to be a bowl of cherries, they were not without pips!

Then all seemed to happen at once.

CHAPTER FIVE

Troublous Days

1937

China was at War with Japan Again

The Japanese had taken Peking, Tientsin and the surrounding areas of the International Settlement of Shanghai. We were not to be spared as Shanghai became the centre of the Sino Japanese hostilities in early August.

*   *   *

Roof-garden Vigilance

There were rumours going around that Japan was going to launch an attack at 6pm on Friday, 13 August, 1937. We had difficulty getting to and from work. Shops were closing their doors as the streets were beginning to get crowded with refugees panic-stricken to get to the safety of the International Settlement. A couple of evenings before the expected attack, Peggy Brewer and Nellie met on the roof-garden of the Embankment, together with other tenants, to see what was going on at the North Station area, Chapei, one of the Chinese suburbs surrounding the settlement, an important connecting point to the rest of China only a mile away from the Embankment. Our flat, number 323, faced Chapei.

From a city enjoying peace – Shanghai suddenly seemed to be surrounded by fires and refugees. Peggy and Nellie were frightened as they surveyed the surrounding areas from their strategic position on the roof. They saw many fires, large and small, and heard guns

95

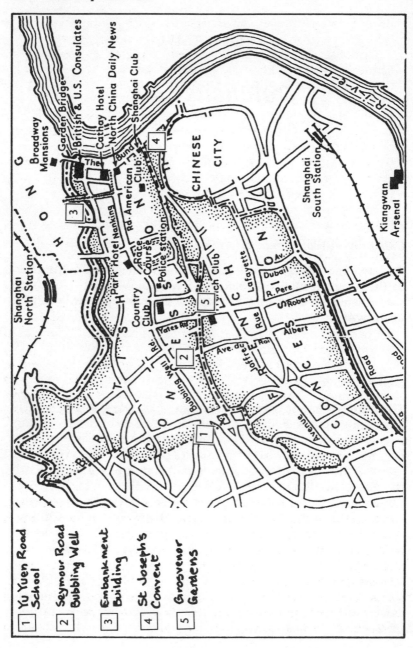

1   Yu Yuen Road School

2   Seymour Road Bubbling Well

3   Embankment Building

4   St Joseph's Convent

5   Grosvenor Gardens

firing between Chapei and Hongkew, another suburb where the Japanese had been making their homes over the past few years.

On looking down over the parapet they watched thousands of Chinese refugees racing towards the settlement. Peggy and Nellie then ran across to the other side of the roof which faced the Soochow creek. There they had a splendid panoramic view overlooking the city area and the creek with all its bridges from Garden Bridge on the left-hand side, through to Honan Road bridge on the right which, in fact, was at the corner of the building. Here the direction of the Soochow creek changed its course – between Honan Road and Thibet Road, further along to the right, and flowed out of sight.

It is believed there were about 11,000 refugees surging across the bridges to reach safety before nightfall – the hour when the attack was due to begin. Parents with babies strapped to their backs, hands grasped tightly to keep together, if possible, were being separated with the crushing and rushing of people carrying a few of their possessions tied in bundles. There really was no room for bundles, and hardly any room left for people. Some chains of hands were broken – the refugees dispersed, families split up. We felt hemmed in as we surveyed the scene but safe when we returned to the four walls of our respective flats.

The map opposite shows where the Embankment is placed in relation to the town. The following is an account of that infamous day, Saturday, 14 August – known in Shanghai as 'Bloody Saturday'. The SVC (Shanghai Volunteer Corp) were called out for emergency duty.

BLOODY SATURDAY

The atmosphere was like the lull before a storm. Little did we know that by the end of the day we would never again live in apartment 323 and that our lives would turn topsy turvy.

Mary left for work, Ivy for her office at Sassoons in the Cathay Hotel building on The Bund – Nellie for her lessons at Mrs Corneck's. Bessie was still in Pei-tai-ho.

At about eleven in the morning a Chinese aircraft appeared overhead zooming around trying to bomb the Japanese destroyer *Idzumo* which was anchored in front of the Japanese Consulate in full view of the Cathay Hotel. From Ivy's office window the aircraft could be seen dropping bombs which were falling short of its target. The office was immediately closed and all staff sent home. Mary and Nellie returned home as well. Business came to a halt.

Ivy's office suggested that she and her sisters should pack up a few items of clothing, leave 323, and move into the relative safety of the Cathay Hotel, thereby avoiding the hassle of the bridges spanning the creek. They were concerned that we lived so near North Station and that it could become a target. Should this happen, and the bridges be closed there would be tremendous difficulty in communicating. They wanted us to be more accessible – for the weekend at least – until things became more settled, or until permanent arrangements could be made. The office would be keeping Dad, who was in India, informed of the situation and meanwhile were looking after us on his behalf.

It was a relief to see each other again. Mary and Nellie were eager to hear Ivy's news that we had been offered a home for the weekend at the splendiferous Cathay Hotel. It was all hurry, hurry as we had no time to lose.

The aircraft, one plane, but many sorties, kept us terrified, and there was incessant firing between Hongkew and Chapei. To speed things along, we each looked after our own packing. Mary and Ivy had to settle things with Amah and Cookboy to make sure they had enough funds to take care of themselves for a few days. They also arranged the welfare of Nellie's cat Tilly.

While packing a few clothes to fill her small bag, Mary had the presence of mind to pack our passports – why we shall never know. Ivy put a few bits and pieces of her own personal effects together. Our cases were very tiny – we had seen the crowds and knew there was no room for extras. Nellie's turn – yes, she perfunctorily packed her undies but first made sure she packed some movie magazines (particularly treasured pictures of Jean Harlow and George Raft) then, turning around to check the wardrobe, decided to wear 'the dress'. Bessie's special new dress – the 'No-No' dress to Nellie! But now, with the turn of events, Nellie felt it was special to her as well and that she should look after it for Bessie. Her suitcase was full – so a quick change was made before leaving the apartment, Nellie's old dress off, and Bessie's new clipsation on. As we were now evacuees or refugees – not too sure which – Bessie would be most upset if she lost her new dress. Feeling extremely snazzy Nellie was ready to leave.

But, before doing so, Mary decided to check what Nellie had packed!
That did it – Mary took over and except for one magazine, Jean and
George were left behind and the space filled with a couple of more
sensible items.

Evacuated the First Time

In all we only had twenty minutes to evacuate 323. When we
reached ground level we decided to hold on to each other – luckily
we knew our destination – the Cathay Hotel. We had no other option
than to move with the crowd crossing the bridge. With the
thousands upon thousands of people who had been infiltrating into
the settlement, all transport had ceased to exist. We moved, shoulder
to shoulder, with the multitude of people heading for the town on
the opposite side of the creek. The aircraft, flying at a low level did
not help. It was an almost impossible journey, but we managed to
make it, literally pushing our way through. We were desperate to
get to the Cathay – we were scared. We felt so alone in the midst
of so many thousands. On reaching the other side of the bridge we
turned left along the creek towards the Capitol Cinema where, for
the first time, we saw the Shanghai Volunteer Corps SVC on duty
– it was good to see them – we knew most of them, they were
brothers of our girl friends, and their friends. It made us feel
comfortable. They were able to give us the latest news and advise
us of the best route to take. A route we thought nothing of most days
on our way to town – but this day it was vastly different. Along the
grape-vine of the (SVC), Mary's then unofficial fiancé, Graham, got
first hand news of our evacuation and where he could find us after
he came off duty.

Eventually we reached the Cathay to be told that a door at the
rear of the hotel would be opened slightly to let us through.
Nanking Road and The Bund entrances were closed. On our way we
recognised other evacuees/refugees – some who had to travel up the
river on tugs to reach the settlement. It was utter chaos. At this time
we remembered the shops, houses, and cinema which we had
passed along the way that had barricaded their entrances from the
masses who by now had reached desperation point.

On entering the hotel we were allocated a room on the fifth floor.
There were many others in the same situation, some evacuees from
the Yangtzepoo area and some of those who had escaped by tug were

also being sheltered in the hotel – unfortunately, not all could be accommodated.

After we had sorted out our meagre possessions – with her faced creamed, her nails manicured and her hair about to be pinned up in curlers Nellie, at her young age of 16, was looking forward to a night in one of the most luxurious hotels she had ever been in – what to wear? (Bessie's dress of course.) She kicked off her shoes and abandoned all worries and prepared herself for a magnificent night out. Mary not knowing quite what to make of Nellie, and not sure who she was at that moment – Ginger Rogers, Carol Lombard or Jean Harlow, – thought some books and knitting would help the time to pass for Ivy and herself.

By this time the aircraft was nowhere to be seen and, as the atmosphere was reasonably quiet, against our wishes Mary decided to go out and buy a few books and some sweets, as well as knitting wool (if possible). Ivy's thought, when Mary returned, was to pop down to her office to see if she could make herself useful.

Fifteen minutes after Mary left, the aircraft started zooming around again, obviously hoping to hit his target the *Idzumo* – it never did. It was flying really low, the ack-ack guns wildly ack-acking at him from the top of the Yokohama Specie Bank – the next door building. A deafening noise but Nellie plodded on to make herself more Jean Harlowish for the evening to come! The plane got a bit too low for comfort – Ivy and Nellie dashed to the windowsill to watch with mixed feelings of excitement and great fear – they hoped to get a glimpse of the pilot! Suddenly the telephone rang. They both threw themselves across the bed to answer it. It was Mary. She rang to say that she had been pushed into a bookshop by a SMC (Shanghai Municipal Council) street coolie wearing a red jacket uniform, and that she was not allowed to leave the shop. All thought of purchases went out of her mind. She rang to let Nellie and Ivy know where she was and that she could not get back, and also to enquire if they were OK. Within seconds of this conversation – it happened.

The Bombs Dropped

The aircraft had been hit – the plane damaged and the pilot knew that he would have to release his bombs before returning to base – Lungwha. To do this, he headed for the river but, too late –

missed, two bombs fell – one hitting the Palace Hotel and falling into Nanking Road, and one hitting our hotel on the 7th floor, also landing in Nanking Road.

Our hotel room filled with concrete dust from the falling debris. We heard voices outside our room – we could see no one as the cloud of dust obliterated people, but we did manage to see a few pairs of feet. Nellie hastily put on her shoes, Ivy picked up her handbag – we passed the cupboard on a shelf in which lay the passports but did not 'see' them, they were left behind. We thought we had better join the voices. We did and, following feet, we made our escape to the lobby. The ceiling of the lobby was glass and was renowned for its beauty – it was shattered. In fact, there was nowhere to shelter, we were afraid more glass would fall, so we huddled together on the stairs thereby having a concrete 'roof' over our heads.

In what seemed an eternity, but only minutes, we were joined by the men from Sassoons' offices. Ivy was soon spotted by the man she worked for. He hailed her and asked her to be leader in yet another evacuation. This time to the Metropole Hotel (also owned by Sassoons) not too far away. Mary was nowhere to be seen or heard. In our moment of shock we had forgotten that she had telephoned us only minutes before.

Evacuated the Second Time

Ivy and Nellie were brought back to reality when they were told by a friend of the family from Yangtzepoo and who was also seeking refuge in the hotel – 'You'll never see Mary again' – because, she continued 'I was chatting to her in the foyer just before she went out to do her shopping – I told her not to go – but she went – then the bomb fell.'

Ivy and Nellie had to act fast and they started to assemble their responsibilities with the help of the staff of the hotel and led the way from the lobby through the hotel arcade towards the wrought iron gates of the hotel at Nanking Road.

Meanwhile the aircraft started to circle around again – sending everyone scurrying back to the stairwell shelter. The pilot, possibly wondering where to drop his last bombs, must have been mortified that he had already caused such havoc and tragedy and still had not completed his mission, to hit the *Idzumo*. He flew on in the direction of the racecourse – he missed – instead of releasing his bombs in the open spaces the bombs hit the centre of the New World fun fair on the corner of the road outside the racecourse where thousands of refugees thinking they had found shelter, were killed.

The Nanking Road bombs killed approximately 300 people and the New World bombs over 1000 – innocent refugees – also hundreds were so mutilated that only time would release them from their agony.

Our reaction? We were devastated and could not believe what we saw. The scene looked like an abattoir. It was wholesale destruction – there were limbs here, there and everywhere – a head elsewhere, and it took courage to pick our way through the bodies and lead our charges towards the Metropole.

Mary's Narrow Escape

After the deafening noise of the blast from the bomb, the doors to shops etc, were slowly opened for inspection and this is when Mary took the opportunity to run out of the bookshop.

She was shocked – bewildered to find that the SMC street coolie, who had pushed her into the shop had been killed. Panic-stricken she ran down the road to the back entrance of the hotel, passed over dead bodies – a Chinese lady pulled at her skirt, then collapsed, dead. Mary reached the back door to find that it had been firmly locked. Someone pointed towards The Bund, the front of the building indicating that that door would be open as it would have been blown in. It was.

Mary, anxiously avoiding people and the lift, took to the stairs – (but unfortunately not the stairwell we were in) – and as fast as her legs could take her she climbed the stairs (five floors) to our room, to find it bare with fallen debris everywhere. Her first reaction was that we had been killed. She rushed into the corridor and into a few other rooms with doors left wide open – all were the same, bare and full of debris. She went up a flight of stairs to the room of a friend – same scene. Now in shock she flew down the stairs to the foyer for help. Someone in Ivy's office recognised her and told her to hurry to catch up with us. We had just left. She was confused and utterly bewildered as she left the chaos of the Cathay to pick her way to the Metropole – alone.

At this stage the SVC were moving in fast and furiously on the horrendous job of clearing the street as quickly as possible. As we had to manoeuvre our way past their trucks we could see they were placing bodies, unrecognisable and incomplete, into their trucks for disposal. At the time it seemed so ruthless, but they had to act that way – to do that clearing up work gingerly would have caused them far more stress than they were able to endure. Most of the young men were in their twenties. They worked tirelessly – a day which would take us all a long time to forget.

The Metropole Hotel, Meeting Place

Ivy, Nellie and their column of refugees reached the Metropole where Ivy recognised a familiar person – the receptionist of the Hotel. She rushed up to him and threw her arms around his neck – much to his dismay she clung on tightly – she did not want to let go. After the horror we had just been through, it was her reaction on reaching safety.

The Metropole residents, guests and tourists, were enjoying their afternoon tea and exchanging conversations in various languages. They were aghast when the dishevelled group rushed through the swing doors, disturbing their peace.

'Yes, they did hear the single aircraft flying overhead' apparently they thought it insignificant ... and, 'Yes, they too, had heard an explosion! ... Oh! it was a bomb, was it?' ... When they connected chattering and the reminiscences with reality, everyone came forward to help in some way or another, offering their seats, a cup of tea – their rooms, to have a wash and rest – their clothes. They cried with us – suddenly all languages were unanimously understood.

From refugees we had become VIPs.

Meanwhile, once freed from Ivy's clasp, the receptionist commenced his massive task of taking down the details of the 'intruders', as word had come through to him from the Cathay that they had to take over the responsibility of our welfare until alternative arrangements could be made.

More Cathay guests were arriving. Telephones buzzed incessantly. Some of the SVC men came in to check if all were safely accounted for and asked if they could be of any further help. 'No?' – back to the streets they returned and through the night and the next day clearing up operations continued. Shops – all of them – with plateglass windows had been shattered and were soon boarded up – there was no looting.

Suddenly, Mary – the loner, rushed through the swing doors. We had put an SOS out for her and so many people were trying in vain to help us find her. In reality she was only yards away, following in our foot steps – but she was about an hour behind us. There was a very emotional reunion.

What were we going to do? We were a group of women and children – homeless and without any possessions. Luckily Ivy had her handbag with her – and so did Mary. Nellie's most treasured possession was 'the dress'!

Word soon got around and it was not too long after Mary was reunited with us that Graham, followed by Jimmy Forbes and Graham's father, 'uncle' Jack, came to our rescue. Uncle Jack accepted full responsibility for the Stead sisters' accommodation until other arrangements could be made and so relieved Sassoons for a while.

Jimmy, who was on SVC duty offered us the use of the ICI penthouse 'mess' for the night in order to give us a little respite until the morning. He was sharing the mess with a couple of other SVC men, also on duty, so it was free for our use. It was in Hamilton House, opposite the Metropole. They were twin buildings – one being an hotel and the other an apartment block.

We went across the road – into Hamilton House, waited for the lift – filled it – and up we went, escorted by Jimmy and uncle Jack. It seemed a never-ending journey up and although the apartment was luxurious and comfortable we immediately declined Jimmy's kind offer. We felt too near the sky and the aeroplane! 'No,' we could not stay. So down we went and returned to the Metropole to do some thinking.

We were greeted by more refugees we knew well who were great family friends. Our number had increased from three Steads to a refugee party of eleven. Uncle Jack decided, for the night, as time was moving on, that we should go to his home on Connaught Road. He telephoned Georgina, his wife, to prepare her. Their home was on the outskirts of the settlement on the opposite side of the town – in fact, it was out in the country off Bubbling Well – considered to be a reasonably safe area, for the time being anyway. Georgina was anxious for news as she felt very cut off.

Safe at Connaught Road

We arrived about 8pm – tired, filthy and hungry. Georgina gave us a warm welcome, offered us hot baths, a change of clothing. 'Help yourselves,' she said, as she rustled around in cupboards etc. Her cookboy had prepared a delicious wholesome meal which we all ate ravenously. After much talking reliving the day's events, remembering things undone, like the passports, we eventually drifted apart to our makeshift 'beds' for the night. We slept wherever we found a space – a camp-bed, settee, armchair, on the floor – wherever. We slept well – and remained, not for one night, as originally suggested, but ten. Our 'refugee party' would only be disbanded, uncle Jack said, when he was happy that alternative arrangements for our safety could be made. As uncle Jack, Graham and his brother, Jack, were away most of the time on SVC duty, we had the use of their rooms as well.

We were so relieved to be together, under one roof. Georgina was terrific, she kept us cheerful. We were worried.

* * *

We looked a motley sight in our makeshift wardrobe of borrowed clothes – men's shorts which looked like Bermudas (not in fashion at that time). 'Uncle's' vests which the children wore, more like mini-skirts, were not fashionable then either. When it had been laundered, Nellie still managed to look snazzy in 'the dress' although, by now, it was stained with coffee, dried blood, and had a couple of snags.

Should the Japanese Swarm In ...

The planes – Japanese now – droned on and on and the news got progressively worse and most of our talk was on what would be the best thing to do should we be invaded by the Japanese – what, for instance, would we do if Japanese soldiers walked into the house? They could, easily – we were on the outskirts after all – but, luckily for us, the wrong side for the moment as the Japanese were battling on the Chapei/Hongkew side of the border. No doubt we would soon be 'next' on their tactics list.

As we passed the days worrying and wondering what we ought to be doing next uncle Jack, unbeknown to us, was receiving threatening letters – some enclosing plans of his home and giving details of who was there, and where in the house they were sleeping. If this and, if that, – they warned – they were going to dive over the house then send in a contingent of men and – well? The answer to that would have been wholesale destruction and mass rape – that was what was on everyone's mind at the time – 'destruction and rape'. These were new words and frightening times. Uncle Jack managed to come home a few nights and we all knew how terribly worried he was. He looked it. He had taken on a lot of responsibility. Us.

One night, as we were assembled around the dining table uncle Jack looked (to Nellie at least) angry. He was worried, very very worried indeed. Soon after the meal started we could hear IT – an aeroplane flying very low as though it were circling around the house and garden – it then disappeared. Uncle Jack stared at Nellie – in such 'anger' – that she thought she had done something dreadful and was in trouble. She felt so guilty although she knew she had done nothing to offend him – then it happened. The plane returned and dived over the house – zoomed up, then disappeared. A warning. As it dived Uncle Jack shouted, 'Under the table'. There the meal ended.

The rest of the night – Jack and Georgina were in deep conversation and by the early morning they announced that we must move. They gave no reasons as to why.

Later, we were told by Georgina that the reason uncle had stared at Nellie – was that he had to make a snap decision if the aeroplane came overhead again. The decision he had made – a dreadful one – was that he would have to shoot us all rather than let us go through the atrocities and rape which the enemy had warned him about – who to shoot first? Nellie as she was the youngest at the table. His wife would be the last, as he knew she would be brave and understand what he was doing.

Hurried arrangements were made by telephone that some of the ladies, particularly those with children, had to go immediately to other friends. Uncle Jack was a target! He was the Senior Officer of the SVC – knew too much, was too efficient and was in the way. Georgina opted to stay at Connaught Road no matter, and so she did. She was very brave.

Another Move – to the French Concession

Sassoons, who were in constant touch with Uncle Jack, took over our welfare once again. The Steads prepared for their fourth move in less than two weeks. We were allocated a room with bathroom en suite in the Cathay Mansions on Rue Cardinal Mercier – French town. It was a private hotel with long-term residents.

By this time the *Rajputana* and *The Empress of Asia* had arrived to transport British women and children evacuees to Hong Kong. A couple of American ships had also arrived to convey American women and children to Manila, in the Philippines. A mass exodus.

Having not been able to contact Dad who was still in India and who had had no word from us, or about us – and with Bessie anywhere, but suppossedly in Pei-tai-ho, we declined the offer to travel on either of these two ships. So we stayed put for a while at the Cathay Mansions and listened to the intensive firing and watched anxiously as the Japanese planes circled round and round dropping their bombs on the Chinese areas.

There was no let up and then after a further week news came through to us that the *Empress of Canada* had arrived to convey more British evacuees to Hong Kong. It was a question of now, or never! Sassoons rounded up more of their staff. Arrangements had been made that their Hong Kong office would take over our welfare. We had a day's notice to get ready to leave.

We did not have much to 'get ready' with – we were still in the same clothes as when we left 323 the Embankment. The snazzy dress was now well snagged, but wearable. Graham, Mary and Ivy managed to get back to the Cathay Hotel to retrieve the passports and what little clothing we had remaining there.

Our final escape – down the Whangpoo – was out to sea to board the *Canada* and hopefully some communication with Dad and Bessie.

EVACUATED TO HONG KONG

There was a truce arranged for a short period in order that women and children could be evacuated. Their last opportunity. We had to assemble at the Shanghai Club, on The Bund. Instructions had been issued to all British residents in the eventuality of an evacuation, whenever, so we were well versed on that. Also, as per instructions, we knew we were only permitted to take a small suitcase of clothing. Never did we ever expect to have to carry out these instructions. But, here we were.

The Shanghai Club was humming with women and children's voices – a NO-NO – as it was a man's club, exclusively – so were we privileged. It sported the longest bar in the world.

Once assembled and accounted for we were handed little cards on which were our details and instructions for the onward journey. Next, to the Customs jetty – opposite the club – where we reassembled ourselves to await launches and other small craft to take us midstream to the British gunboat which would convey us down the river to the ship.

Looking back now, we remember one amusing moment when we had to leave the launch to board the gunboat. Mary, who loathes to be noticed, tried to be inconspicuous and at the same time keep with Ivy and Nellie. On boarding the gunboat she saw a piece of what she thought was rope to hang on to so made a grab at it – no rope – it was the ship's bell and it made a tremendous clang. Mary was beyond herself with embarrassment but Ivy and Nellie couldn't resist a giggle when they looked around and saw Mary's face!

We were directed below deck and as we were going down the Whangpoo past Woosung the Japanese broke the truce and opened fire again across the river – and in the firing the ensign of the gunboat was blown off.

*   *   *

At long last we reached the *Canada*. It was waiting for us out at sea where the Whangpoo ends at the mouth of the Yangtze. It was frightening. All of us, even the little children and mothers with babies in their arms, had to climb up the side of the huge ship on an ordinary ship's gangway with only the sea below us. We had to move very carefully as with everyone doing the same thing, at different speeds, the gangway was swaying. We were scared. The sailors and ship's crew were wonderful as they carried the babies and helped the little children – some crying with fear. When we reached the top and were actually on board the *Empress of Canada*, there were the passengers – waiting to welcome us and give us just everything. We were fortunate as we were given a cabin to share with some other office girls but most of the evacuees – babies as well – had to sleep on the deck. But we were safe. We were issued life-jackets as we boarded and we made good use of them as seating was scarce.

Arrival in Hong Kong

When we arrived in Hong Kong, we were directed to a room in Holland House, Icehouse Street. It was a new Sassoons office block and the sixth floor offices had not as yet been released for renting. There were seven of us from the Shanghai office and we shared one enormous room. We were given two dressing tables, two wardrobes and one chest of drawers between us and had a camp-bed each. There were no curtains. The room was on the corner of the building which narrowed to a blunt-point. There were windows all around us so we each chose a window of our 'own' as our special area and home – for how long no one knew. We had the use of the sixth floor office toilets and wash-basins to ourselves. We were in luxury.

The night after our arrival was horrific – there was a typhoon – the wind roared through Hong Kong at 164 mph. We moved away from the windows, nearer the centre of the room. We turned the light off as the single light in the room was swaying around – so was the room – and so were our beds. We were the only occupants in the building and we were on the top floor. We joined hands and decided to move towards the windows to see what was happening in the street as we could hear the banging and crashing of placards – and what sounded like falling trees. We did not stay too long at the windows – the pressure of the wind halted us. To our astonishment there were leaves in the room – blown in? How? By about 3am we were so exhausted we dragged our camp-beds to the corner of the room, near the door, and tried to get some sleep. Some of us were tempted to move to ground level but not knowing what would happen next we were frightened and decided to stay together.

The next day there was an uncanny calm. We ventured out. The sedan chairs for which Hong Kong was famous were haphazardly stuck here and there on the lower Peak Road. They had been lifted up and thrown by the wind. We went for a walk along the waterfront to see what damage there was down there and found that some junks were sinking; others and some ships had been washed ashore. Even the stern of the *Conte Verde* had been lifted up on to the waterfront.

Soon after the typhoon three of the girls left to stay with friends they had made and the remaining four of us moved into a smaller room. We settled down to await news from Shanghai about our return, if possible. Meanwhile we tried to locate our friends and see if there was anything we could do to help each other. We found that Nina and her mother were housed in one of the stables at the racecourse with hundreds of other evacuees – they were not very comfortable. Other friends were housed in dormitories at the Peninsula Hotel, Kowloon, and seemed to be happy there and had lots of friends around them.

Our impression of Hong Kong was one of utter delight. It was so pretty with the hills and sea everywhere and junks in full sail – so very different from Shanghai. But, we still loved Shanghai the best.

Ivy went into the office to see if she could do any work for them and generally make herself useful for which the office were extremely grateful. Most important of all was that we were able to contact Dad. Still no news of Bessie – most worrying.

Nellie remembers being given her usual pocket money, the same amount as in Shanghai – but a different currency. We quote here part of a letter which she wrote to cousin Hilda when giving her an update of the latest news:

' ... Mary gives me spending money (HK$1.20) – the same as I had in Shanghai. It costs me 10 cents to visit Kowloon on the Star Ferry and 10 cents to come back! I usually visit my friends in the dormitories. My treat is to have a scrambled egg and salad and a glass of milk at Jimmy's Kitchen on Saturday morning and I put 10 cents in the Juke Box and pretend I am at a party ... with the balance I can go to the pictures. I went to see "The Last Train from Madrid" and also "Seventh Heaven" (and cried) – it was lovely though ...'

We visited Repulse Bay and also the Lido for swims and took the opportunity of having a holiday – with no money to spare we managed well.

Opposite is an extract from the article which appeared in The Oldham Evening Chronicle dated the 22 October 1937. The article was a summary of the above mentioned account of 'Bloody Saturday'. As mentioned earlier Hilda presented the newspaper cutting to Nellie 47 years later.

*   *   *

Meanwhile up in Pei-tai-ho Mr and Mrs Sands seemed to be the only people with a radio and a vast number of Shanghailanders would come to their bungalow each evening to hear the latest news. Regular attenders were Miss Alexander and Miss Sutherland, Bessie's ex headmistress and her deputy. It was on one of these evenings, a Saturday, that the news came through about the bombing of the Palace Hotel and the Cathay Hotel. This was certainly dreadful news. And then the newscaster announced the names of the few Europeans who had been killed in front of the Palace Hotel. One was a very close friend of Miss Alexander. She was shocked and naturally broke down. The younger set were asked to find something to do elsewhere while Mr and Mrs Sands tried to console her. Little did Bessie know that Mary had had a narrow escape just by being in a bookshop buying up magazines to stave off boredom.

Thousands of Chinese had been killed by the bombs – they had been pouring into the City for about two days and had become a seething mass from the Garden Bridge along The Bund and up all the streets off The Bund. It was on such a crowd that the bombs fell.

——— HER HOTEL BOMBED ———

Girl Of 16 Tells Of Shanghai's 'Bloody Saturday'

Vivid· first-hand account of the horrors of the war in China has been received in Oldham to-day from a 16-year-old Oldham girl in business in China.

WRITING to her cousin, the girl, Miss Nellie Stead, gives an eye-witness account of the happenings in Shanghai on the day now world famous as " Bloody Saturday."

The cousin, Miss Hilda Stead, of Victoria-street, Chadderton, Oldham, who is employed at Ferranti's, Hollinwood, showed me the letter to-day. Here are extracts from it:—

"When rumour of the war was going around in August more than 11.000 Chinese refugees rushed to the Settlement for safety, blocking the bridges of the Soochow Creek.

"I went on our roof with Peggy to see what was happening at Chapei, but we only saw a few fires, rather large ones, and heard a few guns firing at the Japanese barracks.

"Saturday, August 14, was a very trying day. It is now known as 'Bloody Saturday.'

PLANE ATTACK

"In the morning a Chinese aeroplane flew over the Settlement and anti-aircraft guns from the Japanese gunboats, which were anchored opposite the Bund, were trying to get it down. They could not do so.

There were many Shanghailanders on holiday at the time, all wanting news. Helen, Jean and Bessie decided to compile news bulletins each day and they posted these sheets on the postbox at the bottom of the garden by the gate.

Not long afterwards a British naval frigate, the *Defender*, put in an appearance off Pei-tai-ho. All the British citizens were invited on board to a party – no doubt to boost their morale and at the same time to keep an eye on them. Helen and Bessie seemed to stick together on this occasion. They were offered drinks – white ladies recommended – something neither of them had had before. One sip and the rest went into the nearest pot plant, of which there were many decorating the ship on this occasion. They were too inexperienced to pretend to sip. As their glasses were emptied new ones appeared, receiving the same fate – the crew must have thought them pretty seasoned drinkers – to say nothing of the pot plants the next day.

The Shanghailanders seemed to settle down to the nightly bulletins and making the most of an uncertain situation. All passenger shipping to Shanghai had ceased. They heard that all British residents had been evacuated to Hong Kong.

Helen and Bessie celebrated their birthdays (2 and 3 October) at a wonderful party put on by Mrs Sands. They were given free rein to decorate the patio with grapevine and grapes from the garden – there had been a bumper crop that year. Just about every holiday-maker was invited – quite a party. Unfortunately under the thin veneer of birthday celebrations they could detect the tension amongst the guests – not knowing when they would be able to return and whether or not they would have to spend the winter in Pei-tai-ho. The party was greatly appreciated by all at such a worrying time as it brought some light relief. The only compensating factor was the weather – it was glorious.

Although still bathing in sunshine, the weather was getting decidedly cooler – very chilly in the mornings and freezing as soon as the sun went down. There were fewer walks on the beach. Most of the holiday-makers only possessed light clothing, and with prospects of winter not far away, they searched the market for material to make warmer garments. Bessie picked up some very fluffy beige material which she thought would make nice warm slacks. Home-made naturally – they were a disaster – but who cared they were warm!

MARY, IVY AND NELLIE RETURN TO SHANGHAI

Apart from so-called mopping up operations the Japanese had won the battle for Shanghai and already the Chinese were being pursued towards Nanking – but, we were returning home!

We soon had our names down for return passages and were looking forward to picking up the threads again. There was a long waiting list but eventually we received our tickets. It was a wonderful excuse to celebrate with friends also returning to Shanghai. We had lunch at 'Jimmy's kitchen' and it was here that Nellie was offered her first sherry. We soon noticed that she was quiet and when asked if she felt all right – she was supposed to be the chatty one – she replied, 'My head feels so heavy and my arms are so weak'. She was tiddly.

We sailed in October on the *SS Andre le Bon*, a French ship. Because of a strike amongst the cabin crew there was only a skeleton staff available. The cabin accommodation was good but very crowded. We were fortunate in being able to remember some of our school-girl French. It was a strange trip. We were warned against the drinking water and all meals – breakfast included – were served with red wine or coffee.

Most of the distaff side of the office – Sassoons – were on board and we received a royal welcome on arriving in Shanghai.

* * *

In Hong Kong we had been in touch with Dad. He was very worried about us and concerned about the gruelling times we had been through. He felt we should – when we returned – move from the Embankment as he did not realise that the building, although in the international settlement, was actually on the wrong side of the creek should any further incidents be likely to occur.

Now the most important thing to do was find Bessie. We were not too sure what to expect on our return. Helen arrived back in Shanghai soon after we did. She tried to contact us at the Embankment and eventually caught up with Ivy at her office. She was able to tell her Bessie was safe with the Sands and that they were hoping to get a ship back at an early date. The Sands were insistent that Bessie remain with them and that they travel back to Shanghai together.

CHAPTER SIX

Grosvenor Gardens

1937–1940

Dad had been in contact with Sassoons. There was an empty apartment in Grosvenor Gardens – in the residential area of the French Concession opposite the French Club – which they suggested we might prefer to rent rather than return to the Embankment. The apartment consisted of a dining room, lounge and study (open plan), two bedrooms, two bathrooms, large kitchen and servants' quarters on the top floor. One bathroom was situated between the two bedrooms and was known as the 'House of Commons' – the other, by the front door, was given the title 'House of Lords'. Ivy and Bessie could share one bedroom, Mary and Nellie the other.

We fell for the apartment and soon telegrams were being sent to and fro. Dad was pleased we had made up our minds so quickly. With the exception of Nellie we were all working and felt Bessie would agree we could help by contributing to the overheads.

* * *

The Sands made arrangements to close up the bungalow to be ready whenever a passage became available. Jean and Bessie painted a vast Union Jack on the corrugated iron roof – to indicate to any potential bomber that it was British property. They had to go barefoot to negotiate the roof and it took quite a time deciding which way up the stripes should go – it had to be just right.

Two weeks later they were allocated berths. There seemed to be a great deal of luggage so it was fortunate the train delivered them almost to the quayside. Jean and Bessie were given a double berth cabin, Bessie bagging the top bunk, and there she remained for all the trip – she was suffering from heatstroke, the result of painting

114

the Union Jack on the hot roof. Two days later they were woken by
the noise of the anchor being dropped at Woosung. No one seemed
to know much about the situation. All they had to rely on was
snippets of news from the crew and that wasn't too good. Looking
through the porthole Bessie could see a number of ships waiting to
be inspected by Japanese officials before being permitted to sail up
the Whangpoo to Shanghai.

Everyone felt edgy – Bessie for one disliked the planes flying
overhead. They were flying pretty close – too close in fact. After
passports and inoculation certificates were examined the ship was
permitted to proceed up the river. Once the ship had docked they
were transferred to a tender and were taken to the Customs jetty.

* * *

On their return to Shanghai, Mary, Ivy and Nellie were again
invited to stay with Georgina and Jack. It was good to see them and
catch up on happenings while they were away. Dad had arranged
to take leave of absence to see all was well and see how they had
settled into their new home. It was hoped he would arrive before
Christmas.

We were anxious to get settled. The arrangements were going well
– the movers had been engaged and all we had to do was be patient.
Like all females Mary and Ivy found this very hard to do and
eventually Graham was persuaded to borrow a light van and drive
them over the Honan Road bridge to the flat so that they could sort
out and pack their personal belongings. Whilst there the Japanese
again decided to dive bomb the railway station in Chapei. They were
terrified. Mary was prepared to abandon the trip but Graham and
Ivy having come this far were not. Because of the curfew the bridge
would be closed at 6pm so they called it a day. Graham had
difficulty starting the van – more panic. Eventually after much
tinkering with the engine he managed to get it going and they made
it just in time.

We had to wait a few days before the furniture was delivered.

* * *

We kept in close touch with the shipping company for news of the
Sands and Bessie and lost no time in meeting the next ship. What
a thrill it was to see Bessie amongst the group on the tender as it
pulled alongside the Customs jetty. She seemed to be wearing all

her wardrobe of clothes to keep warm – she looked well padded but not fat. She seemed so desolate but as soon as she spotted us her face lit up and the tears flowed. A very happy moment for us as well as we shed tears of relief.

Bessie did not know that we had moved and it was fun taking her out to our new home. On the way Nellie took the opportunity to confess that 'the dress' she had promised on no account to borrow, had in fact been lived in, slept in, dressed up in and evacuated in, and was now hanging IN RUINS in the wardrobe. She was very forgiving.

Bessie was very taken by all she saw and liked the new set-up very much. Our furniture had fitted in well and there were only a few personal touches to be added.

*   *   *

Bessie found it impossible to sleep that first night – there was so much noise with guns going off all the time – she was scared stiff. We were terrified too but were not going to tell her that – we tried to act very blasé and assure her that the firing was nowhere near and that in time she would get used to the noise like everyone else.

The next night was Halloween and there was a party on at the YMCA. Nellie was going to it with her pals and Bessie was invited along as well. The guns were going off like crazy. Bessie was apprehensive but was again assured by Nellie that it was quite safe. They took rickshaws down to the 'Y', which was opposite the racecourse, and the nearer they got the more frightened they became. The whole sky was constantly lit up by flashes of gunfire. Graham, through the SVC, had heard that something was afoot and he and Mary were worried and decided to join the party – Bessie and Nellie spotted them occupying a table by themselves trying to look as though they were having a good time. As soon as the party was over Mary insisted they all get back home as soon as possible.

In the morning all was clear. What Graham had heard was that the Japanese were determined to get a lone battalion out of a warehouse just the other side of the Soochow creek. Although the 'Y' was on the settlement side of the creek it was only two miles away from the warehouse and in direct line of fire. The 'Lone Battalion', as they were then called, had been routed and the battle for Shanghai was won by the Japanese.

A victory parade was held soon afterwards. There were cheers from bystanders – mostly Japanese – but to us the column looked exhausted and the horses half-starved. We watched from the office window and, when waving to a friend watching from the window of the Palace Hotel across the street, were photographed by a Japanese photographer in the crowd. They were obviously on the look-out for trouble.

* * *

Nellie was looking forward to continuing her secretarial course prior to starting work. Dad was due to arrive from India for his much longed for visit. It was great fun – we were all adults now and enjoyed a special comradeship with Dad. He took us everywhere and was delighted to show off his girls. He gave dinner parties for us to meet or rather renew the friendship of his special friends – the Brownriggs, the Millers, the Caines and many more – others like Auntie, the Vincents and the Loutitts had left Shanghai. Very important to us, he took great delight in meeting our friends. It was such a happy time. We also had fun shopping together – keeping four girls in the lap of luxury was something to be proud of.

The highlight of Dad's trip, after getting us fixed up with furnishings and new crockery – the last lot had gone to pot – was Mary announcing her engagement to Graham. His mother, Georgina, put on a delicious spread and opened up the champagne to wish the happy couple well.

Dad took the opportunity on this visit to sound Nellie out – as he was away so much he had not had the privilege of helping Mary, Ivy and Bessie with their careers. 'Well, now lass', started Dad, as he turned to Nellie, 'Now that you are ready to face the world – what do you really want to do with your life? Some of our friends say you should be a receptionist or, something along those lines, as you have no problem chatting with people, but, the question is, what do you want to do?' With no hesitation on Nellie's part she replied, in all seriousness, 'What I'd really like to do is be either a lowdown night club singer, or a Nun, Dad.' No more was said and soon after Nellie acquired her first post as a junior secretary with the British Residents' Association (BRA).

Meanwhile, never at a loss, Nellie would occasionally spend a Saturday morning making some fudge and, in case it made her thirsty, she would take a little bottle of water, and set off for an adventure on a bus. Any bus route would do – the further into the native area the better. She never took her regular route – it had to be something different and she would excitedly watch out for new things to talk about when she got home. She would pay for her journey to the end of the route, stay on the bus, and then pay for the return journey back home. Sometimes she didn't even know where she was – why worry? One day when Dad was with us on a visit Nellie found the route was taking her down the famous Yates Road. She just couldn't get home quick enough to tell Dad that she had found the perfect tailor's shop for Mary and Ivy. 'Because', she said 'the shop has a sign in the window which says "Ladies Have Fits Upstairs".' Dad really enjoyed that tale and teased Mary and Ivy about it many a time.

A special evening shared with Dad was almost ruined until his sense of humour came to the fore and saved the day, or rather evening. He took us out for an enjoyable meal and then to see a movie at the Cathay Cinema just down the road from the apartment. It was so near, there was no rush – you guessed it, we were late. The lights were out and the movie had started. Mary led the way aided by a shaded torch held by the usherette. The first two seats in the row she was shown into were occupied so she carried on and sat down in the fourth empty seat instead of the fifth. Poor Dad, he came in last and thinking an empty seat had been left for him, went to pull down the seat only to find his hand sliding from a lady's forehead all down her front. He was horrified and furious with us but, once home, we all saw the humour of the situation and had a good laugh.

* * *

When we left the Embankment, Amah and Cookboy, who had seen us through all our growing-up years, decided they were ready for retirement. We were sad to see them go but in their kindly way they found replacements and instructed them as to our wants. The new cook had at one time been employed by an American lady and brought new-to-us recipes with him. However, he still remembered old English favourites and his 'dry stew' was something special. The nearest to it seems to be 'stovies' though he added cubes of meat and the usual vegetables. Though the stew was dry it was still succulent.

Another favourite was his rice pudding made with Carnation Milk and cream. On this trip from India Dad was introduced to the, by now famous, pudding and requested another just so he could watch it being made and so teach Joseph, his cook, on his return to India. He got it all written down and his comment to us later was 'You might well be fat'.

Dad's holiday came to an end and not knowing when we would be together again it was a very tearful goodbye. Dad, must have been lonely in India but it still was not possible for us to join him. We had had a very special time together and prayed that it would not be too long before we would see him again.

* * *

There were many reports in the daily papers of the plight of Chinese refugees who were homeless and in great need. There had been so many wounded and killed during the hostilities that the survivors were having difficulty getting themselves settled. Grace Lavington and Mary decided to start a work party to knit garments and blankets for the refugee children. We called ourselves the Knatty Knitters Klub, in short KKK. There were many alternatives thought up, for example, Katty Kitten Klub and Knatty Knickers Klub. Gradually our strength grew until we were twenty strong. Having our apartment to ourselves – when Dad was away – this became the place where we met every Monday and took it in turns to play hostess. We met after work and spent the evening knitting and sewing small garments – homework was a knitted 6 inch square (15cm x 15cm) to be sewn into a blanket at the next meeting. This we took it in turns to do. In summer, out would come the sewing machines – portables borrowed from parents – and by way of a change we would sew 'split' pants. Our Amah had given us the pattern of this very ingenious garment worn by toddlers. No nappy was needed – the child would squat (outdoors of course) and 'hey presto' the pants would open up very conveniently.

Through the KKK Nellie became friendly with Joy, Grace's younger sister. Their common interest was music, and they thoroughly enjoyed many concerts.

Later, when Nellie had her first daughter, she named her Joy – after Joy Lavington.

* * *

Our new amah was a younger version but just as kind as our old one. We were always finding out new things – this time it was about the amah's 'bound' feet which hampered her movements. We had often seen women with bound feet but this was the first time we had come in close contact with them.

It became the tradition during the Sung dynasty to bind the feet of the upper class young girls. The feet were wrapped tightly and slowly bent until the arch was broken and the heel turned under to produce a foot approximately half the normal size. Small feet were a thing of beauty. Amah actually showed us her feet and we were shocked to see the mutilation – the pain must have been excruciating. During the present century this practice began to die out and was outlawed during 1949.

Cotton or silk socks were worn over the bindings and soft shoes were worn in bed. Special shoes were made – the soles reinforced with stitching and the tops highly embroidered – for party wear and on special occasions such as Chinese New Year.

The regular shoes for both men and women were made of black cloth. The sole – usually 3 cm thick – was made up of layer upon layer of cotton cloth or rags sewn with a pad like stitch to form a very firm and hard wearing sole. This, being flat and stiff, was usually shorter than the upper so that it was easier to walk. Ivy had a pair of these which she took into camp when she was interned by the Japanese – she recommends them for comfort and hard wear.

* * *

Our amah must have had money problems because we used to get frustrated when we were unable to find the clothes we wanted to wear on occasions particularly when the seasons changed from a cool day to a really hot one (spring and autumn). Amah would argue that we left our clothes at our friends' houses – like all youngsters to this day we loved to spend the night with pals rather than travel home in the dark alone. However it was with surprise one day when Nellie was doing her spring cleaning – a hobby she still enjoys – and thought she would give the china cabinet a good do. There was a tiny unused drawer at the bottom of the cabinet. Nellie pulled it out to dust it and out fell a bundle of little chitties written in Chinese. She was about to throw away this rubbish but instead showed it to Mary. On checking through the papers Mary found that they were pawntickets for our clothes. Winter clothes pawned in the summer and summer clothes pawned in the winter – poor amah, no wonder we couldn't find our favourites. Our boxroom being next to amah's quarters on the top floor made the temptation difficult to resist. We retrieved our clothes, sorted them out and disposed of the moth-eaten woollies and forgave her – no more was said, amah never knew what we had done. In fact, we bought her some material for a new pair of trousers for her Chinese New Year celebrations.

*   *   *

Nellie's first job was at the British Chamber of Commerce where she worked for the Secretary of the BRA. She did quite a lot of typing for a Mrs Giles – a charming lady who spent most of her time writing reports. However, one of Nellie's main tasks was to ensure that members of the BRA kept up their membership, by paying their subscription each year. Although it was considered a mundane job it was, in essence, an essential job. Keeping an eye on all British residents in Shanghai was important and records had to be up-to-date. Members who were to be out of Shanghai or on overseas leave were to advise the BRA, and the date of their departure and return recorded. Needless to say in times of emergency this information was vital.

She organised two boxes – one labelled 'Paid' and the other 'Unpaid'. She was learning to be methodical. All subscriptions were due on 1 January. When they came in all Nellie had to do was collect the money, make out a receipt – find the member's card in the unpaid box and enter the date of payment and then file the card away in the paid box for another year. Big deal – yet important. Occasionally the Secretary would check through the boxes and fiddle with the cards – much to Nellie's annoyance. No doubt he was recording deaths, marriages and births (Nellie was not quite ready for that responsibility yet). However, the big day arrived when a gentleman phoned and wanted to speak to the young lady in charge of the membership of British residents. This was it! Nellie was needed to answer a question – hooray. The big question? 'How many British residents are there in Shanghai at the present time?' Nellie braced herself before giving the answer in her most efficient way. 'What would you like to know,' she asked 'the paid or the unpaid members?' Hoots of laughter on the line – it was brother-in-law-to-be Graham's practical joke. Horror. It took a long time for Nellie to live that one down.

Thursday evenings was open house night to some of the KKK girls. Mary had managed to secure the services of a Chinese amah who specialized in manicures and would experiment on anything that would enhance ones beauty. She gave a neck and shoulder massage which was very restful after a stress filled day at work. Another accomplishment was trimming and reshaping eyebrows. This she did by using a long piece of white cotton thread – wrapping it around the thumb and forefinger of each hand to form a figure eight. This was then twisted by a movement of a hand until the 'twist' would trap a hair – sometimes a bunch of hairs – and it would be yanked out by the root. This procedure was used by Chinese women down through the ages. They removed the hair from the scalp to form a very high forehead – another sign of beauty. In time the hair did not grow back so one could relax. Talking about hair – Fridays were known as 'Amami' (the trade name of a shampoo) night when hair was washed and set in curlers, wrapped in a silk scarf in case someone called, and left to dry naturally. This was before the days of household hair dryers. Thursdays and Fridays were popular – by the time the weekend arrived we were beautiful and ready for the tea dances, etc.

A tea dance, usually held at the French Club on Sunday afternoons, was the favourite winter social activity – particularly of the younger set. During the summer months various organisations and clubs would set up bamboo shacks on the racecourse and tennis courts would be laid out. Various competitions were held and as the season drew to a close each club would hold a soiree when a buffet was served prior to the giving out of prizes. The courts were covered with a canvas sheet, coloured lights were strung up and informal dances would be held. There would be much visiting between the clubs as all parties were not held on the same night – dancing out in the open under a starry sky was most romantic, particularly to the strains of 'Deep Purple', 'A-Tisket A-Tasket', and 'Blue Moon' to name a few of our favourites.

Some Saturday afternoons Nellie took it upon herself to tidy up (not the flat as that was kept immaculate by Amah and Cookboy) but Mary, Ivy and Bessie's wardrobes and dressing table etc. They usually came home – fed-up with Nellie's efforts because they couldn't find things – and besides she made sure the laddered stockings were not hers! She had the perfect ones – worst of all was her nagging and being told, yet again 'you'll never make proper housewives if you can't keep tidy...' nag, nag.

'Oh, look!' called out Nellie excitedly one day 'look what's in the cage – I can't believe it – it's a budgie'.

Nellie loved having her own pets so bought herself a canary with a pretty cage. She then proceeded to give the canary singing lessons! She would spend ages sitting by the cage rubbing a cork up and down a bottle of water – which was damp on the outside – until it squeaked. Sometimes the canary responded. Nellie really felt the singing lessons were working – she was ever so proud of her little canary. She would talk to it, clean its cage, and care for it by making little toys for it to play with. Then one morning when she went to take off its night cover, she found a budgie sitting happily alongside the canary on its perch. Although we asked neighbours we could not find its owner. How he got there – the cage was closed – Nellie never found out. He would manage to squeeze himself out of the cage, sit on the top of it, fly around a bit then squeeze itself back into the cage – he was quite tame. So he remained with us for exactly a year when he disappeared as mysteriously as he had appeared. The singing lessons ceased as by now we had a real chirper (besides Nellie) in the family.

* * *

The Palace Hotel in Nanking Road was known for its Saturday morning coffee sessions as well as the usual afternoon tea. A special feature was floor length windows through which the guests could be seen and envied. 'Annie' Caines, spent part of his service at the Central Fire Station, near the Palace Hotel, and his dog soon discovered the advantages of visiting the patrons enjoying tea. They thought he belonged to the Manager of the hotel and gave him the odd titbit. 'Annie' wondered why his dog was putting on weight and put him on a diet – more trips to the hotel.

* * *

There were no 'Follies' in 1937 – for reasons known to you – so Ann had to make quite sure that the 'Follies of 1938' went off with a big swing from beginning to end. We recommended our dancing lessons early in the year when the general atmosphere was back to normal and at long last there was peace and freedom of movement – although there never was any restriction in movements one felt uncomfortable and the Japanese made sure that this feeling continued to fret us.

Bessie and Nellie were chosen to do an extra special number to the tune of 'The Parade of the Tin Soldiers' by Leon Jessel. They had the full stage to cover with their dancing and two sentry boxes. Their movements were stiff – like a tin soldier – and their tap steps sharp, fast and to the beat of drums. The curtain fell after they tapped backwards with fast military-like steps and stopped outside their sentry boxes and gave a smart salute. It was precision work and took a lot of practising in a mirrored studio to ensure their movements were as one – it was really well done – it called for an encore. They always fondly remember the 'Tin Soldiers' routine as their No.1 dance and the uniforms they wore were terrific. Black trousers with a gold strip down the side – red tops with lots of gold braid and tall red hats – more braid and a plume and a gold chain chin-strap.

There were several other numbers in which they took part with the group. 'The Song of India' was an acrobatic harem scene. There was a Russian dance with lots of movement and a high-steppers' dance from Broadway – more top hats, tails and high kicks – rather like the Tiller Girls. The school did their best and Ann put her all into this production not knowing that it would be her last 'Follies'. The war broke out in 1939.

* * *

It was at the tennis club on the racecourse that Nellie first met Barney Maclean and later his pal Bunny Aust, who came out to Shanghai to join the Tramways. Barney's father was also with the Tramways. Nellie and Barney were great pals and Barney was a lovely dancer so Nellie was really swept off her feet. They spent many happy hours at the Palace Hotel Tea Dances. One of their favourite tunes was 'Roll Out The Barrel' – (we'll have a barrel of fun). And, so they did. It was their signature tune and the band usually struck up this melody when they entered the ballroom. They were special pals for a year or so – later Barney left Shanghai to join the services overseas and became a prisoner-of-war. The last we heard of Barney and some other friends was when they were herded together by the Japanese and shipped to Japan. They were battened down in the hold of a ship which was torpedoed by our own people. Sadly they all perished. One of the happy times they shared was when Barney was an usher at Mary and Graham's wedding.

The Cathay Hotel had a large ballroom where we spent many a sophisticated evening. However, the French Club and the Paramount Ballroom were our favourites – each had enormous dance floors which were beautifully sprung and made you feel very agile and weightless. The latter had a very special bar on one side where there was a glass floor over coloured lights – all very flattering for a girl as she glided over its highly polished floor but, as far as the boy was concerned, it was a bit of a headache trying to manoeuvre his girl through the crowd.

After Ronnie Crouch, Bessie became interested in Leo. He was as short as Bessie, a Greek with ever smiling face, one bright lump of gold shining each time he smiled. He was a good dancer and Bessie loved dancing. Their paths crossed later in Calcutta.

*   *   *

Our KKK Group was flourishing. We fondly remember some of the members – Sybil, Grace, Joy, Helen, Amy and Ella Smith (sisters), Beryl Smith, Lorraine and others. We got on well together and soon began to ring the changes by having a quick meeting and then going out for Sukiyaki (Japanese food) which we all enjoyed, or a Chinese meal at Sun Yah, a well known restaurant on Nanking Road. Mary and Ivy were not very fond of Chinese food at this time and would opt for one of the alternatives – curry. Life was becoming very social. Mary was engaged and we each had boy friends.

Mary and Grace – prospective brides – decided they should try their hand at cooking and so planned a dinner at which Ivy, Bessie and Nellie were to be their guests.

After the soup, they served roast lamb with roast potatoes, minted peas and glazed carrots. The dessert was puréed prunes and cream.

It took them hours to get everything ready – the girls were famished and they did justice to the soup and meat course. But the dessert! It was a flop in more ways than one. They had spent their afternoon on a walk in the country and puréed prunes reminded them too much of the cows they had seen ... 'nuff said.

Leslie and Pauline Smith were still at the Embankment. Leslie's description of the girls was that Mary was beautiful, Ivy attractive, Bessie handsome and Nellie pretty. Ivy was enjoying their friendship and hospitality and it was through them that she met Donald Davey again – you will remember Frank Elliott's friend of Yangtzepoo days. Donald was amazed to see the difference between the 'young lady' sitting next to him at dinner and the twelve year old 'brat' who had been such a nuisance. It didn't take long for both Donald and Ivy to make up their minds and they became engaged in March 1939. To re-cap at this moment, Dad being an engineer was known for his technical drawings which were superb. He was also known to draw caricatures, a skill which Nellie has inherited. Nellie is also a mimic and would amuse us all on Sundays by taking off our latest boy friends until we couldn't stand the sight of them. After Donald appeared on the scene it was more than her life was worth to carry on this practice – she got the message.

Donald had three sisters. Two, Gladys and Margaret, lived in North China so Ivy didn't get to meet them until much later. Dorothy, his eldest sister, lived in Shanghai with her husband, Gordon Day and their son, Christopher, and daughter Elizabeth. Dorothy and Ivy were great pals – Ivy loved her dearly. Soon after they were engaged Dorothy had a birthday party for Elizabeth to which Joan Miller was invited. Joan was very upset on hearing Elizabeth call Ivy 'Auntie'. She insisted she was a closer relative. 'I don't care' she said, 'She's my Godsister'.

Graham was always fond of sports, especially running. His best race was the 440 yards for which he held the Shanghai championship. He was invited to represent Great Britain when Glen Cunningham, the world renowned runner, was in Shanghai. Though he was still only a school boy he provided keen competition. While Bessie was working for The Bus Company she decided to join Graham and train along with him. She was doing well and enjoying it until Graham introduced her to eating garlic to keep up her strength.

Graham then turned to riding and thought it would be nice if Mary could join him on rides out in the country. The thought was exciting though she was a little apprehensive after her experience in Peru. Stables near their home had attracted Mary and Ivy to the horses; they loved to watch them being groomed and exercised. All went well and they thoroughly enjoyed themselves until they picked up an insect – a picar – which made its home in the straw. This insect would burrow underneath a toenail to lay its eggs. Needless to say it was a very painful experience – the insect and its eggs having to be dug out and the area sterilised. However, she was determined to give it a go and keep Graham company and was soon able to enjoy the rides in Hungjao outside the settlement.

Graham's horse had to have a red ribbon tied to its tail to show he was a 'kicker' and she soon learnt that it was prudent never to get behind it. One Sunday it stumbled badly, and Graham came to grief sailing over its head. Momentarily he was stunned and asked her to give chase to try and catch his horse – she tried, but very half-heartedly. When Graham recovered he managed to coax the horse back to him, and so they returned to the stables until the next weekend ride.

Mary's efforts encouraged Graham and his next project was to teach her to shoot. They spent many happy hours aiming at floating objects in the stream at the bottom of the garden, or trying to put out a lighted candle. This was too much for Mary – she felt she was reliving a part of her parents lives and couldn't resist telling Graham about Mother and Dad learning to shoot for protection from rebels whilst in Mexico in the early days of 1913 – and also as a safeguard against wild animals. When the necessity arose Mother wore her pistol on a chain around her neck and tucked into the waist band of her skirt. Dad became very proficient and was reputed to be the first man to shoot an earthquake. This was later when the family had moved on to Peru. When he first experienced a tremor and its subsequent noise, he thought someone was breaking in. Dad went on the verandah with his pistol and shot into the air to frighten off the intruders and forever afterwards was teased about being the first man to shoot an earthquake.

Graham's first car was a little Belila Fiat. He was six feet tall and the car so tiny that he was teased about how he got into it or, sometimes, which foot it fitted. However, they loved it and it served them well as in spite of living at different ends of the city they were able to spend a great deal of time together.

* * *

Bessie's love of swimming continued. Vera and family were members of the French Club and, as this was directly across the road from our apartment, Bessie became a swimming member there in order to use the pool which was 50m long and twice the width of the Rowing Club pool. A larger pool is 'heavier' to swim in and thus good experience. In 1938 she finally plucked up courage to enter the championships. The young Dodds were taking part and persuaded her to join them. The championships were held in the YMCA pool and the heats ran each evening for a week. Bessie entered the 50 yards free style and won her heat. She was unlucky in the final swim but the excitement of participating, the atmosphere and smell of chlorine more than made up for the loss.

At this time Jack, Ginger's younger brother, was doing spectacular things with the back stroke – he had gone to Japan to learn the latest techniques. He was a beautiful swimmer, tall and glided gracefully through the water with no effort. Bessie also attempted the back stroke with tips from Jack, though nothing came of it. Her best stroke was the crawl.

Bessie was going steady with Laurence Beattie about this time. She had met him again at the Rowing Club and with Vera and her escort, Francis Carey, formed quite a foursome. On Saturdays the boys played rugby and, as usual, there was quite a female following through the winter months. It was bitterly cold standing about watching the match. The boys were grateful for the support they showed and more often than not an invitation followed to join them for an evening out at their special haunt – the 'Maskee Bar' (a night club) on the 14th floor of the newly built Park Hotel opposite the racecourse.

Summers were taken up by rowing and swimming. Bessie decided to knit Laurence a pair of socks for rowing. She had done quite a bit of knitting in the past but never a pair of socks – that is how keen she was. When she saw them again after a season, and only one wash, her enthusiasm waned. They were a dirty grey, half the size and as stiff as a board.

She was invited by Mr and Mrs Beattie to join them at the Caledonian Ball – Laurence to be her partner. There were four balls a year, St David's, St Patrick's, St George's and St Andrew's, the Caledonian, which was by far the most popular of the four – the Scottish community out-numbering the Irish, Welsh and English. The tradition was for the debutantes to assemble together and line up in front of the President of the Society. They were then each in turn presented to the President. Vera and Jean Todd were also in the line up with Bessie that night. Although Bessie had been 'out' quite a few times, it was her first ball – the official thing. Practices for the reels took place for six weeks prior to the night and each proved to be almost as much fun as the ball itself.

They had special white dresses made. Bessie went back to old faithful – yes, the Kumping Road tailor – who turned out a breathtaking clipsation. It was a white chiffon affair, the bodice consisting of small pleats – no modern pleating machines in those days – with a full circular skirt studded with diamantés lovingly applied by hand. Truly a work of art. Bessie felt and looked a million dollars. The line-up of dresses on the night was so beautiful.

* * *

Although one could say that Barney was Nellie's date, her group of pals kept very much together and Henry was her special friend. Henry was kindness in itself. Having four sisters – he being the youngest of the family – was perhaps the reason why Nellie did not get to know him too well until she was in her teens. The Eardleys lived in the French Concession and later when we moved to that area he was a frequent visitor. His sisters had married or had moved out of the family home to keep up their careers. We suppose we became his second set of 'sisters' – if that could be possible. Henry would call on us on a Sunday morning, after church. We looked forward to his visits. Mary was really taken by Henry because he was the only person who used to call her by her full name 'Rosemary' – she loved that. Nellie – although outwardly boisterous, still very shy – wished the floor would swallow her up when one day Henry called with his camera. They walked around the grounds of Grosvenor Gardens – one picture of Henry by the fountain, one picture of Nellie by the fountain – and so on. He really wanted to have one of 'Henry and Nellie' so thought perhaps Rosemary would take one. They returned to the flat and Mary was happy to oblige, so it was decided to take this special photo on the roof-garden. They stood – almost to attention – side by side waiting to smile for the birdie when Henry whispered to Nellie 'do you like chicken?' Loving her food she responded quickly 'Yes...' to which he answered 'take a wing...' and offered his elbow for Nellie to slip her hand through – Click!! went the camera and poor Nellie was so embarrassed to think that Mary could see through the viewer how 'forward' she was! A lovely age – sixteen going on seventeen!

War Efforts

In 1939, as the refugees gradually became more settled, and needing a change, the KKK decided to work towards a Christmas bazaar. Little did we know that World War II would soon be declared and we would switch our support to the war effort. This brought us tremendous recognition from the British Women's Association who, along with our friends and families, gave us their whole-hearted backing. Lady Clark Kerr, wife of the British Ambassador, arrived in time to open the bazaar at 2.30pm and was received by Grace, our Chairperson.

We were full of importance. We hired the Masonic Hall – a very grand building in the residential district – and decorated it with pot plants loaned to us by the local garden centre. The numerous stalls were attractively set up around the hall, and to add to the afternoon's enjoyment, Santa Claus was very busy walking around and cheering up the little folk. A fortune teller and caricaturist were also at the bazaar and proved to be very popular. A delicious tea was served and during the afternoon an orchestra played, which added to the highlights of the occasion. The majority of the lovely articles on sale at the bazaar were made by members of the KKK and the large crowd present found many ideal Christmas gifts among the selection. The stalls at the bazaar were: home eats, household, linen, toys, tiny tots, milady's stall and bran pie. A very successful afternoon.

Many other charity functions were being arranged as contributions to the war effort – fetes, coffee parties, knitting parties – whatever could be done towards this cause, was done. Graham, Bessie and Nellie were involved in a revue called 'The Dithyrambics'. Graham was partnered in a singing duet – Bessie and Nellie, representing Ann Summer's Studio, were requested to do their Tin Soldier 'parade' dance. The show was outstanding and financially rewarding.

* * *

The KKK was soon to fade out. Late 1939 and early 1940 was quite a time with the various clubs and organisations holding their annual dances early as a farewell to all young men who were beginning to leave to join the forces. There were numerous weddings with 'showers' and celebrations. We had our share and would wrack our brains trying to come up with an original idea for the latter. One worth mentioning was embroidered guest towels. Each one was wrapped separately with a personalised poem attached – the idea being that the donor had to be guessed before the parcel could be opened. Two verses come to mind.

Ivy's – she became engaged to Donald in 1939:

> *She's told by him her eyes are blue*
> *but freckles often obstruct the view.*

Nellie's, our teenage member, was opened last of all!

> *As nutty as a nut tree*
> *though sometimes fairly bright*
> *A good imitation of the 'Dopey' of Snow White*

Mary and Ivy are Married

Dad arrived from India in January 1940 to give his two eldest daughters away in marriage. The plans for the weddings went off smoothly and we seemed to keep our 'best foot forward' as Dad would advise us to do. No hitches were made, nor bricks dropped (not even by Nellie). Dad admitted to nightmares wondering if all would go well. He dreamt that his new suit – which was made especially for the occasion – had only been tacked together by the tailor and as he was walking down the aisle with Mary on his arm, he caught a stitch in his trouser leg and it began to fall apart! Poor Dad had never had a suit made in a day before and couldn't believe it was possible. We know better – the Chinese are wonderful tailors (also shoemakers) and very quick.

Prior to the weddings Dad thought it was time to give his four 'holding down bolts' a few facts of life. He had us gathered round him in the lounge – Mary and Ivy on the sofa, Nellie and Dad in two of the armchairs and Bessie on the pouffe. We assume he thought he had a bunch of potential 'knowalls' for daughters for he talked what seemed to be forever on the subject of 'acting a little dumb'. He maintained that if we did this – and let our future husbands think they knew everything – we would succeed in our marriages. It must have been about eleven o'clock at night when he launched himself into this topic. We were already dead beat, as there had been a number of late nights because of the forthcoming weddings. Bessie sitting on the pouffe, with no thought of a husband in view, could only think of bed. Dad was aiming his lecture at all of us and we had to stay until he was satisfied he had got through to each. The lecture ended about two in the morning. In retrospect Bessie is the only one who remembers this incident – so much for Dad's effort. However, the phrase 'always act a little dumb' did get through. Whether or not we have taken his advice is for others to decide.

Mary married Graham early in February at the Holy Trinity Cathedral. She was attended by Grace, her sister-in-law, as matron of honour, and her three sisters who were bridesmaids. The bride wore a full, ankle length skirt of white georgette with a fine lace top. Her Queen Anne head-dress, also in lace, held a full veil in place. Her bridesmaids wore long frocks in a beautiful shade of clover marocain with silver embroidery at the neckline. Little pill-box hats with a bow at the back completed the ensemble. They carried pink carnations. The bride's bouquet had a lovely mixture of white and pink roses and sprays of stephanotis. The best man was Graham's brother Jack.

A reception was held at the home of her in-laws, Georgina and Jack. Uncle Miller played an important role at the wedding – he toasted the bride and groom both of whom he had known as youngsters.

Ivy married Donald a month later also at the Holy Trinity Cathedral. Mary was matron of honour, and Bessie and Nellie bridesmaids. Ivy wore white slipper satin cut on classical lines – the skirt was full and ended in a short train. Her head-dress was of pearls and orange blossom and at her neck she wore a small spray of orange blossom. She carried a bouquet of Easter lilies. The attendants wore light delphinium blue georgette full length dresses with long bishop sleeves. The dresses had Peter Pan collars covered with tiny rose buds and they carried blue muffs with sprays of roses attached. They also wore a crown of flowers on their heads. Mary wore the same spray of orange blossom and later it was worn by Nellie and then Bessie. Mary and Ivy wore Grace's wedding veil.

The reception was held at the Masonic Hall. Donald's sister Dorothy was hostess and took it upon herself to arrange everything and also decorate the hall. Bertie Baxter was Donald's best man and the happy couple were toasted by Frank Barry a good friend of both the bride and groom.

* * *

The apartment in Grosvenor Gardens was now too big for the two remaining Steads and Dad was very keen to take the two girls back with him to India. He had been alone for such a long time, and now that education had been taken care of, he was looking forward to the company of some family life again. Also, with the escalation of the war, he quite rightly thought it would be safer for them.

Bessie decided to remain in Shanghai for the time being. With the onset of the war in Europe and unable to stand the leering eyes of the passionate accountant any longer, she had applied for the vacancy in the Press Section of the British Embassy. It was hard work but she enjoyed it.

Nellie was delighted to keep Dad company. She realised he must have been lonely being so far away. He was over the moon when she said 'yes' – it was going to be so special. Once again there was upheaval. Dear old Kumping Road tailor, who was now quite an elderly gentleman, was called in to do yet some more 'leettie darts' and 'clipsations'. Nellie was showered with lovely new clothes – handbags, shoes and exquisite lingerie from Yates Road. Dad made one stipulation – Nellie was to have a 'picture hat', with a georgette ribbon around the brim which hung gracefully with a knot and two tails at the back ' ... like Rita Hayworth would wear ... ' he said. Away Nellie went in search of a hat. She was successful and came back home with the perfect hat for all occasions. The georgette band could be taken off and replaced with different colours. It was a brilliant white straw – perfect for the tropics but she soon found out on arriving in India that the European ladies were not quite so fussy and wore a topee! At the time she bought the hat she also bought a fashionable parasol and found this to be the most useful item in her wardrobe. The day for departure soon arrived as Dad had only come to Shanghai for the weddings. A cabin trunk was purchased and packed, and farewells made. So much was happening in the Stead household. We had spent many happy years in Shanghai and during that time had gone through thick and thin together – we were a strong unit, very close. Now the time had come for us to 'flee' the nest and start new lives.

Dad and Nellie were to sail at the end of March on the *Conte Verde*, a luxury Italian liner, to Bombay.

We were dreading the goodbyes – they were going to be traumatic.

CHAPTER SEVEN

We Disperse

1940

Nellie

Dad and I travelled First Class and as a treat, and an extra farewell present, Dad made sure I had a de luxe cabin en suite to myself. The decor was blue throughout – blue linen, bath, bath towels – everything.

Saying goodbye was heartbreaking – it was not until we started to weigh anchor and move slowly towards Woosung did the farewells hit me. I realised that I had committed myself to the parting of ways. Who could tell what life had in store for us.

Sadness enveloped me as I stood on deck. 'No, I mustn't be sad' I said to myself. 'Mary and Ivy are now happily married and settling into new homes. Bessie is happily settled too.' My thoughts were deep and private. 'I must go down to my lovely cabin and decide what to wear for dinner this evening' I decided. But, these thoughts were so different from the thoughts I had when we were evacuated to the luxurious Cathay Hotel in '37. In my cabin, I changed for dinner as 'me' – no Jean Harlow this time. I had grown up.

Also, our numbered days were a thing of the past. Amah and Cookboy, because they would never call us by name, referred to us by number. I was 'No.4 Missey' – but not any more.

Dinner was delicious – meeting fellow passengers great – the journey showed promise.

It was a pleasant journey and everything new to me. My last farewells were made to friends – the boys who had joined up and were in the navy in Hong Kong, particularly my special friend, Henry Eardley. It was a sad goodbye.

After leaving Hong Kong it was a new world and a new beginning for me, aged nineteen years – with seventeen of them left behind in China.

Mary

Graham worked in the Property Department of Sassoons, and after our wedding we lived in a nice small flat in the Embankment. We enjoyed decorating it and setting out our lovely wedding presents, and generally making it home.

After a few months Graham, with many colleagues, decided to leave for India and join the Army there. Only single men were able to enlist at first, and I had no option other than to stay behind, and decided, after getting a job with the Stock Exchange, to consider it my humble effort at war work. I must admit though that when we heard quite by accident that married men were now being accepted to join the Indian Army, we hastened to make arrangements for me to sail with Graham. We only had two days in which to do this – it really was a frantic time, and we only just made it.

Sadly, I was not able to say goodbye to a lot of friends, and left Shanghai with a feeling of nostalgia and apprehension not knowing when I should see Ivy and Bessie again.

Before we left, Graham made arrangements with a Mr Metha, one of his associates at work, to take over the lease of the flat, but leaving us the use of the boxroom where we stored all our wedding presents and other valuables. The key was left with Ivy.

The men were given an emotional send off. How sad were our goodbyes.

Bessie

Having decided to remain in Shanghai, I accepted a kind offer from Vera's parents to stay with them. There was Old Man Dodd (as he was called) and Mrs Dodd – a sweetie – very motherly and always full of fun. Ray was the eldest of the three children and Jackie was the youngest. Vera came in the middle.

The Dodds were very amiable, except at breakfast. I had always been used to plenty of chat – my over-exuberance at that time of day was not appreciated, especially by Ray. Sometimes Vera and Jackie would come to the breakfast table strutting to 'beat me Mama, eight to the bar' or something else from the Andrew Sisters – but more often than not there was dead silence. However, gradually I changed that. I was with them for about nine to ten months. I realised I should have gone to India at the time Dad and Nellie left but I hated the thought of leaving Shanghai and delayed my departure for as long as possible.

1940 was the year of departures. There were two battalions of British armed forces stationed in Shanghai; the First Battalion of the Seaforth Highlanders and the Second Battalion of the East Surreys. There was also one in Tientsin; the First Middlesex Regiment. They were known as the Shanghai/Tientsin Brigade. The final 'Beating the Retreat' on the racecourse was quite spectacular. It was followed by a reception held in the Race Club rooms to which Alastair Moodie (Seaforths) invited Ivy and Donald, Vera, Ian Denby and I. After the reception, Ivy and Donald entertained us at their flat. It was the first time they had spent an evening with Alastair and said they thought he was a very nice chap. My reply was I thought he had no manners. Needless to say I was married to him within two years.

The next day the Seaforths were on their way. The Fourth United States Marine band played them from the racecourse, where they were billetted, down Nanking Road to The Bund and left to the Garden Bridge. Here the Pipe Band of the Seaforths took over and piped their men the rest of the way to the docks and embarkation. The route was lined on both sides by residents waving flags and singing to whatever tune was being played. Alastair being baggage officer was not in the parade. It was a very emotional event and repeated soon afterwards by the departure of the American Marines and the East Surreys.

It seemed inevitable with the departure of the British and American armed forces that British and American citizens would also be asked to leave if at all possible. More and more of Shanghai's young men were leaving to join the forces. Graham sailed with a number of others to join the Indian Army – there was a big send off for them at the dockside – streamers, music playing them out. There was another not so flamboyant occasion a little while later when Laurence and Ray sailed on a cargo ship to Hong Kong to join the Navy. I was no longer Laurence's girlfriend being superseded by a German lass. I went with the Dodds to see Ray off. My poor heart was broken.

I now realised how much I missed Nellie and her mad ways and there was very little to keep me in Shanghai. I hated to say goodbye to Vera and her family – they had been so good to me and I had enjoyed being with them. I have always regretted I never kept up my friendship with Vera. During the war we lost touch. Vera married into oil and I into insurance. I was so involved with bringing up a family I seemed to have no time for anything else.

I left Shanghai by ship bound for Calcutta with plans to travel by train to Bombay. Ivy came to see me off and it was a sad day for both of us. She was now the only Stead left in China – the country where we had grown up and shared so many happy years together.

It was obvious I had bought luggage for the trip. All business-like except for one Hong Kong basket which contained my pillow. Having shared a room with Ivy for years she was surprised to hear I couldn't sleep without my own pillow. Years later when we met up in the UK and I had Alastair with me, plus our two small children, there was no Hong Kong basket! Being a practical mum I had no time for frills. We had a good laugh.

Ivy

In 1940 the family separated. It was the year Mary and I were married. Nellie left for India with Dad, leaving Bessie to follow later.

Donald had not had much time to shop before our marriage so it wasn't too long before I was detailed to buy him more 'jockey shorts'. Donald was always a tease and said 'Now, don't forget I always dress left'. That did it. Off to Wing Ons I went. I examined the shorts and decided the angle was wrong – I still can't tell my left from my right. Explaining my doubt to the salesman he was taken aback and exclaimed 'Ah Missey, this never can do'. Here endeth the first lesson! Was my face red.

Our honeymoon was delayed until September as Donald had to wait for a replacement to arrive before taking any leave.

We sailed north by Japanese steamer and after twenty four hours arrived at Tsingtao, a delightful holiday spot where many retirees from Shanghai and other eastern ports settled.

The Japanese were always very health conscious and when travelling to Japan a sample of 'stool' had to be produced before landing permits were issued. It was not always possible to do this with the result the ship's cat was followed and the 'find' cut up and shared out.

We didn't fool the authorities for long. We had only been underway a few hours when we were told to report to the Medical Officer's cabin. Filled with curiosity we all complied and actually formed a queue trying to peek into the cabin to find out what was happening. We had met one of our friends on board and we lined up together. When my turn came Donald kept all the peepers at bay. There was a white sheet hung across the cabin hanging to within eighteen inches of the floor – the doctor was on the other side with a porthole behind him. A perfect spot for a bit of shadow acting! One had to drop one's pants, bend over and in a flash the doctor inserted a glass tube and, hopefully, obtained a sample which, when developed, would prove whether or not one had dysentery. Only if clear would you be allowed ashore. Our friend was very short but luckily the sheet was low enough to hide all. The exclamations of the passengers as they left the cabin were varied, from 'Oh my', 'Mama mia', 'Mon Dieu' to 'Ai-yah'.

We stayed in a guest house run by a delightful couple – he was English and she was Russian. Her cooking was superb and being a new bride I tried to get some of her recipes. She was very obliging but as everything (seasonings, cooking times, etc) were 'to taste' it was not very helpful.

Sybil and Geoff Forestier were staying at the same place. Sybil was an old friend and member of KKK, and Geoff and Donald were both members of the Shanghai Rowing Club and had known each other for years. We had some lovely outings and picnics together – unfortunately their holiday was almost over before we arrived. When they left they kindly left us their cholera certificates – we had forgotten to get ours before we left Shanghai – which meant we could visit the town without having to dodge through shop doors to avoid a Japanese armed with a huge syringe ready to inoculate anyone without a certificate. The sight of someone advancing towards me with a needle in his hand still gives me the shivers – be it a legitimate injection as when I had to be piggy-backed home from Dad's office in Yangtzepoo, or even the Kumping Road tailor coming at me with a pin. A communal needle turned me to jelly. It was rather like Walt Disney's rubber stamp – 'You're done', 'You're done'.

Sybil's Dad had worked for the Chinese Maritime Customs and one of his colleagues – Mr Pezzini – had retired in Tsingtao. It was through Sybil that we renewed our friendship with the family. I first met Erminda (fondly called Minda) and her sisters, Leyda and Leitcha, when we attended St Joseph's convent but we lost touch when she left to attend university. They were all very musical and we spent many a happy evening under the stars listening to Minda's mother singing – she had a beautiful voice. Leyda was a pianist and played with the Shanghai Municipal Orchestra.

* * *

Donald and I started our married life living in a small apartment he had furnished before we were married. As people were starting to leave Shanghai we were soon able to move to a larger apartment in one of Sassoon's estates on Avenue Petain at the corner of Zikawei Avenue. In addition to one bedroom and a lounge we now had a dining room and also a large enclosed verandah.

The two battalions of British armed forces and the battalion of American marines stationed in the city were withdrawn in 1940 to serve elsewhere. We hated to see them go but took a deep breath and, as best we could, gave them a happy send off.

Mary and Graham and many other young people were soon on their way to join the forces either in Hong Kong or India. It was while Bessie was staying with the Dodds that she met Alastair of the Seaforths. Donald and I met him at a final reception held for the battalion prior to their departure and after which we enjoyed a meal together. Towards the end of the year Bessie decided to join Nellie and Dad in India – it was then we heard the Seaforths were now stationed there!

Bessie married Alastair in 1941 but not before she had been an attendant at Nellie's wedding to Michael Poole who was, at that time, serving in the Royal Indian Navy Volunteer Reserve.

Meanwhile, Donald again tried to be released from the company only to be told he was expected to remain at his post and act as Head Office for the Far East. The company had agents in Hankow, Tsingtao, Tientsin as well as Hong Kong, Singapore and Manila. As all mail was sent by sea at that time, and ships were continually being sunk, it was necessary to have someone on the spot who could take charge. Presumably nobody expected the Japanese to play such an horrific part in the war – Shanghai being an international settlement would not be affected!

Donald was kept terribly busy – business in Shanghai was being conducted as usual and with his added burden he could only keep up with things by working at home every evening. I was lonely, I missed the family and found the days long. A lot of my friends had already left so when I was offered a job at Jardines – Shanghai's top import and export company, I jumped at the chance.

We were both busy. Life continued on in this way with the news of the war getting worse day by day. Donald was not happy about the situation and booked a passage for me to join the family in India. After a lot of argument on my part we finally settled on a date, after Christmas 1941, the earliest I would leave.

CHAPTER EIGHT

Too Late!

8 December 1941

Japan attacked Hong Kong, Singapore and Pearl Harbour. The western powers declared war on Japan. Ivy, now the only Stead sister left in Shanghai, takes up the story – of her ordeal as a prisoner of the Japanese.

SHANGHAI TAKEN OVER

Geoff Forestier, who was living downtown, told us he was almost blasted out of bed by the big guns on the *Idzumo* tied up half a mile away from the Garden Bridge which spans the mouth of the Soochow Creek. She had been there since 1937 and was part of the scenery, or so we thought. The *Idzumo* was firing at the British river gunboat *HMS Petrel*. The American gunboat, the *USS Wake*, had already surrendered but the *Petrel* had returned fire and refused to surrender and were making efforts to blow it up. Most of the crew jumped overboard and swam to the French Bund where they were taken into custody by the French police and interned in a hospital in the French Concession. France had not declared war on Japan. Geoff immediately turned on his short-wave radio, which he always kept tuned to San Francisco, and heard President Roosevelt announce the attack on Pearl Harbour.

Living in town Geoff tried to get his car to safety at his office. However, the Japanese had already taken over and had their sentries on many of the downtown intersections. With difficulty he managed to get through only to find the Japanese were already at the office and he and his colleagues were not allowed to leave for three or four days.

It didn't take long for the news to filter through to us; being a fair distance away we had heard bangs but had no idea what they were about. The news was absolutely shattering. We had been invaded, overrun and lost our protection all at the same time. We were desperate.

You cannot imagine what a horrible thing it is to be cut off from the rest of the world with no means of communication; no access to funds whatever your bank balance may have been. Just a big blank and big questions: 'What will happen to us?' 'How are we going to manage?' 'Where is our next meal coming from?' However, we were not alone – there is strength in unity. All British and Americans in China were congregated in either Shanghai or Tientsin and before long we were allowed to cash $20.00 (Chinese dollars – not American) per week; we were issued with red armbands with a large 'B' for British which had to be worn at all times. Donald was No. 904, I was No. 905.

Motor cars were seized; cameras, radios etc were confiscated and all private dwellings were searched and ticketed so no furniture could be removed. We were not allowed on public transport, and were not allowed in public places such as restaurants, cinemas etc. Residential accommodation in town was immediately commandeered by the Japanese. Fortunately our one bedroom apartment was in the French Concession and not immediately needed by the Japanese – as friends were turfed out of their homes, we were able to help.

* * *

Once Geoff was able to leave his office – the Shanghai Telephone Company – he came to stay with us. We fixed up the enclosed verandah for him and let him have our garage, now empty, for storage.

Geoff continued to work and in September was called down to the manager's office only to find two Japanese military policemen waiting to arrest him. The manager had already been arrested. Working for the telephone company they would find it easy to tap wires and relay vital information – they were therefore picked up as political prisoners. The Japanese took them to their headquarters – Bridge House – known for its torture chambers. (Bridge House was behind the Post Office on the corner of North Szechuen Road where Bessie and Nellie picked up the school bus when we lived in the Embankment.)

After a few months a Chinese gentleman came to see us – he had just been released from the same cell as Geoff. He was scared to say too much but told us they had been in a cell with ten others – men and women together – with a bucket used as a toilet in one corner. Geoff had been wearing shorts at the time he was arrested so had no warm clothing – there was very little we could do about this. However, with our visitor's help we arranged for a restaurant in town to send in a meal daily, if possible. This had to be things that the guards would enjoy and some things which they didn't like and would hopefully leave for Geoff.

After the war we heard that one parcel was received – we provided clothes including a pair of heavy socks with reinforced soles sewn in, invaluable as all shoes had been taken away from prisoners. The restaurant packed food but Geoff only received two apples and a square cake of camphor to keep the lice away. The apples were camphorated and could not be eaten. Of the warm clothing only the socks were received.

* * *

After Geoff was picked up four other friends came to stay. We kept our bedroom, a couple had the dining room and the other couple the enclosed verandah – we all used the living room. We were very worried people but somehow we managed to get on together for the best part of a year before being interned. Even with expenses divided six ways we found it difficult to manage and soon started selling off private belongings – at a dreadful loss as we had no bargaining power.

We became very economy conscious trying to make ends meet. They did once in rather a peculiar way. Our next door neighbour's wife had been shopping and found a very wide piece of elastic. 'Ah' she thought 'just the right thing – I need a new girdle – yes, I think I'll have a go.' She found a zip to match, got out the sewing machine and was surprised to find how simple it was. She stitched the zip to either end of the elastic thus making a perfect cylinder. Her husband was delighted with the amount of money she had saved. Unfortunately she demonstrated her new garment with the zip down the centre front and couldn't take it off. It took her husband all afternoon to cut her out of it. Such a ticklish job could only be done by manicure scissors.

With the uncertain situation we started to hide away a few of our treasured possessions. Ours were packed in a camphor wood carved box – a wedding present from my three sisters – and taken through a guarded check-point on the back of a Gas Company truck. It was covered with an old blanket, the idea being the Japanese would think it a gas stove. It got through – our treasures were looked after by Minda for the rest of the war.

The only way I could collect Mary's effects stored in the boxroom of their first home in the Embankment was to walk across one of the bridges, armed at all times by Japanese sentries, and fill a small basket suitcase with a few items. I mingled with the crowd and luckily was never searched. In spite of varying my route it was a few months before I had cleared everything which we then packed and left in Graham's name with one of the Swiss storage companies. Mary and Graham received their belongings at the end of the war when they were stationed in Singapore.

*   *   *

You will remember as a child I had never been able to master the art of riding a bicycle. Now that the war had started in Shanghai and we were having trouble with transportation there was nothing else for it – I would have to make another attempt. I sent a boy out to hire the shortest bicycle he could find; in the meantime I got myself dressed up in an old pair of Donald's slacks (I didn't possess any) and waited. Imagine my chagrin when I found he had brought back a child's bicycle. However, I had a go and rode off down the road hoping to get my practice over with before Donald returned – if I couldn't manage he need never know. He was on his way home with a friend and I all but bumped into them. I think I made their day – they had never seen anything so funny as me trying to ride with my knees reaching my chin. I was happy though – I could reach the ground without using the brakes or falling off.

Eventually I did manage to ride. I even did the shopping on my bike. I would buy the week's supplies, hanging the eggs on one of the handlebars. Luckily I hadn't been shopping when I had my worst accident. I was mortified – I fell off and, don't ask me how, I got my leg caught in between the cross bars. I couldn't get it out either.

* * *

We existed as best we could. There was much loss of face after the fall of Pearl Harbour, Hong Kong, Singapore, and Manila. There were spies everywhere and it was a relief when we were rounded up and sent to internment camp. We would have accommodation and enough food – according to the Geneva convention. How wrong we were. The Japanese soldier wears a rice filled bandolier, with the help of which he lives off the land. We couldn't be better fed than their own men but, as we couldn't live off the land, vegetables and occasionally a little pork were provided.

INTERNMENT

Haiphong Road

In 1942 the Japanese opened Haiphong Road camp (to the west near Connaught Road). This was the first of many camps and it was here that a cross section of the business community were interned together with political prisoners – four hundred in all. Jimmy Forbes and Geoff were political prisoners – Geoff was transferred from Bridge House and we didn't see him again until the war was over. It was strictly a male camp where conditions were very tough and where the inmates suffered many atrocities. This was the first camp on its way to the gas chambers in North China when the Japanese surrendered. They were taken to Fengtai – outside Peking – in February 1945 and later rescued by an international team in late August. They were then moved by a US cruiser via Tientsin and arrived back in Shanghai in October.

Yangchow

In February 1943 Donald and I were part of the first contingent of civilians to be interned. Our friends continued to stay in the apartment until they too were interned. Geoff's things stored in the garage were intact when we left.

We were allowed four packages each – one a bed which would be transported, the other three – suitcases – to contain food for four days and our clothing. One suitcase was filled with sou'westers and wellies – very essential as in the country there would be no more macadam roads or paths, just plain mud. One of our doctors suggested that we include salt and yeast tablets in our packing, two very essential items – the latter to stave off beri beri usually caused by a lack of vitamin B.

We had to find our own way downtown and assemble at the Holy Trinity Cathedral. There we were labelled – showing, of all things, sex and, much to the delight of 'friends', age. There was a host of people seeing us off principally because they wanted to know what would happen to them when their time came. They would come up and say 'Hello' just to see how old you really were. There were no secrets. We thought this rather funny until we realised that we were in for a long stretch of no secrets, no privacy and, in fact, no anything.

There were 375 people in our group, including twenty children. We were rounded up and marched down to the docks each carrying our three pieces of luggage and boarded what we used to refer to as a 'chicken boat'. In case you are wondering we carried a suitcase in each hand with a strap over the shoulders. We then had a knapsack for food. I would have enjoyed a walking stick to help keep the balance and have had permanently sloping shoulders ever since.

The berths – two foot by six foot (60 x 180cm) – were like wooden boxes, three on either side of an aisle and three tiered. There was a rough mattress – rather stained – no sheets or other type of covering, and no pillows. You had to climb over one bed to get to the next – real fun and games. The men were in a separate area and only had room to sit on a tatami (straw) mat. Washing and toilet facilities were communal – men, women and Japanese guards all together. We spent one night on board – it was enough. The ship sailed down the Whangpoo and up the Yangtze river as far as Chinkiang where we disembarked. From there we were taken by junks across the river and up the Grand Canal to a place called Yangchow.

Yangchow is a walled city in the heart of China known as Marco Polo's city. It was here that the China Inland Mission had run a hospital and where their missionaries learnt Chinese before going out into the field. The complex was fairly large – the missionary houses had been walled off to accommodate the military, leaving the hospital as an internment camp. In other words we were walled in within a walled city with the military in between the two walls.

There were several dormitories – previous wards – and a few separate rooms which had been converted from bathrooms. We were fortunate in being allocated one of these rooms which we shared with our good friends, Molly and Frank Smith. (Molly, nee Cormack, worked for Sassoons.) We had just enough room for four beds – one up one wall, two across the top and one down the other side. This gave us each a corner to face for dressing purposes. We are still very good friends – rather fantastic when you consider the strain we were under.

Our arrival at the camp was very dramatic. No beds had arrived. We were all exhausted and had to muster and be lectured to – we were given a notice pointing out all the 'do's and 'don't s' and stating the penalties for disobeying or trying to escape. We were still trying to feed ourselves and it was a very hungry group that bedded down on the bare floor to get a few hours sleep.

There were two outhouses built at either end of the camp. One, a toilet, was divided across the middle – one side for women and the other for men. Each had commode type facilities and were twenty seaters. The other was a wash house which had a long cement trough down one side for washing – face, body or clothing. There was no running water – what we used came from the canal – and during one particularly dry spell we were restricted to one gallon of water per person per day. A good excuse not to wash.

Not knowing what to expect in the way of toilet facilities I had taken a 'potty' with me – a highly decorated enamel one which we christened 'buttercup'. Some people made their own seats – one was made from three strips of wood and the owner would wear it like a bracelet, saying 'I'm going to frame the Emperor'!

All plumbing, pipes, fittings, etc, had been stripped from the original bathrooms. We had to manage with the facilities mentioned above. If you wanted a wash-down you used cold water in a bucket and tried to find an isolated corner – usually the toilet. We soon ran out of soap, toothpaste, deodorants, cosmetics – you name it, we didn't have it. Washing powder was unheard of. You swilled your clothes in water and hung them in the sun hoping that would freshen them. Tattletale grey was the order of the day. After a few months and lots of complaints the Japanese found the dismantled pipes and our men fixed up a type of shower room. We had a reed fuelled stove (we also used reeds for cooking) to heat water behind a partition on which the plumbers fixed the shower heads. The water was on for ten minutes and there were three or four bodies to each shower. No cubicles. We took it in turn to wet, rinse, etc, all at the double hoping to get rid of the dirt before the water was turned off. It was the first warm shower we had had in five months. Absolute heaven.

* * *

Our calorie intake was worked out at 900 calories a day consisting of congee – a watery rice, no sugar or milk – for breakfast and usually pork soup for dinner. You were fortunate if you found a piece of pork in your helping but Donald did better than that – he was 'lucky' enough to find someone's bandage in his soup. He had no dinner that night but though I had the next serving I wasn't put off! Occasionally we had fish instead of pork and once we had a ration of eggs – I forget how many – but they were to feed 375 people. The kitchen crew did well – with the aid of some flour from our iron rations they made pancakes for us all. It was the only time we had a dinner queue. We had to watch that the servers didn't favour their friends – the serving hatch was kept almost closed so that only the dish appeared and not wiggly fingers to give the show away.

To supplement our diet we were issued with brown – almost black – bread. A minute loaf each per day. If it was not eaten it turned green overnight. On one happy occasion we were issued with everlasting jam. I think it was made with turnips or swedes, artificially flavoured and sweetened and was in a constant state of fermentation. If you had a spoonful it increased a spoonful overnight! The taste was appalling but we loved it – it was sweet and helped to satisfy our cravings.

Our beverage was plain green tea which went right through us, though the size of our mugs may have had something to do with this. We all had taken in large mugs thinking we would get our fair share of whatever was going – we paid for our greediness. Tea was our only drink – plain cold water could not be drunk as this came from the canal and was polluted. Coffee was a thing of the past. Once we had an issue of fresh milk, just about enough for two cups of tea. I was so excited about this that when I had received our portion I spilt it running up the stairs and we had to sit and watch everyone else enjoying theirs.

Another memory is being so hungry that we raided the guards rubbish bin for the pork rind. This we boiled in a tin set in the smouldering reed ashes and then let it cool. We called it 'brawn' but it would not have won any prizes. However it was food and filled a corner.

* * *

It didn't take us long to settle into a routine. We were divided into groups and each group did the same chores in rotation. One incident sticks in my mind, that was when Donald's and my details clashed. He was on water carrying duty keeping a tank of water filled in the kitchen so that we could use the taps. I was on kitchen fatigue. Our food ration that day was forty fish which had to be cleaned and gutted – no mean feat and, needless to say, we were covered with fish scales. The vegetable was bean sprouts – a veritable mound of them – which were brought into the kitchen and dumped on the not too clean floor. The sprouts had roots on them which we had to 'tail'. Our supper was watery fish soup – the only way to feed 375 people. Donald and I smelt of fish for days.

Home was a square building with a V at the end. There was a basement which was kept locked until the summer when we had a dysentery epidemic and it was turned into a hospital. We had one doctor and two nurses – all missionaries and used to working under primitive conditions. One wing of the V was for women and the other side for men.

Donald had malaria and was the first male patient – I was his nurse. As the wards filled up I was still involved. It was a long walk to empty potties – down a long corridor, upstairs and out in the garden to the outhouse. We soon rigged up a box to act as a step and climbed through the basement window to the toilets just outside – very precarious but time saving. The only medication we had was aspirin which we could only use in an absolute emergency. The dysentery patients were fed on a diet of what we called mountain potatoes, brought in specially by the Japanese. They looked rather like a horseradish and were slippery when being peeled. They were rather bland but seemed to do the trick and gradually patients recovered. Donald's temperature was brought down by artificial perspiration – I was taught how to bathe him in cool water which immediately evaporated with the heat of his body, thus reducing the fever. It was very successful but it took Donald a long time to get his strength back.

* * *

We were shocked one day to see a peculiar type of dark cloud overhead. 'What kind of storm is this?' we wondered. As it got lower and lower we were inundated with what we called 'stink bugs'. A three-cornered hard shell type of insect – approx. 1 inch (2cm) square except that it was triangular – with the most dreadful odour. No matter where you stepped you couldn't help treading on them – they were in your clothes, in your hair, in fact everywhere.

In spite of all the chores time still dragged. Some of us had managed to slip in a pack of cards amongst our effects so learnt to play bridge. We had one or two excellent players in camp who very kindly gave lessons, but when to play? It was decided that the only thing to do was to use our quiet time, between two and four each afternoon. We had to be very quiet and played in a kind of sign language which was rather fun. We made a fist for clubs, pointed to the ring finger for diamonds, the heart for hearts and made a digging motion for spades. Passing your hand quickly from left to right under your chin meant no trumps.

Another form of entertainment was 'In Town Tonight' – I believe an imitation of a BBC radio programme. We had people with us from the outports and even one who had been a lighthouse keeper. They talked about life in their various fields. All very interesting and entertaining – particularly at dusk when our infamous 'stink bugs' became active and took off like planes flying on a mission. This was a nightly occurrence until happily one night they didn't come back.

* * *

Conversation was mostly about food. What we were going to cook when the war was over; have you tried such and such – it's delicious; my favourite meal is steak and kidney pudding, etc. I only knew one person who had other things on her mind – Ann, who wanted to go into 'her bedroom' and lock the door. Lack of privacy was a big problem.

The Japanese being fond of children would round up our group of youngsters and take them over to their gardens to play. They had a great time – there was room to run and even kick a ball around. Imagine our envy when they returned one day and told us they had enjoyed a 'beer'. Many mouths were watering – how we envied them.

Then there was inspection day when a Japanese dignitary arrived in Yangchow and was shown around our camp presumably so he could see the wonderful condition we prisoners were in! He was accompanied by the Japanese commandant, our representative, the doctor and our interpreter – a young girl of eighteen who had been brought up in Japan and knew the language. Our representative was asked if anyone was pregnant. 'Oh no' was the reply 'we don't do things like that under such conditions.' The doctor corrected him 'Oh yes, there is one pregnancy' 'Who?' our representative wanted to know. 'My wife' was the reply – so much for Ann's privacy.

The above was wonderful news. It gave us all something to look forward to and work towards. Out came those matted sweaters (all had been badly washed) and knitting pins. Hours were spent prising out stitches and then making baby clothes. Colour didn't matter. One girl actually knitted a hundred stitches, took them out and measured the wool, then worked out how many stitches she could knit with the amount of wool she had. So the size of the garment was determined. We managed quite a layette before we were all sent back to Shanghai where the baby was born.

We were a funny looking lot of people. Clothes didn't fit – if it was cold you wore everything you possessed, as long as you could get it on you wore it, holes, stains no matter. We were all in the same boat. I think the ladies looked the worst. We had no shampoo, no hair dye, no perms. Hair grew out naturally but in the process the grey roots grew longer and longer and where you always thought Mrs so-and-so had beautiful hair it turned out to be straight and mousey.

* * *

Understandably we became depressed from time to time – the main culprits being the lack of news and, of course, food. We only knew about the several defeats in the Pacific field – nothing about the happenings in Europe.

A very well known judge from Shanghai suffered greatly from this depression and had a mental breakdown. The Japanese commandant, our representative, the doctor and our young interpreter visited him to assess his condition. He shared a room with others but when the officials entered they found him alone, stark naked and standing in an empty enamel wash basin, thinking he was having a shower! Our interpreter was shocked and didn't know where to look. This was only one of his many activities and we all breathed a sigh of relief when he was transferred to 'C' camp. We had got rid of our handful but 'C' camp were not amused. 'C' camp was a larger camp also in Yangchow where there was a makeshift hospital. Occasionally medical supplies were received from the Swiss Red Cross. Our friend now disliked buttons and cut them off all his clothing (this was before zips!) and if he saw a used commode he would upend it!

* * *

Because of the lack of running water the worst chore of all was toilet cleaning. Carts were brought in into which we 'decanted' and then, with almost no water, tried to clean the commodes. We would do one toilet – twenty seater – and then march round the camp to the other toilet and try to clean that too. About the last time I was on that duty we had just heard that our camp was going to be disbanded and we were returning to Shanghai. Great excitement. Fantastic. At this stage we had been in Yangchow for seven/eight months and there could only be one reason for this new development – the war was over and we were going to be released. In the excitement we marched to the second toilets to the tune of one of Souza's military marches using our little brooms as batons and – I got something in my eye.

Yu Yuen Road

The rumour was partly true. We were going back to Shanghai but not to be set free. We learnt later that there had been a prisoner exchange between Japanese on the west coast of America and Americans in China, and that had left many vacancies in the Shanghai camps. There were three camps in Yangchow, 'A', 'B' and 'C'. Parts of 'A' and 'B' were in the first group to return – the ones left behind had the job of cleaning up their camps; 'C' camp, the hospital, remained in Yangchow until the end of the war. We had our usual morning roll call – all hands on deck, so to speak, to be counted off. We had already packed our bags – beds had been shipped days before leaving us stiff and sore from sleeping on bare floors. However, we made it down to the canal where we were once again boarded on junks for the trip to Chinkiang. We were packed like sardines on deck and the only toilet facility was a lean-to shed on the poop deck which hid a large hole through which the Yangtze river – noted for its strong current – could be seen. I assisted a young girl of ten, hanging on to her like grim death, but never had the nerve to use the chamber myself.

At Chinkiang we were marched to the Railway Station and put on board a train for Shanghai. We had been issued with bread and water to last the trip and after a night's train travel we were a very sorry looking sight – tired and famished.

On arrival we were boarded on to trucks and taken to different camps to fill up the vacancies left after the exchange of prisoners. Donald and I ended up in the Yu Yuen Road camp, previously the Shanghai Municipal Council school where Bessie and Nellie were pupils. I shall never forget the welcome we received. The inmates expected us but didn't know who was in the group and it was a lovely surprise to find we knew many of them. They had a special welcome waiting for us and we sat down to a hearty meal of tea, bread and margarine – the latter we hadn't seen since our internment. We hadn't eaten properly for days and wolfed everything down until we saw Doreen, a friend of mine – watching us with tears in her eyes.

We were now in a much larger camp – the girls school, the boys school next door and at the end of the playing field a group of Nissen huts which had originally been erected to house the British troops who had at one time been posted to Shanghai. This was quite a complex. We had no heating at all but we were able to walk around the grounds and do a little basking in the sun – actually the only way to keep warm.

Donald and I shared part of the kindergarten with another couple from Yangchow. We had running water, group showers – usually cold – and a delightful Soochow Tub. This is like a huge flower pot – approximately ten feet in circumference and about three feet deep. You can only sit in it but filled with warm water it makes a wonderful bath – I got to use it once before it was out of bounds. Compared to Yangchow we were now living in luxury – Shanghai was a very modern city. No longer did we have to rely on water from a canal – we had filtered, chlorinated, running water, albeit turned off at times as was the electricity.

Unlike our special welcome party we soon found that the normal fare was not very different from our Yangchow diet – roughly 900 calories a day – mostly carbohydrates which seemed to affect the women differently than the men. We puffed up but they soon looked like walking skeletons. Donald was only just over 8 stone when we were released.

* * *

The Yu Yuen Road camp was about two miles away from the Great Western Road Hospital – a very modern hospital which had also been taken over by the Japanese and which they ran assisted by Russian, French and German doctors and nurses. Being so near, anyone who was desperately ill with a contagious disease, or having a baby, would be sent there – no visiting allowed. There were a lot of children and this rule also applied to them. Our first case of measles was a little five year old girl. She was sent out of camp by ambulance all on her own. Very upsetting until we heard one of her pals say to another 'Its not fair, now she will come back with a baby'. I was one of the expectant mothers sent out. Our child was stillborn and I shall never forget being kept in solitary confinement and deprived of a visit from my husband.

Cooking facilities were now easier. There was a coal burning stove in the kitchen so, after our 'dinner' when the stove was allowed to cool down, one could – if on kitchen duty – use the oven. I remember having a yen for a rice pudding. The nearest I got was using some of my saved millet from breakfast (there was a shortage of rice at this time) adding salt instead of sugar and using soya bean milk. It looked like a pudding having a lovely 'skin' on top, but there the similarity ended.

After the loss of our child I was rather ill and Donald and I were moved to a part of one of the Nissen huts. Having been erected as temporary accommodation these huts had no insulation and were perishingly cold but our cubicle was our own little home. Any water in the room overnight would freeze but we had privacy and welcomed the change. It was here that I was allocated an 'egg' a special treat to help build me up. We hadn't seen an egg since the pancakes of Yangchow so it was very precious, but how to cook it? It had to be cooked secretly as sharing an egg with Donald was one thing but having to share it with friends quite another! Donald came up with a brilliant idea. The egg would be fried in an old battered sardine tin over a candle in our own small corner. Great.

We drooled and licked our chops and started. Unfortunately once we got going there was an air raid warning and the lights went out. We hastily covered a small table with a blanket and crawled underneath – Donald, myself, sardine tin, egg and candle, and continued to cook our beautiful egg. What we hadn't thought of was that when the 'frying pan' was over the flame we were in total darkness. The egg was delicious – nothing has ever tasted so good. The after effects were hilarious – when the lights came on we found we looked like a couple of piccaninnys. Our hands, faces and clothes were covered in greasy candle smoke.

* * *

The Swiss Red Cross now started to send in parcels. There was nothing regular about them but it sure was wonderful when your turn came and you were lucky enough to find cigarettes inside. We continued to play bridge and enjoyed it more and more though the cards were getting very moth-eaten. Occasionally we would have a special party bridge evening and a prize – a cigarette – would go to the ones who bid and made a grand slam. A good incentive which often paid off. The cigarette would be smoked there and then – passed around the table from one to the other it would soon be red hot. The cigarettes came from the non-smokers who had received parcels and had done a swap. On one occasion a girl friend and I – both beginners – had to play two experts. This on one of our special evenings. Andree was so nervous that when we all threw our hands in as being useless, she took one look at the cards and said 'Oow, we all 'ave an Ass' in her little French accent. That broke the ice!

* * *

Yangtzepoo Again

As time went on the camps had a red cross painted on the roof to distinguish them from the Japanese military camps. This was arranged by the Swiss Red Cross so that should Shanghai be bombed our camps would be safe. I think this gave the Japanese ideas and once again we were on the move. It was early in 1945 and three of the Shanghai camps were transferred to a large military camp in the Yangtzepoo area while the Japanese moved to the safety of our prisoner-of-war camps. We were transported to the corner of Lay/Yangtzepoo Roads and from there had a long walk carrying all our belongings except beds. The guards were tough and we just had to keep up. Many a piece of baggage was discarded on the way.

Our new quarters were an old hospital – dirty and bug ridden after having been well used – and we were very cramped. Twenty couples to a large ward, families of three in another ward etc. No cubicles or curtains. Again it was fun meeting the prisoners from the other camps. When you are cooped up with the same people for months on end it is refreshing to have someone new to talk to and, of course, we had lots of notes to compare. However, it was not easy to adjust to the new living quarters. One had to get dressed in bed and as we were all on shift duty it was not unusual, on waking up, to find your neighbour, who had just come off duty, enjoying a mug of tea and at the same time watching your antics. I often thought of the lady who had said all she wanted was to go into her bedroom and lock the door.

Toilet facilities were almost nil but we did have a Japanese innovation to serve each building. This was a shed with a slit running down the middle of the floor over which you crouched astride – the oldies had trouble getting up again and one often heard a cry for help.

JAPAN SURRENDERS

Some time in June or July our camp was strafed on more than one occasion by, we presumed, the Americans. They always came at night which was lucky for us as we had a curfew and being indoors there were no casualties.

Shanghai is a twenty four hour sea journey from Japan. We were mesmerised by a terrific hail storm around the middle of August, 1945 – the stones were the size of tennis balls and one had to duck for cover as quickly as possible. We didn't know, of course, that this was the effect of the atom bomb on Nagasaki. We had no idea what was going on and that the Americans were very active in the Pacific. Soon after this we woke up one morning to find the Japanese guards had all left – Japan had surrendered. Can you imagine the excitement, the wonder, the tears of joy – we were stunned. We just didn't know what to do. We were too far away to be able to walk into town and we had no money for transportation if there was any.

Gradually other foreign nationals found our camp and news began to filter in. Minda bicycled about eight miles to see us, she had looked after our dog, a wirehaired terrier, and brought him with her in the front basket on her bicycle. He recognised us, he remembered Donald's special whistle. The children were curious – they hadn't seen a dog (or didn't remember) and tried to guess 'was it a cat?' 'No'. 'Was it a pig?' etc. It made you realise what they had been missing. Also, we soon found they didn't like milk or butter or rich foods which we thought would be a treat – they wanted soya bean milk which tasted like raw beans, or dry bread with occasionally a little lard spread on it.

French friends invited us to a victory party and though it was a wonderful celebration the loveliest memory of all is the weekend that Minda put her flat at our disposal and spent the time visiting her sister. Her servant was in attendance and we had a roast beef dinner, complete with wine. Luxuriating baths and comfortable beds. It was a wrench to have to go back to the camp as we still hadn't anywhere else to go.

Suddenly everything was happening at once. Have you ever felt like a millionaire – we did. Chiang Kai-shek's representative turned up one day and issued all of us with a small hand towel with the words 'Happy Good Morning' written in red and also a million Chinese dollars. We were rich, or so we thought. On the strength of this windfall Donald and I walked to Yangtzepoo Road to catch a tram to the nearest shopping area – Wayside – for an ice cream. We spent the lot on our special treat and arrived back very tired but pleased with ourselves. A very expensive ice cream.

Once the Americans had touched down at Lunghwa airport they started to fly in food and medical supplies. These were packed in large cartons and drums and dropped by parachute. Some dropped in the camps but lots of them landed outside the camp and were enjoyed by the local people – Chinese – who had also had a very hard time .The food parcels were something special. We all received a carton which was divided into four – each section being one day's supply of food. It was in tins or packages and was scientifically worked out as regards nourishment, including such items as spam, chicken, vegetables, coffee, milk powder, sugar, jelly and intriguingly a small packet with three cigarettes and one stick of chewing gum. We never figured that one out! The parachutes themselves were made of nylon, in beautiful colours and made lovely clothing – very cheerful and just what was needed after our drab existence.

The British were not far behind the Americans. The British Consul and entourage arrived from Chungking while *HMS Hermes* (now at rest on the River Thames, London) arrived from Hong

Kong. An old flame of mine from my teenage years was with the Consul – a wonderful opportunity to hear news of old friends and how they had fared during the war years.

REPATRIATION

The British Consulate was opened up and repatriation was being arranged. A friend, Muriel, and I volunteered to work at the consulate and were provided with transportation – eight miles there and eight miles back on a wood-burning truck. There was no gasoline available at the time and some ingenious Chinese had found a way of burning wood logs to provide the heat or steam to fire the engine. Muriel worked for the passport consul, I was archivist and another girl, Freda, was the consul's secretary. Soon we received very welcomed salaries.

There was a lot to do getting everyone sorted out, tracing people and so on – lots of enquiries and telegrams to and from abroad. Nellie's 'paid' and 'unpaid' trays would have come in useful at this stage. Around this time the commander of *HMS Hermes* invited the consul for dinner but as he was too busy with another 'repat' ship his secretary was asked to go and represent him. I was asked to accompany her. We were still living in the camp; Freda and family had moved out of their camp and were living in the opposite direction, but nearer town. As transportation was difficult it was decided that I would spend the night with Freda but, how to let Donald know? Eventually a signal was sent to the consulate from the ship to phone the camp and notify him. It sounded good. The call got through all right but very late and the lady who answered the phone (she had moved into the empty Japanese office and had the use of the only phone in camp) had to go down two flights of stairs across the compound into the building we occupied and find Donald in the dark. Needless to say she was not pleased and woke Donald up with 'Your wife is spending the night on the *Hermes*'. I went straight to work the following day and had quite a bit of explaining to do when I returned.

Things were looking better. We soon got rid of the grime and with borrowed clothes from Minda we started to perk up and feel more 'with it'. Donald's brother-in-law, Alastair Clark, the Assistant Military Attaché to the British Embassy in Kunming, sent funds which enabled us to move back to our apartment – a complete shambles which had to be fumigated and scrubbed out. Donald's sister, Dorothy, and family arrived from 'C' camp in Yangchow followed by Margaret and son – Alastair's family. It was a happy time though a very emotional reunion. Gordon, Dorothy's husband, had died on his release from camp and Dorothy with her daughter and son were being evacuated to Australia. This was recommended for education purposes but as far as we were all concerned they were going off into the unknown. It was good advice, however – Australia was a great place to be at that time – and they have all done well.

Donald's other sister, Gladys Barnes, and family were interned in Tientsin and on their release were repatriated to England. We looked forward to seeing them later.

In October 1945 news was received of the Haiphong Road camp – they had been rescued and were on their way back to Shanghai. They were due to arrive at the Embankment on the 11th – they were given a tremendous welcome. It was wonderful to see them again though they did look tired and dishevelled. Donald copied Chiang Kai-shek's gift and handed Geoff a million dollars just to see his face. He was delighted with the reaction and Geoff's 'How could I ever repay you?' He left for San Francisco in November.

I have only mentioned the camps in which family and friends were interned, but there were many others.

Transportation was still difficult but we did manage one memorable evening out. The Grand Theatre was showing special news clips taken during the war years and we attended with Molly and Frank Smith – the couple we shared a room with in Yangchow. I can only describe what we saw as fantastic – we were overwhelmed and left with a feeling of awe and a dose of goose-pimples. We had to stand through four national anthems – British, American, Russian and Chinese. Later Molly and Frank retired to Nassau, Bahamas.

Having no children we had to await our turn for repatriation. Donald was busy getting his business affairs sorted out and I continued to work at the consulate – becoming the consul's secretary when Freda was repatriated. (I also worked for the ambassador when he was in town.) Our turn was coming up and we were trying to collect a few decent clothes to wear on arrival in England. I felt so clever when I found a panty girdle. What a find – there was nothing like that available after the war. I was assured it had only just arrived from America – I was privileged to be given the chance to buy it, I was told. I kept it for months until the right moment arrived and within hours all the elasticity had disappeared.

Donald too had his failures. He was given a pair of American army boots which had cleats on the bottom. They were nice looking so he took them to the little Chinese shoemaker who cut them down to look like shoes and filled the holes where the cleats had been. Donald kept them for his first visit to head office in London. As luck would have it, it rained and his feet were soon wet through. We found later that the holes had been stuffed with matches.

There were few cars on the road and we used pedicabs – an open cab or chair pulled by a bicycle. I remember seeing one wealthy Chinese couple obviously on their way to a party decked out in their finest, diamonds and all. Not having a car they had had a small car made, not unlike the children's toy cars, and were having a great time peddling away and steering at the same time. Unfortunately they only had two speeds – 'stop' and 'go' – but that didn't matter, they had transportation and were proud of it.

Our Turn has Come

We sailed in March 1946 on board the SS *Strathmore* – a mixture of happy and sad people – apprehensive but sure of a happy future. After years of restriction and internment we were on our way to freedom. Freedom of movement and speech ... what could be better than that? We were sad too. Donald had been born in China and I had spent twenty four years in Shanghai. It was our home. We had many good Chinese friends and although we were now aliens – friends are friends. They were there to bid us farewell as were Donald's compradore and Joe, our cookboy, and his son who had looked after us so well. Little did we know we would not meet again.

In 1943 the Western powers agreed to renounce all extra-territorial rights in China. This meant that when the war ended the international settlement and other treaty ports would revert to Chinese cities. Shanghai, the gateway to China, was one of the most cosmopolitan cities in the world. It was also one of the largest ports – Hong Kong and Kobe were its only far eastern rivals. The population included Jews, Annamese, White Russians, Filipinos, Japanese, Indians, Germans, Austrians, Swiss and Spanish to mention a few as well as British, American and French nationals. Now this was all gone.

Yes, we were sad – also bewildered. It always surprises us, even now, when we read of the vice in pre-war Shanghai and how it was ruled by the 'British Raj'. Vice can be found anywhere. As for how the diplomats lived and behaved, it was never a British Colony as so many still believe – it was an international settlement and ruled by a Municipal Council.

There was a wonderful, friendly and caring side to Shanghai that we shall never forget. Yes, there were many incidents with fierce fighting amongst the Chinese people and then the Sino-Japanese hostilities – but for the Europeans, or rather 'foreigners' as we were called, we escaped their wrath, that is until 1941.

It was a thriving wealthy city. Dad must have done a lot of soul-searching before leaving us there. He missed a lot during our growing up years but some of his conscientiousness must have rubbed off on us as we all turned out to be good at our jobs. We trained to be stenographers – we had a good education, admittedly no chance of making university status, but then that did not seem to be so important in those days. As children we would have hated living in Hankow and later India.

* * *

But I digress. The ship was ready to leave. We stood on board in disbelief as our thoughts nostalgically relived the past. We watched until we could no longer see The Bund – the buildings too small, the people just dots. We were travelling a reverse journey from the time Mother and her four children sailed up the Whangpoo on the *SS Teiresias* to meet Dad twenty four years ago. The scenery was much the same but there the similarity ended – where the trip out had been a new beginning filled with hope this was the end of an era. 'All gone' as we might say today to a child when the sweetie jar is empty – 'All gone – our Shanghai'.

Donald was allotted a hammock in the bowels of the ship – he had quite a tale to tell when one night one of his neighbours had a nightmare and set all the nearby hammocks swinging. I had a funny story to swap. The ladies were in the regular cabins which had been rearranged to accommodate more than the usual number of passengers. I was in a cabin for six – three bunks on either side. I knew four of my cabin mates – the sixth was a nun. She had the bottom bunk, I had the middle and the top bunk was occupied by a girl travelling alone. One particular night she was homesick (I think) and had a couple of drinks. We were supposed to be a 'dry' ship so she was lucky. She was a little the worse for wear and it was quite a struggle for us to get her up into her bunk without waking the nun who must have had a giggle or two while pretending to be asleep! Nothing was said the next morning.

There was great excitement one day. We were given 'ditty bags' issued by the Swiss Red Cross but, for convenience, packed by the Canadian Red Cross. The men had their special bags. The ladies' bags contained such items as note paper, envelopes, pencil, soap, flannel, tooth-brush and paste, lipstick, face powder, brush and comb. What fun we had making ourselves 'pretty' girls and swapping lipstick until we got the right colour.

Graham was now stationed in Singapore and came on board to see us – we were not allowed ashore. He had lots of family news for us – Mary and their two children, Wendy and Graham, would soon be on their way to join him. We would not meet for another few years. Dad had retired to England. Bessie and Nellie and families were still in India – hopefully they would soon be on their way to England where we would meet up.

We went ashore in Egypt – below the Suez Canal. We had a short train ride to a military camp and were served tea in a large marquee and entertained by a band of German prisoners. They greeted us by playing 'God Save the King' very badly and out of tune but excelled themselves when playing 'Lilli Marlene'. It was the first time we had heard it and were fascinated. We were then taken to another marquee to be fitted out with new clothes!

Next Stop – Southampton

Dad and a friend had come from Eastbourne by train – it was wonderful to see their smiling faces. They had had quite an arduous journey to Southampton and we were all terribly disappointed to hear visitors were not allowed on board. We had to remain until the following day when we would travel by boat-train to London.

When we arrived the station platform was crowded but we soon spotted Dad waving frantically. What a welcome – out came the hankies – everyone crying they were so happy. People had difficulty in finding each other in the crush and we were asked more than once 'Do you know so-and-so?' 'Is so-and-so on this train?' Everyone desperate to meet their loved ones.

Correspondence

On arrival at Southampton we all received a letter from King George VI – this is very special to me.

During these war years correspondence with the outside world was unheard of. Before we were interned the rumour went around that the Swiss authorities were trying to arrange something, and on the strength of that I typed several pages – single spacing – and sent it to Dad, in India, giving him as much news as possible. The Swiss did eventually arrange that we prisoners be allowed to write twentyfive word letters. The recipients could write twentyfive words on the reverse side and the letter would be returned to us. I always hoped that my letter had got through so you can imagine my surprise when, after more than a year, I received a reply to 'extracts' from my letter. These were in a Continental handwriting and puzzled Dad so his reply didn't convey much. From my letter the family now knew I could ride a bike and could even carry the shopping home on it – eggs as well.

Officially, we only had one opportunity to write a twentyfive word letter and by trying to save words my letter seemed more like a poem. Dad thought it was a coded message and spent days trying to decipher it. The war ended before I could receive an answer.

Before we were interned Bessie, in India, sent me a letter through a friend of hers who was travelling to Kunming. The letter was opened up and readdressed in a distinctive Chinese envelope with my name printed on it in Chinese characters – 'Daywee Tietie', translated this means elderly woman of the Davey house. Unfortunately there was no way I could reply – but the news made up for this. Bessie and Nellie were both expecting their first babies.

Another letter I received was very sad. It was after our release from internment and was forwarded to me through official channels with the note 'Found amongst Ft. Lt. Henderson's effects'. He had been killed on a flight over the 'hump' into Kunming. That letter was from Nellie.

* * *

We had a letter from the British Ministry of Pensions and National Insurance in Ottawa, dated 20th May, 1955. The letter seems to wrap up our war years in China, TRULY – 'ALL GONE – OUR SHANGHAI'

Plate 1. Mother and Dad on their wedding
day in 1912.

Plate 2. Pingliang Road, Yangtzepoo – our new home in 1926.

Plate 3. Dad's dancing girls.

Plate 4. Auntie Cameron.

Plate 5. Outside Shanghai – a typical
Chinese village scene.

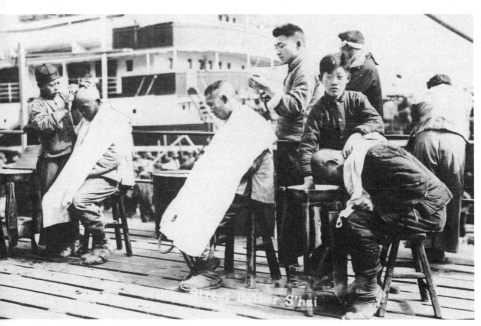

Plate 6. Barber's shop in the street.

Plate 7 (*above*).
Fires at Chapei,
August 1937.

Plate 8 (*right*).
Evacuation to
Hong Kong.

Plate 9 (*below*).
Soochow Creek looking
towards Garden Bridge
from Embankment
Building.

Plate 10 (*left*). Dad in 1937.

Plate 11 (*above*). Uncle Miller.

Plate 12 (*below*). The four of us with Dad at Grosvenor Gardens.

Plate 13. Henry Eardley
and Nellie on the roof of
Grosvenor Gardens.
"Take a wing . . ."

Plates 14 and 15.
Bazaars became a way
of helping the war effort.

Plate 16 (*below*). KKK.

Plate 17 (*top*).
Ivy and Donald's PoW armbands.

Plate 18 (*above*).
Identification card issued by French Concession.

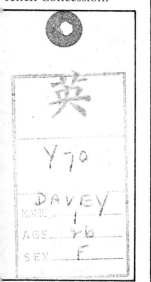

Plate 19. Ivy's name tag.

Plate 20 (*right*).
Letter from the King.

BUCKINGHAM PALACE

The Queen and I bid you a very warm welcome home.

Through all the great trials and sufferings which you have undergone at the hands of the Japanese, you and your comrades have been constantly in our thoughts. We know from the accounts we have already received how heavy those sufferings have been. We know also that these have been endured by you with the highest courage.

We mourn with you the deaths of so many of your gallant comrades.

With all our hearts, we hope that your return from captivity will bring you and your families a full measure of happiness, which you may long enjoy together.

George R.I.

September 1945.

Please address
your reply to
THE MINISTRY REPRESENTATIVE
And refer to file: 8314

THE BRITISH
MINISTRY OF PENSIONS
AND NATIONAL INSURANCE
168 Charlotte Street
Ottawa 2, Canada

20 May, 19 55.

Dear Sir/Madam,

I have been advised by the
Minister of Pensions and National Insurance that
you qualify for payment of £43, representing your
share of the final distribution of Japanese Assets
in the United Kingdom.

A cheque for the above amount
is enclosed.

Yours faithfully,

Ministry Representative.

Donald Lawson Davey, Esq.,

16 Fifth Avenue,

Pointe Claire, P.Q.

Plate 21 "All gone – our Shanghai."

AFTER SHANGHAI 1946–91

CHAPTER NINE

Ivy and Donald
Meet Family Again

1946–1947

Dad took us back to Eastbourne where he had arranged for us to stay with his friends. This would enable Donald to visit his Head Office (Yorkshire Insurance Co. – since taken over by General Accident) in London. Meanwhile we would have a reunion and relaxation period and spruce ourselves up a bit.

Donald's parents were missionaries – the China Inland Mission – starting their sojourn in China at the Mission in Yangchow (where we were interned). They had been married at Holy Trinity Cathedral in Shanghai where, years later, Donald and I were married. I never met them – by the time Donald and I were courting his Mother had died and his Father was retired in England. He was an air raid warden in Exeter, Devon. Donald worried about his elderly Father all alone in England and was looking forward to seeing him again and introducing me to him. We didn't know until after the war that he had been killed in 1942 during a raid.

DAD TELLS OF HIS RETIREMENT IN 1946

It was a happy relief for me when my time for retirement came. Suddenly I felt the need to be released from chronic loneliness.

Kovilpatti was cut off – Nellie and Michael visited me when they were expecting Joy and we met again when Nellie was sharing a bungalow 'Mirabel' with Mary – up the hill at Kodaikanal – that was all I saw of her.

Likewise, Bessie could almost have been on the other side of the world – near the Himalayas she couldn't get to see me, nor could I visit her. India, although a lovely and interesting country is so widespread – places inaccessible – transportation difficult.

Mary, bless her, made her home with me when Graham went off to serve with the Indian Army in Burma.

I spent hours alone on my large verandah at nights just thinking about the past – my days with Mother in Mexico, then Peru – the days in Shanghai – now India. My children? Everywhere, alone too as Graham, Michael and Alastair were serving elsewhere. My biggest anxiety was Ivy and Donald. They were never out of my thoughts. Had they enough food? Were they keeping reasonably well under the conditions of an internment camp life? Oh! how I longed for some news.

Yes, for my own sanity I had to move on and retirement was a goal to look forward to.

Kovilpatti, approximately 200 miles from Tuticorin – India's most southern point – was a sleepy mill station. It consisted of the mill and its workers and a missionary couple who lived some distance away but in the same area. I was visited by Ada and Fred Ford who lived at 'Tuti' and they became my greatest pals. They were good companions. They would visit me as often as they could and bring their friends with them, especially at Christmas and perhaps a couple of times during the year to celebrate a birthday.

It was through Ada that I persuaded Mary to take Wendy to Kodaikanal, a beautiful hill station, to get some relief from the constant heat of the plains. They were going to share a holiday house together for a few weeks. They started their journey from Kovilpatti (the Fords drove up from 'Tuti' to collect them) and Fred and I drove them to Madura from where they travelled up the hillside by taxi. It was a steep drive with lots of hairpin bends. Fred and I knew that although the taxi driver was familiar with the route he would not give his passengers much confidence as he tackled the bends and anything else that got in his way! He would be reckless. They got there. Apparently Mary's first impression of this beautiful hill station was the wonderful smell of wood smoke from the fires they enjoyed – the feeling of coolness at last – having rings slip around her fingers because they had lost their puffiness. The lovely fresh mountain air and the smell of the eucalyptus trees. It made me feel good to hear her reaction.

In 1945 Nellie joined Mary at 'Kodai'. They were both expecting again. There were other visitors as well including Georgina and Jack Shotter who were en route to the States. I went up to Kodai for a holiday to see them, together with the Fords.

Nellie's Diana was born on 5 July, and young Graham on 29 December. Joy and Wendy were apparently overjoyed at the new additions and became very motherly and protective.

Soon after Diana's arrival Michael, who had been posted at Chittagong, was transferred back to Bombay where Nellie joined him. When the war ended he joined Boots Pure Drug Co. Ltd, in Bombay.

Graham is now making arrangements for Mary to join him in Singapore where he was posted on his transfer to the British Army – his life's ambition. They are planning to set up home there, for a little while at least. Mary and the children have to wait for permission to be granted before they can officially join Graham as it is not too safe there and accommodation is difficult to obtain.

Bessie and Alastair likewise, are making arrangements to move on – after Alastair's demob leave. He was in Burma. They should be home soon.

So ... the time had come ... Joseph, my cookboy – they all seem to be called 'Joseph' in India – and I started the laborious task of packing up the last Stead home in the east.

I planned to start my new life in 'Square One' among family and friends to await news of my girls. I did not want to put down my roots until I knew what they were all going to do, and where they were going to settle. It's interesting, it has taken me nearly thirtyfour years to complete my journey – starting off in Lancashire, on to Mexico, Peru, China and India and now, here I am again – doing what comes naturally to we 'Brits' – settling in good old Blighty!

After a few months rest I have taken up advisory work which I much enjoy.

BESSIE

Hearing Bessie and family were well on their way to Liverpool, Dad remained in Eastbourne so we could travel up north together to meet them. He also arranged a party for us to meet relatives I had never met with the trip to welcome Bessie. We stayed with a cousin and after living a life denuded of personal relatives – as opposed to honorary 'Aunts' and 'Uncles' – I was amazed at the number. They were two deep around the room and I found it very difficult to sort everyone out. Three young girls, Myrtle, Hilda and Edna, the mannequins used by Dad on his leave in England, sat on the floor and, as only they could, held the party together. They are an important part of our real family.

We managed to see Bessie but, like the time Dad came to meet us at Southampton, no one was allowed ashore.

We couldn't stay overnight – lack of accommodation – and Bessie and family had to travel by train to Glasgow so we waved goodbye and said farewell to Dad who returned to Oldham.

Once Donald's affairs were settled he was given a year's leave to recuperate and get fit. What better place to spend it than in Kirn, Argyll, where Bessie and Alastair were staying with his parents.

Dad joined us for a short holiday. We were staying in a nice guest house – 'Duncrag' – the food plain but plentiful. Whereas we had been rationed to one egg per week down south we had eggs and bacon for breakfast each morning.

The weather was perfect – long lazy summer days when we would go off on a picnic, by bus as we didn't have a car, and enjoy the scenery around Loch Eke. I think the name was part of the attraction. Young Alasdair was slow in starting to walk and we would spend hours out in the garden propping him up and trying to encourage him. Dad was thrilled to be with his own once again and revelled in his grandchildren.

Donald and I put on weight and soon looked like our pre-war selves – it was a super summer in more ways than one.

Bessie Tells Her News

I left for India on a slow cargo vessel, calling at Hong Kong and Penang and arriving at Calcutta two weeks later. At Hong Kong I met up with Lawrence and Ray who showed me all over the island and the New Territories.

At Penang we took on board two Shanghai lads on their way to join the Indian army. Penang was to give me the first insight into what life could be like further west. I was given a tourist guide of the town and countryside. Penang was lush and beautiful – no modern buildings there then. I was in a mood to compare everything with Shanghai, which was in every way modern, and so I did not appreciate the quiet lazy town. I was not happy at having to leave Shanghai at all.

The ship put in at Calcutta and I was on my way to Bombay the same night. I was given a tremendous welcome by Nellie. Dad had an apartment near the mill – a good way out of Bombay and in rather a congested suburb.

Nellie had met Jean Guthrie and occasionally we would spend the whole day in each other's company, but this had to be planned as transport had to be arranged – all very restricting. I decided to get a job and life became less boring. I hated India and if I could I would have returned to Shanghai on the next ship. I suppose this was only to be expected – everything was so different and I was homesick for my friends.

Soon after my arrival Nellie met Michael Poole. It was a whirlwind romance and they were married in May 1941. Not long afterwards Dad was transferred to south India – I refused to go with him as the thought of burying myself in a yet more remote place was too much for me. Instead I stayed with Nellie and Michael in a little flat in downtown Bombay.

Suddenly the war was almost on our doorstep. I had a visit from Alastair on holiday prior to going into action – he was the Seaforth Highlander I had met in Shanghai – one of the gang at the Rowing Club. We hit it off almost immediately and decided to waste no time in getting married. Dad said Nellie's courtship was a snail's pace compared to mine. Alastair had to return to Agra after his holiday and, because he was under age, had to get permission to marry. His Commanding Officer probably thought the worst had happened – however, permission was granted. We were married on the 20 December, 1941, at the Scots Kirk. Nellie was my Matron of Honour and Mr Harper, a good friend of Dad's, gave me away.

The wedding took place at 10am and the reception was held at Nellie and Michael's flat. Unfortunately Michael was transferred to sea and was unable to act as bestman. Nellie did us proud. We made our exit at about 2pm and arranged to keep out of sight until the evening, as we were being given the loan of the flat for the remainder of Alastair's stay and Nellie wanted to see the guests off and arrange to move out.

Being in the army Alastair had the use of the Bombay Club and we went there for tea and a swim. We then went to the pictures where we met Pep Farmer from Shanghai. We had a drink together at the interval and asked him back to the flat after the show. We were so pleased to meet someone from Shanghai we had forgotten it was our wedding day! Poor Pep. It came out casually in conversation that we had been married that morning. Well I never saw anyone move so fast. He hurried out of the flat and I have never seen him since. Pep, as his nickname suggests, was never a fast mover.

Alastair only had time off to get married and had to return to Agra to be ready to go to the Front. His plans were changed and instead of going to Burma he was sent to GHQ, New Delhi. I was able to join him in January.

Living in India was so completely different from Shanghai. It was war time, we were all in the same boat and had to make the best of it. We had eight moves in New Delhi before Alastair did eventually go to the Front. Our accommodation varied from being 'paying guests' (an Indian expression) to a suite in the Grand Hotel; 'shamianas' to glorified pigeon holes.

Ivy May was born in New Delhi on 7 February 1943. Like all first time expectant mothers I was apprehensive about having to cope with something so small and fragile. When I first saw her I reckoned I had nothing to worry about – she had shoulders on her like a boxer, a very straight back and weighed in at 8lb 10oz. She had no wrinkles and looked just like a porcelain doll.

After Alastair left for Burma I went to stay with Nellie and Michael again – they were now attached to a navy establishment on Manora Island, off Karachi. I was there for about a year. Alastair made the long journey to see me on his first leave and we decided it would be better if I found accommodation somewhere closer to Burma.

So I was off on the move once again. I proceeded to Darjeeling and there I remained until the end of the war. It was a very tedious journey especially with a young child. The train had problems. Our water tank developed a leak and we were without water for most of the trip. We had a night in Calcutta and then an overnight journey by train to Siliguri, and from there a bus ride up to Darjeeling. The bus ride was hair-raising, everyone talking at once and gesticulating, including the driver, and no one watching the road.

I got accommodation at Alice Villa, a boarding house. The accommodation was adequate (by this time all luxury of Shanghai was forgotten). There was no flush – just a thunder box and you had to remember to leave the back door open after use. I guess whoever did the emptying must have listened in until the coast was clear. We bought our water from a 'beestie' – he carried water in sheepskins. Water was heated at the back in a mobile boiler and when ready emptied into the bath by bucket.

Being in the hills and amongst the clouds most of the time, it was pretty damp. We used a huge basket affair, like a crinoline hoop on which to air nappies.

I met Adeline Kelly at Alice Villa. Later Adeline and her husband, George, and Alastair and I were to become great friends throughout the whole of our stay in India. George was a tea planter and after the war went back to Assam.

Darjeeling was very beautiful. I eventually got a flat on the other side of the hill facing the lower snows and Kanchenjunga – especially beautiful to see first thing in the morning when pink with the glow of sunrise.

Young Alasdair was born in Darjeeling on 10 April, 1945, at the Sanitarium. He was not as robust as Ivy, weighing in at only 8lb 2oz and he kicked up hell from the start. I was glad to have had Ivy first to help soften the blow of motherhood – Ivy was placid and very easy to manage, Alasdair was very demanding.

At the end of the war Alastair came to collect us. We went across India to Dulali to assemble for a ship home and were there for about three weeks. We sailed from Bombay. The sea voyage to England was horrendous – I shared a cabin with eleven other mothers and their babies and nappies.

When we docked at Liverpool two weeks later there was Ivy with Donald and Dad to meet us. Next we spotted Alastair's sister Joyce in wren's uniform. She looked very smart and our attention was attracted to her because she was getting so many whistles from the troops on board. We were not allowed ashore and it was only through a lot of sign language we were able to introduce each other. Unfortunately, as there was so much congestion with the crowds on board and those on the dockside, we were not able to get close enough to have a word.

Joyce escorted us to Glasgow where my mother-in-law was waiting to welcome us. I was a bit apprehensive about meeting my in-laws but found them extremely kind and most hospitable. We made our way to Kirn where the Moodies had rented a house for the summer. It was a sad time as my father-in-law was dying of cancer. He had only just retired from the Bank with no time to settle in a home of their own.

NELLIE

Nellie and family were the next to arrive and were staying with Michael's parents in Guildford. Donald and I had returned south by this time and spent a few days near them – a whole new family to meet. Dad had, of course, already met Nellie's in-laws and it was good to hear they got on together famously.

Our first view of Nellie was seeing her chase Diana – a toddler – and trying to catch her as she ran out of the gate and almost into us. A strange but welcomed meeting. It seemed like only yesterday that we had seen her off on the *SS Conte Verde*. Apart from two adorable youngsters following her around she hadn't changed a bit. It was the first time we met Michael – they seemed very suited to one another and very happy.

Nellie Tells Her News

It is lovely seeing Ivy and Donald again but, oh! dear, it will be sad hearing their news firsthand. Michael and I returned from India a couple of weeks ago and – for me, it is the first time in England since I left as a baby in '22.

After leaving Shanghai the *Conte Verde* stopped at Hong Kong where we met up with the Mr Dodd, Ray and Henry Eardley. Henry invited me out for lunch and it really was so special as he had taken particular care in pre-planning our meal – all my favourite dishes! He really made me feel a VIP. It was sad saying our goodbyes. Once more Dad and I sailed off – this time we called at Manila in the Philippines. New people, new national dress. I found it strange to hear the locals speaking with a flawless American accent.

Singapore was our next port of call. There we visited the Botanical Gardens and fed peanuts to the monkeys. I wanted to keep them all as pets. They were cheeky and so daring – I could easily identify ourselves with them, when I remembered Dad teasingly say to us, as kids 'You're worse than a barrel load of monkeys'. We ended our sightseeing with a cool refreshing drink at the famous Raffles Hotel where we admired the two fan-shaped Travellers' Palms at the entrance to the hotel.

Next stop, Colombo, Ceylon (now Sri Lanka). My first introduction to the Singhalese/Indian ladies in their beautiful saris. We were awestruck as, like most tourists, we visited the jewellers' shops to admire the precious and semi-precious stones of Ceylon.

Bombay – our destination. It was hot and humid – the people noisy and friendly. It was not long before I had become acquainted with the beetlenut vendors and the red juice which they spat out and from which stains remained.

We were met by Dad's neighbours, Nellie and Sid Hayes. Dad was so proud to show off one of his daughters and, for him, I wore my Rita Hayworth hat – but I soon found myself wearing a topee like most of the other European ladies.

Home was in a mill compound off Patel Road where the mill 'Lines' were and where the mill workers lived in what seemed to me, in hundreds. To keep cool the workers slept in the street and because of the camber of the road they slept with their feet towards the gutter and their heads in the centre – both sides. Not easy to manoeuvre a car in what little space was left.

It was going to be a lonely life.

The first thing I did on arrival was to go to the loo – where my introduction to creepy-crawlies began. I hardly got settled when a lizard fell off the ceiling and ran down my leg – I had been initiated!!

* * *

To recount the story of my life from the time I left Shanghai to meeting up with the family would take forever so I shall try to give a brief resume of what I did between 1940 and 1947.

* * *

Mary and Graham arrived from Shanghai. It was wonderful to see them and to hear news of Shanghai – being so lonely, I hung on to their every word. Then Bessie came to join us – fantastic. Bessie hated Bombay and soon got a job. She was lucky in that she had experience. All I could do was look after the Paid and Unpaid boxes of the BRA membership list. Ivy, on re-checking her POW armband, noticed that it was stamped with a 'BRA Stamp'. I guess I may have been promoted to stamp those armbands of the 'remaining' British residents had I stayed on in Shanghai.

Somehow I met Michael – backstage. Bessie and I had little opportunity of meeting young people but through Jean Guthrie and Barbara Stott (both their fathers were also mill managers) we were involved in a show put on for the war effort. We were dancing again and happy to do so. Our contribution was our favourite 'The Parade of the Tin Soldiers'. Luckily we both still had our costumes. Jean sold Michael a ticket for the show. He came backstage and that is where and how I met him. After a whirlwind romance of three weeks we were married at St Andrew's Cathedral, Bombay. Not only did I acquire a super husband but a most attractive sister-in-law – Josephine – better known as Josie. Josie was married to Johnny Skelton in the States and naturally I used to day-dream and wonder when we would meet.

Michael was a Sub-Lieutenant in the Royal Indian Naval Volunteer Reserve. Needless to say I joined the Navy as well, as a Chief Petty Officer in the cipher office. I enjoyed the work. It was exacting and my forte there was working out corrupt messages. The other girls did not have the patience – I enjoyed the challenge. Ultimately the corrupt messages were kept for me if I was to be on the next watch.

Soon after Michael and I were married Dad was transferred to Kovilpatti near Tuticorin – the tip of south India. Bessie came to share our flat. We lived in Bombay town and met lots of people of our own age and life became more like 'Shanghai-days'.

Alastair arrived in Bombay for his vacation and it was not too long after this when he and Bessie were married. Her wedding dress was out of this world. It was a full length ice-blue chiffon dress. I was matron-of-honour. A small reception was held in the flat but as Michael was transferred to sea, he was unable to act as best man.

News Flash! The Japanese attack: PEARL HARBOUR – MANILA – HONG KONG – SINGAPORE ... next ... CEYLON?

Japan at war with the USA – Britain – the World? What was happening? How would Shanghai be affected? So many unanswerable questions. What would happen to Ivy and Donald? – we were naive enough to think that they would be safe in the international settlement. After all, we had been safe there so many times before. How ignorant can one be? No news – no letters – no messages. What could we do? Nothing. We were all so worried. None of us could begin to imagine what life would be like under the Japanese.

Michael had been transferred to a minesweeper. Alastair joined his unit and Bessie moved on to be near him. I sold up and closed the flat and left for Colombo to be nearer to Michael. Colombo was his base for the time being.

Michael's ship was at Rangoon and was the last ship to leave, helping with the evacuation of Rangoon, after the fall of Singapore as the Japanese headed towards Ceylon. He met Tommy Brewer (Peggy's brother) on the dockside as he was helping to empty the warehouses of whisky and other alcoholic stocks. The cars which had been abandoned by the escapees were being pushed into the Irrawaddy River rather than leaving them behind for the Japanese. They got talking and Tommy told him that he had walked out of China via Chungking. Michael told Tommy that I hailed from Shanghai. He took one look at Michael and said – 'You must be Nellie Stead's husband'. Tommy was offered a lift to Colombo but he declined as he said 'I've come so far under my own steam – thanks, I'll continue'. His aim was to reach Britain somehow. His last words to Michael were 'Love to Nellie'. We heard later that Tommy did arrive safely, but had quite a journey – unfortunately he was killed in a car crash in London soon after his arrival. So sad after his Herculean effort to escape from China.

* * *

Before leaving Bombay for Colombo, I was given a letter of introduction from Lt. Comdr. Harry Bird, Chief Signals Officer, Bombay, to his opposite number in Colombo.

I travelled by train from Bombay to a port near Tuticorin, changing at Madras, where I spent a night in the Station Hotel. On arrival at the port I boarded a small ship which ferried between India and Ceylon. On arrival at Ceylon I had another train journey to Colombo. My possessions consisted of a trunk and a handbag. I did not know anybody in Ceylon but I did remember the jewellers' shops and knew more or less what to expect. Firstly, I booked myself into an hotel. Secondly, I got in touch with the Navy Office and produced my 'chittie'. I was introduced to some of the girls there who found accommodation for me at Framjee House – a guest house with a railway line at the end of the garden which ran along the coast.

My Colombo home was quaint. It was in the 'turret' of the guest house. It consisted of two rooms, one above the other, with a staircase leading into each room. One ascended the stairs at the end of an enclosed verandah to my sitting room. It was a useless room. The staircase leading into this room and the second staircase leading up to my bedroom took up much of the space. A plank of wood acted as a roof to the second set of stairs and was used as a shelf or, dressing table.

My bed filled the room leaving a small space at the foot of it with about five hooks on the wall for my clothes. An ironing board, which the guest house provided, lived under my bed with my trunk. There was a small bedside table and lamp – and that was it. When I wanted to iron I would put up the ironing board, but had to sit crossed-legged – yoga style – on the bed to iron as the board took up the floor space.

Being a 'turret' there were four windows one on each wall – so I had lovely breezes – north, south, east or west – I certainly had a room with many views – the sea on one side, the main street on another not to mention the coast line and a window from which I could watch the local train snake its way up country. But, I could not use my light at night as to do so I had to close the windows which were painted black and draw across them heavy black material – regulation blackout fabric. I had a choice, I either sat in the dark – or closed the window and stifled in the heat. I chose to sit in the dark and listen to the waves lashing the shore, and the little local train puffing on its way with an occasional hoot – and dream my dreams. I was never lonely – the peace at these times of solitude were glorious.

After the fall of Singapore and as the evacuees started arriving in Colombo, with other girls from the office I would visit the Quayside offices to search the registers of arrivals in case a familiar name turned up and we could be of some help. Where to start? We each took a register in a different letter of the alphabet and ran our fingers down the register – not knowing anyone in Singapore didn't help.

*   *   *

Unbeknown to me Uncle Miller had resigned from the Shanghai Fire Brigade in 1940 – after I had left – and had joined a similar organisation in Singapore. The Millers were together until 1941 when Emily and young Joan were evacuated to Australia. By the time Singapore fell, uncle had become an invalid and was put on the last ship to leave Singapore. When he arrived at Colombo he decided to leave the ship to await another one for Australia. Having only what he stood up in and no access to funds he managed somehow to get in touch with Dad by telegram at Kovilpatti for financial help. Immediately Dad telegraphed me to arrange to get some money from the bank, find uncle and give him as much help as I could. I eventually traced him to the YMCA only to be told that he had left two hours earlier. He had managed to get a berth on a ship going to Australia. My downfall was going to the bank first.

* * *

Michael's ship was re-based to Bombay where he was transferred to the Signal School in Colaba. I left Colombo to join him. The Navy had taken over a super apartment block on Marine Drive and we were so lucky in being offered a one-bedroom flat.

Joy – full name, Helen Leslie Joy – was born 3 February 1943, at St Elizabeth's Nursing Home, Malabar Hill – weighing in at 7lb 10oz. She was our bundle of joy. We so often laugh at our ignorance. Michael was getting concerned as to how he would be able to visit me in the nursing home when the baby arrived. He was working on shifts and it was monsoon time and we did not have a car. It was a long uphill bicycle ride – needless to say he would be saturated if he was caught in the rain. Henry Boas, our neighbour said to Michael 'Oh! don't worry about that – there is no real need to see the baby for the first week – it will be like the pups – their eyes don't open for a week'! We looked at each other in disbelief – was that true? We lacked the courage to ask – so had to wait until 3 Feb! Joy had big blue eyes – and seemed to be looking at us as if to say 'There you are – see?'

* * *

From Bombay we were transferred to *HMIS Bahadur* a training establishment on the island of Manora off Karachi. We travelled from Bombay across the Sind Desert. It took three days. Michael, Joy in her little cot, Sophie Marie our Goanese nanny, Sue our bull terrier, and I – all packed in a two berth railway carriage. We had a tiny loo. The carriages were individual with no connecting corridors so once the train set off – you just had to stay put. We had to take all our own boiled drinking water – bottles of it, as well as boiled water to bathe Joy. The guard would telegraph the next station for our meals which were popped in through the window at various stations. There were no covers for the dishes – mostly curry and rice and a nice beef stew for Sue – by the time we received it it was congealed. Michael had to hurriedly exercise Sue at the various stops – not too plentiful but fortunately with long waits so it all worked out very well except it was extremely hot. We also had in our compartment an enormous block of ice on which a tiny fan played – that gave us 'air conditioning' in its most primitive form. Joy slept on the block of ice in her little papier maché bath which was filled with nappies as a mattress.

We loved Karachi or rather Manora once we were settled in. We were housed in an old house – the only house on the establishment which was not built especially for the navy. Newcomers had to live there before moving into the new houses, when they became available. This house was called 'The Chapel'. Three days after our arrival Michael fell ill with dysentery and was taken to hospital in Karachi.

Before Michael went into hospital, I sensed there was something not quite right with the house – strange things were happening but being so busy I passed them off. Once I was alone – with nanny – and particularly when I was completely alone in the house I realised that there was a poltergeist. The fun and games started. In all seriousness, I felt that someone was in the house trying to frighten me – and no way would I allow myself to be frightened. However, from then on, I was never alone! I was 'followed' up the stairs. I used to say to myself 'I'll wait until I get to the top of the stairs, turn round, and say BOO'. I was determined to frighten whoever it was – but, of course, no one was there. Likewise as I bathed Joy in the big bath I used to sense someone standing at the end of the bath watching – similarly, I would quickly look up and say 'BOO'. I felt a fool, because no one was there. This went on for a month. I was beginning to feel a bit worn.

It was most difficult to convince Michael about the poltergeist. However, five years later when we found ourselves in Calcutta (as civilians) we met someone at a party who was talking about the poltergeist at The Chapel on Manora. Michael looked at me and said. 'So, it was true!'

I must tell you of the last thing that happened to me. It was when I decided to arrange the house differently when Michael was due to come home from hospital. I had long since realised that my 'friend' did not like pictures on the wall because each time I hung one up, the next morning it would be placed neatly on the floor under the nail from which it had been hung. This last night I went to 'town' and hung all my favourite pictures up and placed a portrait of Ivy on a table. With everything nicely set for Michael's return the following day Sophie and I decided to retire for the night. It was then that I confessed to Sophie that I would be really glad to have Michael home as I was beginning to feel uncomfortable. We chatted about our experiences. She had them too, but we had never discussed this subject before. On going to our separate rooms – she slept in the nursery with Joy – we both felt so nervous that I suggested we carry Joy's cot into our room and all sleep together. We settled in bed. After I had turned the light off there was one enormous crash (up to this time there had been no noise). Sophie and I – shattered – crept down the stairs, armed with a curtain rod to see who had intruded into the house – no one. But, all the pictures were on the floor in the usual way with the exception of one, which had obviously been thrown across the room. It was found behind the settee in the corner on the opposite wall to where the picture had been hung. Ivy's portrait had been neatly placed face down.

* * *

We were soon allocated our new quarters and before long Bessie and little Ivy May came to stay with us for a while. It was lovely to have her with us and it was great for the cousins – except for four days, Ivy and Joy were 'twin' cousins. We celebrated their first birthday party together which ended with quite a bang-up celebration ending at about two in the morning.

Alastair came across to Karachi to spend his leave with Bessie and Ivy May but as we were so far away from his unit's area, Alastair decided that it would be much more convenient if Bessie lived nearer to him. So, once again Bessie was on the move – she settled in Darjeeling.

* * *

Later in the year Michael was transferred back to Bombay prior to being posted to Chittagong, near Calcutta. I followed him and joined the Navy Office in Bombay. I was expecting again and soon decided to join Mary at Kodailkanal – not only because it was a lovely place to be but also because, on my own, accommodation and expenses to run a flat would cause too many problems.

Along came Diana Jill, on 5 July 1945 – tipping the scales at 9lb 10oz. Diana was born in an American Mission Nursing Home run by Dr Otto. Kodaikanal is a superb hill station in South India. The nursing home is beautifully situated and from my gorgeous all pink (for a girl) private bedroom I literally felt on top of the world as I had a clear uninterrupted view of the plains below. Mary and I were at that time sharing 'Mirabel' a bungalow at Kodai while Graham was in Burma. Young Graham was born a few months later on 29 December. Mary enjoyed the blue room, for a boy.

Michael and I were so lucky – our family was complete. We had the two daughters we always wanted and for myself – I can now tell you that when we were first married, I used to wonder when and how I'd meet my mother-in-law. We corresponded regularly and were great pals. I used to day-dream of our meeting and I finally settled on it – long before I even became pregnant. I hoped so much, and then I knew, that I would be greeting her holding the hand of a little girl with blond hair, blue eyes and slightly crooked front teeth – holding in my arms another daughter about two years younger with dark brown hair and brown eyes. Isn't that fantastic? That's exactly how it happened. Here they are!

* * *

Wonderful news – the war had ended. Michael was being demobbed from the Navy – we had to start all over again – and presumably we were going to go 'home'. But, where was home? No doubt we were all thinking the same thoughts – Dad for sure was making his arrangements to retire and settle in Britain. Ivy and Donald posed quite a question mark. Would we meet up just to say 'hello – how are you?' on some quick visit. Would the family split up again, for ever – never to meet up again? We would just have to wait and see. At this stage I had never given a thought to 'home leave' and the like.

* * *

We returned to Bombay and the accommodation situation had worsened – no more Navy flats available. We lived in an assortment of homes from one room where we slept, cooked, ate, and each corner of the room 'allocated' a name (by Michael and I) – one corner the dressing room, one the kitchen where we had a tiny Baby Belling stove. So it went on for Michael and I, two gorgeous daughters, and Ayah who lived in. We also had an Indian bearer who worked by day – he did the household shopping and cooking in our 'kitchen' (ha). I had to get a job to help with the finances.

Then one day Michael came home to tell us that a Ronnie Hall was looking for a family to help him run his flat as his wife was in Britain making school arrangements for their children Judy and Antony. Selina, their youngest daughter would be returning to Bombay with Ursula as soon as all was in order. And this is how we made life-long friends with the Halls. We moved into Ronnie's flat – it felt like a palace compared with what we had been used to. He later built a delightful beach shack on Madh Island about twenty miles out of Bombay. On and off we stayed with Ronnie until we were officially repatriated to Britain.

*   *   *

The timing of our arrival here – and Bessie and Alastair's is perfect for a family reunion. Dad is with us too – a pity Mary, Graham and the children are so far away in Singapore.

We are staying at 'Relugas', the home of Michael's mother, Lady Robertson and Sir Benjamin. Sir Benjamin – usually called 'Barts' – is retired. He was Governor of the Central Provinces, India – he is a great Scotsman.

Michael is now with Boots, India – based in Bombay. We are learning to become 'civilians' whatever that means.

We arrived at Southampton having been repatriated on a troop-ship which conveyed prisoners-of-war back to Naples, Italy. That was touching. Families and friends waiting to meet up with their loved ones and it was too sad to watch any further when you could see some leave empty-armed as some PoWs had died en route. My heart ached for them.

When we arrived Michael decided that we should take a taxi as a treat to Guildford. It cost us £5. We were broke. It was when we were ringing the doorbell at 'Relugas' that it suddenly occurred to me that my dream had come true – I've already told you that little story.

Lady Robertson is bedridden and has been for twelve years with Parkinson's disease and so she has quite a handful of people help look after her as Sir Benjamin is not too fit either. They are delighted with the children.

I am not a 'tourist' at heart and, on the first sight-seeing outing, by the time I had got dressed up into all sorts of strange borrowed clothes – I was only used to tropical wear – I was most uncomfortable.

Whichever way I surveyed myself in the mirror, I looked wrong. Can you imagine me wearing not one, but two fox furs at the same time? No, I can't either – but I did, and with something that resembled a top-hat on my head. But it is fashion (not mine) and the sight of me hanging on to two children must have caused many a laugh. Luckily Michael and I could see the funny side to this as well.

*   *   *

Before Ivy and Donald left 'Relugas' they told us all about their internment. We talked, too, at great length about our growing up days at Yangtzepoo, Pingliang and Grosvenor and about the Brownriggs and Auntie Cameron.

*   *   *

Dad joined us at 'Relugas' for a few days from where he took us up to Blackpool for a little holiday before we travelled around to meet up with others in the family. Even though Myrtle and Hilda were so special to our family, sadly I did not meet them at that time. Edna had left for Canada. We had a lovely time and it was fun becoming a real-live relation – not a 'paper' one through correspondence.

We left Dad and travelled up to Moreton where Bessie and Alastair had rented a house. Myrtle came over for a day. She was just as I expected her to be – special. The four cousins – Ivy May, Alasdair, Joy and Diana were good company for each other and enjoyed playing together.

Bessie and I had not seen each other since our Karachi days when Joy and Ivy were a year old. We had lots to catch up on and to share our news and thoughts of Ivy and Donald. We were becoming more 'with it' familywise.

From Moreton Michael travelled to Nottingham – Boots' head office – to sort his future out and I travelled on by train to Reading where I was met by Elva Rush, a friend from Bombay. Michael joined me there. We were going to share a home for a few weeks with Elva at Nettlebed. What a train journey! This time, with the same darn top-hat, borrowed coat (fortunately minus fox-furs) plus – somewhere – amidst the luggage two children and, Oh yes! my sandwiches. I'm sure the gentleman opposite didn't know whether to laugh or cry for me. Anyway, hours later I arrived at Reading where Elva, looking extremely smart in her sensible clothes and brogues, met me. She took one look at me and said 'Not quite Reading'! The top-hat was hastily discarded by Elva.

Michael and I shall be leaving for Bombay as soon as his demobbed leave is up. I suppose we shall all be in the same boat now that we are in 'Civvy Street'. Our Shanghai – all gone, for sure.

I hope we will be able to see each other as often as we can although it will be difficult if we find ourselves in different countries.

Back to Bessie

Alastair was demobbed and after a short holiday went back to his old job with the Liverpool London & Globe Insurance Co. in Glasgow. He wanted to go abroad again – as far east as possible – and was soon sent to head office at Liverpool.

We went to live at Moreton in the Wirral. We were there for about four months. Ivy and Donald came up to spend Christmas with us – my first attempt at stuffing a turkey and I think Ivy's also, so we gave it full measure by stuffing it at both ends to make sure we did it right. Nellie and Michael had already been up to see us and I got a ticking off from Nellie – she said I would never make a decent housewife because she had found a number of stuffed suitcases under her bed.

Alastair got his posting overseas – to India, but I think he was hoping for China. We sailed on the SS *Franconia* on 27 February, 1947, the day the thaw set in after a very bitter winter.

Our destination was Calcutta. I was expecting again. It was pretty hot in Calcutta and with no permanent accommodation there it was decided I should take the children up to Darjeeling and stay there until I had my baby. Craig arrived on 4 June, 1947, weighing in at 8lb 6oz – Ivy was still the record holder.

Soon after Craig was born the children and I returned to Calcutta to be with Alastair.

MORE REUNIONS FOR IVY

Donald's sister Gladys and family were also on the list of arrivals and we spent some time near them – all of us in digs in London. Their daughter, Barbara, had recently announced her engagement to Steve Thirtle and it was a happy time helping Gladys make preparations for their wedding. Not an easy task as ration coupons were still the order of the day. Unfortunately we missed the wedding having left England a couple of weeks before the happy day.

We also saw Margaret and Alastair. They arrived soon after Gladys and joined us in the digs in London. Their son, Graeme, was about four. He was a cute little guy and only spoke Chinese until he left China. When I looked after him, while Margaret shopped, we enjoyed the automatic lifts down to the Underground – we would go down one and up another at the next station. I would then reverse the procedure just to hear his joyful exclamation 'by he self he do'.

Donald now attended office spasmodically and agreed to go to Hong Kong rather than Shanghai to resume the Far Eastern business. We were due to leave in March, 1947.

There was still one member of the family missing from our year of reunions – Mary who was now in Singapore. We looked forward to seeing her on the journey out. Again we sailed on the *SS Strathmore* – she had been refitted and was no longer a troop-ship but once on board we felt we had never left her.

We had the same stewards and cabin crew. We were no longer a 'dry' ship which was fun and, of course, we were allowed ashore at all ports. The ship's destination being the Far East we knew a lot of the passengers and it was just one big happy party.

At last we berthed at Singapore. Mary and Graham were on the dock to welcome us and take us back to their home for a lovely evening hearing all their news – not having met since 1940 there was a lot to catch up on. It was lovely to meet the young Shotters – Wendy a long legged fairy and Graham a sturdy 16 month old who was determined to go everywhere on his own.

We enjoyed our stay and natter. We returned to the ship and continued our journey to Hong Kong where we lived for the next four years. At that time most companies sent their employees out east on similar contracts – Donald and I looked forward to meeting Bessie and Nellie on our next leave.

CHAPTER TEN

Mary the Hostess

1948–1952

In 1948 Graham was posted to Blackdown, near Aldershot where we gradually began to feel more settled – so much so that we were able to invite Dad to come and make his home with us.

He bought himself an Austin Seven and had fun touring the country visiting his sister and other relatives in the north. He had only been with us a few weeks when he took off to visit his sister, Aunt Ada. This trip became one of his favourite stories. The way he told it 'The young Shotters got a big surprise when they received a card from Land's End and then another from John O'Groats, before they got my letter saying that I had eventually arrived at Ada's'. We became anxious about his long journeys and asked if he ever got tired. 'When I feel tired, I just pull into the kerb, or lay-by, shut my eyes and have forty-winks. I wake up as fresh as a daisy – you must remember me doing that in the old Shanghai days. Don't worry – I know when to stop.'

We had a lovely home at Blackdown and delightful neighbours. Wendy and young Graham settled happily into their new school. There was lots to do and lots for me to learn in an entirely new environment. Having been used to cooking being done for me, my efforts had disastrous results on more than one occasion. However it made good story-telling and lots of amusement for the 'veterans' in that field. Dad joined the 'army' life and enjoyed every moment too.

Nellie was the first to return. She contracted typhoid again – the two types at the same time – whilst Michael and she were in Calcutta. She was a very sick girl and spent many months in hospital before she was eventually invalided to Britain to stay with us. She was flown home on an Air India Constellation as a stretcher case – she was too ill to have the children with her. It was a very weak and worried Nellie who arrived – she needed a considerable amount of nursing, but with Dad's help we managed. Bessie and Alastair, who were also in Calcutta at that time, helped Michael to look after Joy and Diana. Later, when Michael's first overseas leave became due, Bessie fitted them out with clothes. for their return journey by sea, with Michael. Unfortunately their plans were changed at the last minute as the children developed chickenpox and instead of sailing they had to wait until they were well again before flying home.

Meanwhile Graham was posted to Aldershot proper – and so we moved *en famille* and were soon settled into a much bigger house – Salamanca Lodge. Michael returned with the children. By now we had quite an extended family and it was simply wonderful all being together. We had so much in common it was a happy household.

Ivy and Bessie both wrote to say that they too were returning for their first overseas leave and were planning to visit us. Unfortunately Graham would not be around to see them as he was posted yet again, this time to Korea. However, he was happy to know I would not be alone and would have family for company. What could be better. The burden of being parted from the children and I was lessened as he knew in no way would I be lonely!

After Bessie and Alastair's visit with the children – Ivy May, Alasdair and Craig – they moved on to Scotland where they stayed near the Moodie clan.

Ivy and Donald arrived last of all and announced that they were on transfer from Hong Kong to Canada.

According to Ivy, postwar Hong Kong was very different from the Hong Kong we knew. The war had caused much damage and all the houses had been stripped of wood – floors, ceilings, windows, in fact anything that could be used as firewood. All had to be renovated and in the meantime residents were living in hotels – accommodation was very difficult to come by. Before leaving England they were advised that the shops had been denuded so had purchased most household goods prior to their departure. They had been unable to obtain crockery – that was for export only – so put their name on a waiting list and hoped the next shipment would be large enough to include their order, if not they would have to go on waiting. They eventually were allotted a Wedgewood tea set which was used as everyday ware – nothing else being available!

They eventually moved out of the hotel to a house on the Peak which the Company (the Yorkshire Insurance Co.) purchased and turned into three apartments for staff. Donald had the fun of redesigning the inside of the house, aided of course by an architect, an old friend from Shanghai.

It was in Hong Kong we again met Lorraine – a former KKK member – and her husband Leslie Money. We spent a lot of time together mostly at weekends on Leslie's boat when we would sail to one of the outer islands and spend the night. Their friendship made such a difference to our stay in Hong Kong. We met Leslie again in England but we were too late to see Lorraine – sadly she had died of cancer.

Molly and Frank Smith had returned to Shanghai after the war but when the communists were in power they left for Nassau where Sir Victor Sassoon had transferred his assets. At that time one had to have an exit visa before being allowed to leave China. After a long wait they received theirs then travelled by train to Canton and so in the back way to Hong Kong – no doubt due to the lack of foreign shipping at that time.

They arrived soon after Donald had left to do a business trip across Canada while Ivy remained to catch a Blue Funnel cargo ship which would get her to England a few days before Donald was due to arrive. It was a pity Donald missed seeing Molly and Frank again – they must have had a lot of news to catch up on – news of families, friends and the company. When Ivy arrived in Singapore en route their ship was still in the harbour so they had another lovely time with them

It was a long relaxing trip home, visiting Manila, twelve days in Singapore, where she was able to visit other Shanghai friends now stationed there, Penang, Colombo, Port Said and so on home to Liverpool. It was a well timed trip as she was only with us a few days before she travelled up north again to welcome Donald.

Nellie was gradually becoming stronger and having the children with her again helped tremendously – she had been lost without them. Now that she was able to get about a bit more she was enjoying Michael's leave. Like their friends in India, Nellie and Michael realised they had a problem – the education system there was not the best and as they, like their colleagues, dearly wished to do all possible to ensure the girls had a good beginning in life, they enroled them into Clare Park, a boarding school in Crondall, Farnham. They were not entirely alone as Carol and Katie Garratt (of Calcutta) and Margaret Rush, Marion and Rosemary Fletcher (of Bombay) were also boarders at Clare Park.

Bessie and Alastair were of the same opinion – unfortunately there was no option for parents in India. After thinking things through they enroled their children in the Dollar Academy, Scotland. Bessie came south to join us when Ivy arrived in the autumn and we were able to enjoy a first 'all together' reunion since 1940 in Shanghai when the family first split up.

*   *   *

It must have been about fourteen years since we had seen Auntie Cameron of Yangtzepoo days so we took this opportunity to have a special treat. We decided on the spur of the moment that we would take advantage of being together and visit her. We drove from Aldershot to Herne Bay, Kent, by taxi, to see Auntie – alas alone – Mr Chandler had died two years after they arrived in England.

There we were – the four of us – with Dad, once again at Auntie's tea table with lashings of goodies – toasted teacakes and, oh yes! strawberry jam. Dear Auntie was nearly blind and so very deaf. We wept, we laughed and we 'reminisced' and we just loved her all the more. We left her with her very good friend to keep an eye on her – her little guide dog. It was the longest taxi ride we had ever had: it cost £20 (£4 each) but we just felt the special occasion included comfort as we were not familiar with train journeys and cross-country travel in Britain. Besides we had to get back to Aldershot for the children's supper – Michael was looking after them for the day which was great.

If we could repeat such a trip it would be well worth it even at today's inflationary prices. What a beautiful memory we have of our last tea party with Auntie. A wonderful dream come true.

*   *   *

We had a good few months visiting friends and relations – in between times the men, Donald, Alastair and Michael finalising their new contracts. Alastair and Michael were going back to India – Donald to Canada. Graham was still in Korea – but hopefully he would return before the final departure of the family. He had missed the reunions and had a lot of catching up to do. But, it was not to be so.

Michael and Alastair – coincidentally – found themselves booked on the same ship returning to Bombay. Bessie and Nellie had to remain in Britain and had the sad task of placing the children into boarding school. However, on the lighter side it was fun and exciting for them arranging brand-new uniforms for the children with trips to London and Edinburgh in order to get this and that – just right – according to the long lists of must-haves and must-not-haves which the schools requested. The children, although looking back now must have been bewildered and overwhelmed by their new lifestyle to come, accepted the change in different ways.

On reflection Nellie admits now that she would not do it again – it was not of her choice – it was a *fait accompli*.

So our extended family diminished in size to myself – still hostessing – with Dad, Donald and Ivy, Nellie, Joy and Diana and, of course, Wendy and Graham for company. And Graham to return soon. Great. The four children were fantastic together, until one of them was punished. The 'punisher' received worse punishment as the other three acted in sympathy and protected the offender.

It was around this time of holiday/recuperation that Nellie decided she would learn to cook. She had not had much chance whilst out east and I guess seeing me active in the kitchen gave her ideas. The time soon came when I had to attend a meeting and left her in charge. The menu included a stuffed marrow. 'Right,' she said 'I'll do that – no problem'. Or so she thought. In fact it was quite an experience best told in her own words.

'It was at a time that meat was not that easy to come by – and it was expensive. So, the very thought of me possibly ruining our main meal – there were nine of us to feed – turned me into a 'monster' with two left hands and an empty head – in short, I got the hee-bee-jee-bees!

The household departed in different directions and I was left in charge with only 'our Mrs Smith', who was busily putting the house in order.

To cut a long story short – and like this story – I seemed to 'short-cut' the marrow as well. This is what happened. .. I placed the minced meat on the kitchen sink and placed the marrow – plonk – there as well ... and proceeded to cut both ends off

Why? I now had three pieces of marrow ... I had a peep inside before proceeding to stuff When 'hang on, there are pips inside' said me to me. So, to make it easier to de-pip the marrow I decided to cut it lengthwise as well ... *voila!* ending up with four pieces of marrow – no pips and some minced meat for stuffing. So far so good ... (I thought).

I edged a little closer to the sink, placed one end of the marrow up to my chest, with my left arm (elbow resting on the sink) I made a 'short-arm' and held the lower half of the marrow and wedged the upper half on the top – seemed the correct thing to do – so, I then did the same with my right arm – two 'short-arms'! The going was great – all I had to do now was stuff the marrow. With the minced meat placed near at hand (well planned!) the stuffing was easy – though messy – and the bits and pieces which oozed out along my arm, on my blouse and down the sink were efficiently scooped up with my right 'short-arm' and – Hey Presto! – one green marrow was stuffed and ready to place in the oven. How to get it there .. (in the oven that is?) Help!

Me.	Mrs. Smith?
Mrs S.	(Rushing into the kitchen). Ooo – ooh – ye all right?
Me.	(Draped over the sink – hugging one well stuffed marrow with two 'short-arms') Could you please get me a bandage from the bathroom upstairs.
Mrs S.	(Thinking I'd chopped my arms off – had no idea I was trying to cook a meal – which she knew I couldn't do!) Ooo – ooo – ye – yes – dashed at the double up the stairs muttering 'Oh dear'.
Me.	(Calling after her.) Make it a 4" bandage!
Mrs S.	(Returns.) Flying down the stairs – two at a time, – it was great speed at this stage – but when I asked for scissors to cut the bandage she realised what I had done and collapsed into peals of laughter and left me 'hugging the marrow'!

So I continued with great determination and gusto to tie the bandage around the marrow thus ... being a reasonably methodical type, only the best would do – so the bandage had to be in neat rows – each ending in a neat little bow – no way would I just 'bandage' my now well cared for marrow. Done, and into the oven it went.

The sink and I were soon sorted out and cleaned up and, I was smiling brightly when the family returned home for lunch. My sister had such a happy smile of success written across her face when she was told ... 'all's well ... its in the oven ... and I did it!'

We still remember, all these years later, with lots of laughter – the pathetic marrow laying in the oven under a neat row of burnt bows! But it tasted good.'

* * *

On the eve of Joy's ninth birthday, Dad went to bed early as he said he was tired and felt an early night would do him good. Nellie stayed up late to decorate some swiss rolls for a birthday cake for Joy's little family tea party the next day. It was to be a swing! Being no baker she bought the rolls and made a good job of her swing – only she would have tackled the almost impossible – with a little doll waiting to be pushed between the candles. Quite a balancing feat.

There was no birthday party on the 3 February 1952 – dearest Dad had a massive stroke. We were all in shock. We had been apart for most of our lives but we felt so blessed that we had been together one way or another during the past year and that we were able to share some family life together. We were so privileged that Salamanca Lodge could accommodate us all as it did. Aunt Ada and Bessie hurriedly came down to Aldershot and together the four Stead sisters with Aunt Ada and her son attended Dad's funeral at Brookwood, Woking. Donald looked after us admirably and relieved us of the formalities that take place at such a sad time and of which we were quite unprepared to handle.

* * *

Ivy and Donald departed for Canada. Bessie remained in Scotland for a few more months. Nellie flew out to Bombay to join Michael on his tour of office in India. Graham returned from Korea – having missed everyone. But it was lovely to have him home and to be a complete family once again.

The past year had overflowed with a potpourri of memories for us all – happy – sad – everlasting.

CHAPTER ELEVEN

Finale
1952–1991

BESSIE

I joined Alastair in Calcutta and we were to spend the next twenty years on the Indian sub-continent. Our first contract was for six months leave after four and a half years. This was the norm at that time. However, this changed and we actually proceeded on leave after four years – our next leave was after three and a half years, decreasing to two and a half years and then every eighteen months when flying back and forth became available. Our six months leave usually necessitated renting a property and taking with us bed linen and towels for five. For this we had a large black tin box which weighed a ton – this over and above personal baggage and brown paper bags for oddments (it meant someone having to count the pieces of luggage at each stage of our journey). Later we were able to make arrangements with Joyce to keep the box for us between leaves, and much much later we bought our own flat in Edinburgh for the children to live in once they left school and for use during our visits to Britain.

Accommodation always seemed to be a problem for us. (When I first agreed to contribute to this book I called my section 'Of no Fixed Address'). Firstly, there were the seven moves in eighteen months in Delhi. Then there was Karachi, Darjeeling, Kirn in Scotland, Moreton on the Wirral and then back to Calcutta and Darjeeling where Craig was born.

When Craig was robust enough to do the trip back to Calcutta, Alastair managed to get us a six months let in a block of flats called Chowringhee Mansions. While in Darjeeling we had employed a wonderful Nepalese girl called Jetti to be ayah. She remained with us until the children went to school in Scotland. She was only a tiny little thing, not much taller than Ivy at the age of eight. Craig, of course, was her baby. She looked after the children well and was a great help through our accommodation problems.

Our next move was to a two-roomed apartment in the Kanani Estates – one room as the living room and the other slept five with wardrobes used as a division. It was a bit cramped to say the least. After about eighteen months we were fortunate to get accommodation in Tivoli Park. I say fortunate because by this time flats were difficult to come by with landlords cashing in on exorbitant sums as 'key' money. Tivoli Park had large grounds attached and was well situated for the school. The children were happier there. At this time Nellie and Michael were transferred to Calcutta and the cousins had many opportunities to get to know each other. I joined the Deputy High Commission and worked for them for the next ten years or so, resigning each time I went on leave and rejoining when I got back – whether it was Calcutta or Bombay. After our leave in 1951 I remained with the children and took a flat in Dollar. The children and I were there for about a year, at the end of which I entered the children as boarders in Dollar Academy.

When I returned to Calcutta the firm had allocated to us a flat in Alipore Road just across the way from where Nellie and Michael were living. From then on our accommodation problems were over. The firm provided furniture with the flats. There were many take-overs in the insurance world at this time along with rearrangement of staff. We were able to move about more freely now that we were housed and the next ten years saw us in Bombay, Karachi, Bombay and then back to Calcutta. In 1967 we were transferred to Singapore where I stayed until 1971. Alastair remained there until he retired.

India was full of exciting times. The night before Craig was born the news came through that India was to go independent on 14 July. A couple of years later on 14 July we felt in Calcutta the earthquake which devastated Assam. The tremor lasted a full two minutes; time enough to discover it was an earthquake because the fans were swinging; time enough to go through to the children to get them up and prepare to descend; time enough to look out of the window and see the trees swaying. We were on the fourth floor of a block of apartments. We had only moved in that morning – a temporary refuge from Tivoli Park where polio had hit and we were under doctors orders to move to somewhere where there were no children. We were very grateful to Piere Menut for taking us in.

Alastair bought an old two-seater Ford (similar to the one he shared with Ian Denby in Shanghai). The children loved to crowd into the dickie with Jetti. In fact they became most popular with their friends who also wanted a shot in the dickie. At sometime or other we became members of the Tollygunge Club and it became a ritual to go out there on Sundays for afternoon tea (cucumber sandwiches and all). Years later it was at Tolly we caught sight of the first sputnik orbiting the earth, and we were out there listening to the whole of the Queen's Coronation relayed by radio, sitting outside under the stars, when a violent nor'wester struck the moment the crown was placed on her head and we had to take shelter in the club house.

We were at Tollygunge, fortunately this time without the children, when we heard of the assassination of Mahatma Gandhi. We thought it best to return home. It was a long journey back to town and we were very vulnerable in our open two-seater. Our way was through a very congested area, the atmosphere was tense; no one shouting but a multitude of voices murmuring. We were stopped and asked for a lift, very politely, and we had no option but to agree. In no time at all we had five in the dickie and about another five clinging on to wherever they could. All they wanted was a lift to Chowringhee.

Bombay, our next move, was quite different from Calcutta, as it was by the sea and less dusty. We were able to go for pleasant picnics to the beach at weekends and it was lush. We·were only there a short time when Alastair was posted to Karachi for six months.

Karachi we liked from the start. It had been hinted by the office that Alastair was earmarked to take over as manager when the present one retired. It was a smaller place and everybody seemed friendly.

I joined the British Women's Association (nothing to do with the Shanghai one). It was a going concern, open one day a week for members to meet and have a chat and coffee. On other days there was a children's library, baby clinic and servants' clinic. On Tuesdays besides coffee there was a dress exchange for all those mistakes one buys in a hurry whilst on leave, and an arts and crafts stall. One never missed going. I also joined Paddy Ralph's work party. She was chairman of the Children's Aid Society which helped homeless children. We used to meet once a week and make Christmas decorations to be sold at a grand sale in December each year. It was at Karachi that I first became interested in painting – I managed to sell a painting at a BWA exhibition and have had the bug ever since.

We went back to Bombay for about a year and then were posted, as we had hoped, to Karachi, supposedly permanently. There were a few more take-overs and the inevitable rearrangement of staff, and we found ourselves after two and a half years back in Calcutta for another period of five years.

During our second stay in Karachi the children were flown out for their summer holidays. Ivy left school and remained behind until we went on leave. Craig and Alasdair came out again for the holidays when we were settled back in Calcutta.

I would go home once between leaves so that I could see them more often. This did not help our marriage: finally during our stay in Singapore we decided to part. I returned to England to stay with Mary in Oxford. Craig had emigrated to Australia a few years earlier. Ivy and Alasdair were now married, Alasdair to Iris Gray – they have two children, Claire and Graeme; Ivy May married Roddick McCall – they have twins, Gillian and Grant; Craig married Lesley Roche, a true Australian girl and they also have a girl and boy – Robyn and David.

I moved up to Scotland to be nearer the family and bought a house with a delightful garden in Moffat. Betty and Adam Gray, Iris's parents, very kindly put me up whilst negotiating the purchase of 'Hillview'. I lived in Moffat for about ten years before moving to Edinburgh, where I have lived ever since.

I remember a fortune-teller coming aboard the ship at Penang all those years ago who said I would marry someone who would always be moving. He suggested someone in the army – as it was war time that sounded feasible. I have often wondered, as it has turned out, whether there was something in that prediction, and whether there will be yet another move for me.

As a family we use any excuse for get-togethers. We have had some great times – trips to London, narrow-boat trips on the Oxford Canal, a holiday in Wales with Wendy and David, and just 'at homes' with me in Moffat besides many more with Ivy and Nellie at Kings Sutton – but our most memorable one was the narrow-boat trip in 1984 because Mary's young Graham had come over from Australia especially to celebrate her 70th birthday.

NELLIE

It was late 1952 when I joined Michael in Calcutta. As accommodation was extremely hard to come by Margery Garratt said to Michael, 'Nellie is not to stay in any more guest houses – you must stay with Guy and I at Alipore'. This sounded ideal, and it was. We had both entered our girls (they Carol and Katie) into Clare Park, England and were so very lost without the children. We had lots in common – we were a compatible foursome. The men worked hard during the day – Margery and I kept ourselves busy – in many ways doing nothing. We looked forward to our evenings spent on the back verandah when we shared the children's letters and we spent a great deal of time laughing. We were happy.

Bessie and Alastair were also in Calcutta but at Tollygunge – we saw them at weekends when the men were home and had the use of the company's car to visit. Then, of all things, Bessie and Alastair moved into a flat – right opposite us at Alipore – it was great. It made us realise what a small world it was. Two sisters from Shanghai finding themselves living in flats opposite each other in Calcutta!

Disaster struck. It was a very black afternoon. I had been resting on my bed – afternoon siesta – the shutters were closed. We always closed our shutters from midday to evening to keep out the heat. On getting up and opening mine the sky looked forbidding. The whitewashed buildings stood out dramatically against the black-black sky and I remember thinking to myself 'I would hate to have to fly in a sky looking so angry'. It was frightening.

Guy and Michael returned from work. We turned on the radio to listen to the news as we usually did in the evening. A news flash came on that a BOAC Comet had crashed. The aircraft, on a stop-over from Singapore, was bound for London. It had taken off about the time my shutters were opened. It was rumoured that perhaps the pilot thought he would be able to rise above the turbulence within seconds of take-off, but he didn't. All perished in the disaster – the crash remained a mystery.

The following day we received news that Michael Collins of Boots, Singapore, was one of the ill-fated passengers – would we do our utmost. What could we do – we tried our best. We arranged floral tributes from his wife and mother, family and friends. We tried to represent the family and company in some small way when we attended the mass funeral service the following day. A moving service as all were buried in an enormous communal grave – a coffin for each passenger and member of the crew. The service was conducted by priests and ministers of all denominations not knowing the religious background of the passengers and crew.

My Michael was, at this time, instrumental in closing down the Calcutta office as he did not feel the business potential was good enough to warrant an office – fully staffed. It was a sad time for him. He did not like doing this – it also put him on a spot as, in essence, he was doing himself out of a job as well – but it had to be done. Sadly we said goodbye to Calcutta and our many friends. We knew we'd meet Bessie and Alastair again – but it was quite dreadful leaving Margery and Guy – perhaps our chances of meeting again would be at a Clare Park parents' day – if we ever were to be in Britain at the same time.

We had no idea what Boots had in store for us. We returned to England for our leave to await further news.

*   *   *

We travelled 'home' on a P&O ship and headed straight for Clare Park, Crondall, near Farnham. It was a delight to see the girls – all of them, and some of the Mums and Dads from India – the Fletchers, as well as George and Elva Rush.

Part of our holiday was to be spent in Truro, Cornwall, where we had hired a caravan for a month. It was super and time was not a problem as we had our own 'caravan time'. The ruling was, whatever time we woke up it was 7am – much to the confusion of our neighbours as we would be having breakfast at their lunch time on occasions.

From Truro we drove up to Penicuik, Midlothian, Scotland, to visit Mary and Graham – they had moved there from Aldershot after Graham's return from Korea. As mentioned earlier the Shotter and Poole 'kids' were made for each other and their friendship was very special.

At the end of our leave we were posted to Hong Kong. Michael was to take over from Len Ayres who, in turn, was to fill the gap in

Singapore created by Michael Collins' death. This move was to change our life-style completely.

India was lovely and the way we lived there was natural. Accommodation was restricted simply because there was a shortage. Calcutta, at that time seemed to be an unhealthy city. Dysentery, cholera, typhoid (as I knew only too well) plagued us, besides chickenpox, measles and the like. However, memories of our days spent there were superb.

We were among the first batch of civilians after the war – the second and subsequent batches were a different kettle of fish. They had air conditioned apartments/houses with not only one, but two air conditioned bedrooms and, in some cases, an air conditioned lounge as well as an air conditioned car. We had fans. Life-stylewise, we were not competitive amongst ourselves – we were all in the same boat, permanently broke. Although we would have no doubt enjoyed the luxuries – looking back – I'm glad we didn't. We would have been spoilt too early. Life in India at that time was a challenge and we had fun making the best of every situation – fortunately with a sense of humour. More treasured memories.

* * *

Hong Kong changed us in many ways. It was obviously so different from how I remembered it as an evacuee in '37 – let's face it that was 17 years ago. We were now living a very sophisticated life – my wardrobe changed – and I enjoyed the change. Clothes properly made – well fitting – shoes once again made by a Chinese shoemaker in whatever material I chose, with a bag to match if I wanted it that way. We could purchase almost anything in the food line. We lacked nothing. Hong Kong had it all but, the simple things we enjoyed in India were not there, and never would be.

* * *

Joy and Diana flew out on their first flight alone – it was a long trip and entailed an overnight stop en route. They were two very tired little girls with no smiles on their arrival at Kai Tak airport. Joybelle (my pet-name for Joy) did not enjoy the trip and looking back I realise it must have been very hard on her having the responsibility of looking after Diana as well. It's not easy being a big sister, I'm sure.

I worked for the Hong Kong Police in the Narcotics Bureau and Anti-Corruption Branch. The work was most interesting and, being methodical, suited me greatly. Finding the different aliases to the Chinese names of the suspects/culprits kept me busy for the longest while. It took me back to the corrupt messages which I dealt with, almost exclusively, in my navy days. I usually stayed in the office to have lunch and the office I worked in was a 'cage' within a cage. The detainee awaited interrogation between the two cages. The haul having been placed with us in our inside cage. It was sad to see the guilty party of an opium haul awaiting interrogation – it used to make me feel a heel – but that was what it was all about and compassion could not be considered.

As I had to continue my work with the minimum leave whilst Joy and Diana were with us it did not make much of a holiday for the girls but somehow we managed and had fun. What could parents do? We just did not have funds available for extras like sightseeing. Some might say – 'I envy you your lovely happy exotic life in the east'. Yes, some may agree with that comment but it was not a family life. We had little choice. We were lucky, extremely so, that we had what we did have. But regrets? There will always be some for most of us – but how many admit to them? Few.

* * *

Two years later Michael was transferred to Singapore to work alongside Len Ayres. We moved into Michael Collins' home and Len into the bigger house next door. Boots looked after us well and we had a delightful home where we spent many happy years. Here I worked for – my favourite 'boss' – Charles Wechsler a diamond dealer who also dealt with Cadillacs, Rovers and Volkswagens – luxuries galore! Singapore was beginning to become sophisticated – a different life-style to that of Hong Kong – but equally as good. I guess we were adaptable – we had to be out east – wherever we were.

Gee and his wife Sim, were our cookboy and amah. They had four children. Teh Han, Lee Feh, Lee Lee and little Teh Boon their youngest son who was born when they were living with us. We were a big family and Sim became my best friend. We had fun. She did not understand my English too well but we got on great with our Pidgin English. Christmas day was our special day because I personally entertained them in our home – in our reverse position – employer/employee – they got a kick out of my amateur baking for the special occasion. Then we would exchange gifts from under the Christmas tree decorated with tinsel and baubles – these were fun times and became quite a tradition. It was so different for them and soon they began to understand the Christmas story.

*   *   *

During our time in Singapore the overseas companies began to realise the difficulty their staff were having in trying to live a family life without family. Contract terms became more realistic and eventually it worked out that we were able to see our children every year. Joy and Diana would fly out and spend their summer holidays with us and the next year we would see them in Britain.

Wonderful news! Josie had suddenly decided that she was going to fly over to meet us all before we departed for Singapore where we could easily find ourselves in remote parts of the world – never meeting. England being closer to the States was too much of an opportunity for her to miss – so she virtually just turned up.

I found it quite remarkable how she and Michael resembled each other – they could easily have been twins. Josie has been a wonderful aunt to Joy and Diana and every year at Christmas time we receive most interesting letters giving us all her family news. We look forward to these letters very much. Unfortunately, I regret to have to admit I am not at all good at reciprocating – but the girls do. Josie, being Josie, always forgives me.

When Joy finally left school to join us and start on some career she asked if she could have a holiday with a friend of hers en route, to which we said 'Of course you may'. She got off the aircraft at Bahrain with her friend where she spent a delightful weeks' holiday with her friend's family. We met Diana on arrival in Singapore. They were good days too but unfortunately Diana had to return alone to go back to Clare Park.

Meanwhile when Singapore became independent Michael and I had to become Singapore citizens as most expatriates were advised to do – thereby having dual UK/Singapore citizenship. It also resulted in the fact that work permits had to be obtained as only Singapore citizens were permitted to work. Joy lost out on this. She would have to be a resident for three years before qualifying for citizenship thereby being able to work. To fill her time, I worked – earned money – she worked for me – earning a little money. She had several paid jobs such as, (*a*) managing the house as well as doing the household shopping (*b*) caring for the animals – Pimms and Waggles, our two dogs. She made her own clothes and studied shorthand and typing at some outlandish school in the Serangoon area – an area out of bounds to army personnel as it was not considered a good area to be out and about in alone. Poor Joy had a rough time as she had little company. But she did a wonderful job of her life and never once complained. She was involved with some charitable organisation when she was asked to look after the little children backstage at some show. Loving children she much enjoyed this. A young gentleman also helping out, with the lights, was Norman Drake. They fell in love and that was it! Looking back – that was how Michael and I first met – backstage!

Joy and Norman announced their engagement. Soon after Norman returned to England – he had been doing his National Service stint in Singapore – he returned to his profession as a teacher and plans were made for a first Stead grandchild wedding – and all who could turn up did so for this momentous occasion. Joy and Norman were married at Tonypandy, Rhondda, Wales – Diana, Wendy, Ivy May as well as Lesley Knight were her bridesmaids. Her wedding gown and the bridesmaid's dresses were made in Singapore. Mary and Graham, young Graham and David Andrews (Wendy's fiancé) attended. Ivy flew over from Canada. But the Steads were in the minority – Bessie and Alastair were in Calcutta with Alasdair and Craig at the time and were much missed. Joy and Norman were so honoured when Craig sent them a piece of music which he had composed especially for their wedding. No matter how one could have tried we could never have outnumbered the tremendous response from the relations of Norman in Wales – they were ALL there. Norman's Mum and Dad (Alice and Roy) – his brothers, Geoffery and Harry as well as Geoff's wife, Marion – such a big family for us to meet. A fine time was had by all – it was a great occasion.

Joy and Norman now have four children – Helen Leslie, Ashley James, Ruth Elizabeth and Joanna Lynne (at the time of writing this they are all in their twenties and doing very well indeed).

* * *

When Diana eventually left Clare Park she was with Joy for a little while in Singapore before Joy left to live with Norman's family in Wales to make their wedding arrangements. There was still a restriction on work permits and Diana found it next to impossible to settle down and do nothing. Besides she was missing Joy very much indeed. Diana decided to return to Britain to stay with her best friend Isabel in Farnham – which she did. Later she shared a flat with four other friends in London where she met and fell in love with Llewellyn Hilton Jones – it was not too long after this that they became engaged and married.

Michael and I were on leave for their engagement but unfortunately we were unable to be at their wedding which they chose to be at the Kensington Registry Office followed by a reception at an hotel and then a small buffet party in their new flat for family only. This time Bessie, Alasdair and Craig (big Alastair still overseas) attended the wedding besides Mary and Graham – who gave her away and acted as proxy for Michael. Wendy and David and their young son, Martin, were also in attendance besides Joy, Norman, Helen, Ashley, Ruth and 'expected' Joanna. Another Stead grandchild wedding.

Diana and Llew sent the first tier of their wedding cake out to us in Singapore which we were asked to keep to celebrate their first anniversary. I thought I had found a safe place to hide this cake from temptation but ... in due time when Sim and Gee arranged a special supper for Michael and I to celebrate this long-awaited anniversary ... the cake 'tin' was produced by Sim, and on opening it I found it empty! One very guilty looking Michael standing by! He sheepishly admitted that throughout the year, when he used to stay up late to listen to his much loved classical music – he'd secretly open the 'tin' for yet another nibble – how to confess this to DJ (as I called Diana) and Llew – they would be waiting for a letter giving our reaction to our little anniversary party. We all had a good laugh and Michael was forgiven. I never tasted the cake.

Diana and Llew have three children – Jennifer Ann, Anthony Thomas and Ian Michael (twins) – very sadly baby Sonia was only with us for three short weeks. At the time of writing this Jennifer, now sixteen, is interested in drama and catering, and the boys are up-and-coming athletes.

*   *   *

Time went on happily then one day I thought 'Oh! no, not again – I can't believe it – another 'Bloody Saturday' '. The world seemed to crash around us – it was a time-bomb which had been planted on the mezzanine floor of MacDonald House – owned by the Hong Kong & Shanghai Bank. This was at the time of the Indonesian confrontation when one never knew when the next bomb would go off.– in a telephone booth? – near a car?

In my case, the events which led up to this incident were quite coincidental. At that time Michael used to do a considerable amount of travelling for the company and about six months prior to this horrific day, he was away touring Malaya on business. His last words to me were something like this ... 'Please don't start changing the garden this time – I like it as it is'.

I was known for planning major changes in the house when Michael went away – be it new curtains, re-arranging the furniture, the garden or buying a new carpet. Michael hated changes and so, if I really wanted to change something badly, I would plan well in advance and await another business trip. This time it was going to be landscaping the garden. All had been arranged, so I could hardly go back on my plans.

Michael was hardly across The Causeway between Singapore and Johore Bahru when in came my contingent of garden workers. It was a Saturday and all was going well. New path laid and an arbour erected. All we required were some new plants. I knew Michael would enjoy the change, once he got used to it. He usually did.

Salamat, the company driver was my No.1 for the day – I had full use of the car and it was great. Salamat and I set off towards Bukit Timah and Dunearn Road to shop around for plants and shrubs to put the final touches of colour to the new flower beds.

It was extremely hot and we were tired. On our way back to the house in Windsor Park Road, I thought it would be a good idea to buy a nice big block of ice cream for Sim's children – which we did. Half way home, I thought ... 'that's not fair – what about Salamat's children'. So we turned round and went back to the ice cream shop and bought another block. It was decided that as we were nearer Salamat's house, we had better give his children their ice cream first.

In Malaysia the Malays live in kampongs. This is a compound where the whole family live together, in different houses, of different sizes and in this case Jay, Salamat's nephew, had the more respectable house. Jay was young, doing well as he was working in an office. He was affluent. He sported a carpet – not often used in a kampong house. He had a three-piece suite and a radio – in fact, he lived well. I was offered the best seat – which happened to be the settee and soon all the kampong kids were peeping through the open windows and generally big-eyed wondering why I was there. Then out came the ice cream – with two blocks, we just about made it. Not only Salamat's family but I should imagine all the children from near and far kampongs came around just for a wee lick! Little did I know then that I was probably sitting on a detonator.

On the day of the bombing – Michael was away again, this time in Manila – as was the usual practice I could utilise Salamat's time to purchase or arrange maintenance on house things. I was planning to have some lamps re-wired. I particularly requested Salamat to purchase white wiring – not brown. He would have the purchases ready in time to collect me at the office to go home – about 5 to 5.30.

At about 3pm I received a frantic telephone call from Salamat. He was not at all his usual self – which was polite and calm. He was most irritated, rude and off-hand when he told me he could not get 'mauve wire' – he was in a panic and worse still he could not tell me what he really wanted me to do – that was to escape. When I tried to calm him and say that it was white, not mauve, wire – there is no such thing – he hastily hung up on me.

At four o'clock there was one tremendous blast! The detonator had gone off – the lift shaft was shattered and one of the lifts ended up in the street. Two ladies working in the bank had been killed – their office in the bank was on the other side of the wall on the mezzanine floor. My office was on the floor above. Salamat obviously knew about this. Although he was not a guilty party to the incident his nephew Jay was – very much so. We later read in the newspaper that he had all the 'gear' for this day planned and the explosives – or whatever is used for a time-bomb – hidden in his house at least six months before! (I often wondered if it was hidden underneath the settee!) Jay ended up in jail.

* * *

When Michael and I retired from Singapore we decided to settle in the Seychelles – the most idyllic country I have ever lived in. It is beautiful – and the life-style there has a charm of its own – simplicity. The Seychellois are delightful people and they know how to make the best of every situation. They are not greedy for possessions. They are never in a hurry – they live, one day at a time – usually 'tomorrow'. Stress, nervous breakdowns are unheard of there.

Our first 'own' home was built at Anse la Mouche on the slope of the mountain and because it was on a gradient it ended up in three tiers. My only regret is that Joy and Diana and their families never saw this dream-home.

In order to keep myself occupied I decided to try to teach the young teenagers how to make something out of nothing. My raw material was broken and dead shells picked up off the beaches. I had never worked with shells before but somehow we managed to start a little cottage industry called 'Coquillages Exotiques' – meaning exotic shells in Creole – which ran a successful seven years. With the help of the young Seychellois we were able to welcome the first jet visitors when they arrived off the BOAC inaugural flight with a lei made up of shells and seeds – it took us 463 hours to make these garlands.

Saturday morning was purchasing day and the little children who had been picking up shells during the week used to come with their little plastic bags of shells – needless to say none were turned away. I would record their names in order to remember them the next time and so I was able to put two and two together and remember families as well – I had 129 little children and spent a fortune! But, oh! it was all so worthwhile.

Ivy visited us – in fact she was with us when we heard the news of Jennifer's birth. Cable & Wireless telephoned the message to the house – we shed tears of happiness together. Bessie and Alastair also visited us for a short holiday in the 70s.

It was in 1973 that I became more interested in the church and then became a Christian. I started to go to Bible studies with Rev. Charles and Dorothy James – my dear friend Winifred Gass – Jacky Riley of AIM (the American Inland Mission) and Brian Adeline who is now ordained. I was baptised in the Indian Ocean, off Anse Royale, Mahe, in 1982. We shared some wonderful times together – the Lord working through each one of us in different ways.

In '82 I decided that it was time for another visit to Britain to see the girls – unfortunately Michael had no desire to leave the Seychelles, even for a minute. I travelled on a jumbo jet – a superb aircraft. How wonderful it was to see my Joy and Diana and their families – they were all so happy and busy and well. Ivy treated me to a trip over to Canada to visit her and of course I met up with Bessie and Mary.

Whilst I was in Britain – Michael suddenly died in November '82 – I was devastated. I had a lonely journey back to attend his funeral and close up our lovely house. As transportation would have been a very costly thing I had no option other than to leave our worldly possessions behind. Fortunately I was able to sell the house – albeit at a great loss. With 44lb in weight of clothes I departed the Seychelles taking with me many happy – and sad – memories – praising the Lord that he was there helping me at this turning point in my life. I feel exceedingly privileged to have been able to live in such a lovely country.

Once again I found myself at Ivy's in Canada. Bessie and I travelled over together. We were sorry Mary missed out on this reunion. She was with Wendy in Wiltshire. Unfortunately Bessie had to return after two months. I stayed on for another four and decided to take this opportunity to visit my sister-in-law Josie and her husband Johnny. What a thrill for me. I travelled alone from Montreal to Denver then on to Colorado Springs where Johnny and Josie were awaiting me – what a reunion. They were fantastic and could not do enough for me and it was lovely meeting all their friends. It was a beautiful day and the scenery superb. During my short stay they took me almost everywhere – I visited Will Rogers' memorial hall, and saw many of his movie-stills in frames on the wall. We went for a train ride where we saw masses of Aspen trees with their 'gold dollar' shaped leaves shimmering in the breeze. One of the most fantastic trips was when I actually walked over the highest suspension bridge in the world at the Royal Gorge – and I *hate* heights! That was something and I enjoyed every moment! It was fascinating peeping over the railings at the Arkansas River over 1,500 feet below, and watching a train creep by – resembling a caterpillar more than a train. Wonderful days and memories I shall always treasure.

I was sad to leave – my journey back took me to Denver again then on to Chicago and I was met by Ivy and Edith at Toronto for a reunion with the Canadian side of the family, namely 'Langley & Company'. Ivy and I then decided we would share a home – we returned to Britain and bought our little home in King Sutton in '83 moving in during '84.

I am now retired near the family and am able to enjoy the closeness of loved ones. Diana's special interest is in caring for children – she runs a successful child-minding business. Joy excels herself in helping Norman run their own business in Oxfordshire. Her businesslike acumen is something to be admired – and her energy. Both girls are excellent cooks – a gift not inherited from me!

IVY

After our leave we sailed for Canada where we spent the rest of Donald's working career. We left thinking we didn't know a soul there and were pleasantly surprised to find several friends from Shanghai, some last seen before the war. We had lost touch with Minda who had married a German during the war and then been repatriated back to Germany. Communication was difficult and unfortunately we lost touch. We hadn't been in Canada long before Minda appeared on the scene again. She had remembered the company Donald worked for and wrote to the head office to try to trace us. We were put in touch with each other – Minda was in Toronto and we were in Pointe Claire on Montreal Island. Minda's marriage had failed and she had taken her daughter, Rose Marie, and joined her brother in Toronto. It was a delight to have them visit us and renew a very precious relationship.

Geoff Forestier had settled in the United States, had remarried and now had a son – Ian. He invited us to join them on a holiday at Mountain Top Inn in Vermont. It was our first trip into the States. It was a very special reunion, we had met briefly in London just after the war – there was so much news to catch up on – our lives had changed considerably, with Geoff now residing in the States and we in Canada. It was a memorable occasion exchanging news of mutual friends and the time just flew.

The next and last time we met was when they visited 'Man and His World' – Montreal's Expo 1967 – and spent a few days with us. We still keep in touch.

We had a nice surprise in 1968 when Bessie decided to travel home to Scotland from Singapore via Canada. 'Man and His World' was still going strong and we spent several visits there. She was the first member of my immediate family to visit us in Canada and I enjoyed taking her around and introducing her to our many friends.

Only one branch of the family came to Canada while we were there – Barbara, Donald's sister Gladys' daughter and family – remember the wedding in London? Barbara and Steve (Thirtle) and their two daughters, Barbara Ann and Susan came to live fairly near us. We were very close and spent a lot of time together. It was in Montreal that Sylvia was born and not long afterwards they emigrated to the United States where they have resided ever since. It was while they lived in Buffalo that their daughter Wendy was born. We spent many lovely holidays visiting them there and recently Susan – now Dunleavey – invited Nellie and I to visit them in Connecticut. That was a another special holiday and a tremendous reunion with all Barbara's family present – their daughters and two grandchildren. At the time of writing this has been increased to five and we hope, one day, we will have the pleasure of meeting them.

On Donald's retirement in 1970 we had a three week holiday in Britain visiting relatives and friends on a whirlwind tour.

Sybil Forestier was a family friend – she was a prominent member of our KKK group and participated in our famous war effort bazaar. Sybil and I have kept in touch over the years – Christmas card with letter attached. When Donald retired we visited his family in Australia – travelling there and back by cargo vessel sailing through the Panama Canal. We had to catch the ship in New York and were met at the airport by Sybil and her mother before continuing on to the dock for embarkation. This was our first meeting since 1940 when Sybil left Shanghai. Our next meeting was here in England when we had the pleasure of meeting her husband Ted.

Having rented out our house we were able to spend about ten months 'down under'. Margaret and her husband, Alastair, kindly put us up on their lovely Avocado farm in Kuraby just south of Brisbane. Their son Graeme and his wife also had a cottage on the farm. Dorothy, now widowed, was living not too far away, as was her daughter Elizabeth and husband and their two daughters, Sally and Penny. Dorothy's son Christopher and wife Gwen, and their four children, were in Papua New Guinea at that time so we were not able to meet. However, not long afterwards Christopher and Gwen visited us in Canada and so made the reunion of families complete.

Donald hired a car and we motored south where we stayed with Joyce (Moodie) and her husband in Melbourne. Also there were Graham Shotter and his bride and, of course, his aunt – Grace (Lavington) Shotter, Mary's sister-in-law. On our way back to Brisbane we stopped at Sydney where we did a spot of sightseeing and visited Uncle Miller and family. Joan was now married and had a lovely family. We returned to Canada also through the Panama Canal.

In 1972 I was widowed. Margaret, Donald's sister, was on a trip from Australia to Britain, and flew to Canada to spend a couple of months with us. She was with us when Donald died and was a tower of strength. I couldn't have managed without her.

In 1974 I got itchy feet. I realised that I wasn't getting any younger and, having the opportunity to rent the house for three months, I decided to do just that and fly out to Australia for a last trip to see relatives. It was quite an undertaking and once I had made up my mind I decided to include ALL the family – it became a flying trip around the world!

I left Montreal for Vancouver and a change of plane to Hawaii where I spent the night. Next on to Fiji for another night's stopover. From there I went to Sydney where again I had to change plane – this time for a smaller inter-state flight to Brisbane. I spent several weeks there with the family and then flew to Papua, New Guinea, not to see Christopher whom Donald and I had missed on our previous trip – he had retired to Brisbane – but to meet up with Margaret's son Graeme and his wife who were stationed there with the Australian army.

The next family members I wished to visit were Nellie and Michael in the Seychelles. To do this I had to fly from Papua to either Hong Kong or Singapore and thereon to the Seychelles. I chose Hong Kong – having lived there before I felt it would be rather fun to look up old friends. What a disappointment – I had forgotten how long we had been away and found that our friends had retired or moved along. There had been so much building, reclamation of land, new roads and even a tunnel linking Hong Kong island with Kowloon that I was virtually a stranger. I spent two quiet days on my own, my only excitement being a look at the shops – what a temptation – and going on a couple of tours from Kowloon, where I was staying at the Mirama Hotel, through the tunnel and over to Hong Kong. I naturally wanted to see the house on the Peak where we had lived and found a tour much easier than trying to find my way through a maze of new roads.

From Hong Kong I flew to the Seychelles via Colombo which was just a quick stop. I spent three very happy weeks with Nellie and Michael. They had a beautiful open planned house high up on a hill and overlooking the Indian Ocean. The view was out of this world and we spent many a happy hour just sitting on their verandah chatting and admiring the scenery and beautiful sunsets. Nellie and I went on a side trip to La Digue which was rather fun. We flew from Mahe over to Praslin Island in a very small plane – a ten seater, each seat having its own door rather like a limousine. Praslin is noted for its Vallee de Mai, its black parrot and its famous coco-de-mer which has male catkins and giant female fruit – double coconut representing the pelvis. The residents maintain Praslin is the original Garden of Eden and it could well be.

We proceeded by boat to La Digue – our destination – and stayed in an hotel owned by friends of Nellie and Michael, Cabines des Anges. A very interesting island where there were only two cars. We were confidently walking down the country road when one of the cars backed out of a driveway and I was almost run over! There has only been one nasty accident on the island and that was a head-on collision by the two cars. The drivers must have been admiring the scenery too. The islands are noted for huge turtles and one day a fisherman called at the hotel and wanted to know about a tag he had found on a turtle he had killed – the natives eat them and use the shells for ornaments. The tag had been attached to the turtle in Florida and it should have been protected – this wasn't known by the fisherman. What interested us was how it arrived there – had it come round Cape Horn, the Cape of Good Hope or through the Panama Canal – we'll never know.

The Seychelles is made up of a group of eighty-odd islands and several schooners sail from one to the other delivering cargo and taking tourists. While we were on La Digue a schooner arrived and delivered seventeen passengers from a party of eighteen. The captain thought they had all gone ashore when in fact one was still down below fast asleep. Poor guy, he had missed his stop and would have to continue on the round of islands!

I was sorry when I had to leave, but leave I had to. The next stop was Heathrow Airport, where I was met by Norman and Mary. Christmas was spent with Mary and family and then I travelled north to have New Year with Bessie and her family. I arrived back in Canada on 4 January – tired, happy and with lots of news for my pals.

I was a curler – a very active sport particularly when participating in bonspiels (matches between clubs). Then I was also a member of the IODE – Imperial Order Daughters of the Empire – or as husbands called it 'I Often Don't Eat'. We kept busy on various events to raise money for charity and public speaking and art scholarships. It is impossible to mention all my friendships here but I still keep in touch with Dorothy Penney and her daughter Barbara, Betty McLaughlin, Marion Selyan, Helen Bird, Trudie Fuller and Millie Cavey who taught me to drive without dual controls and still remained calm.

I also keep in touch with Peg Seller, my back door neighbour in Pointe Claire. It was she who instructed me in the art of gardening and taught me many of the fancy names. Peg was also a curler but her fame lay in synchronized swimming – used in the famous aquacade at the Rowing Club of Shanghai days. Of all the people honoured in Canada's Hall of Fame, Peg Seller is the only one known to me personally – we are all proud of her.

I remained in Canada and in 1980 I met and married Charlie Alfred Gallagher. He was a Toronto lad and we made our home north of Toronto in a place called Stroud, where a niece of his, Margaret McKinnon, also lived. This was in a senior citizens estate – Sandycove Acres – where we all had our own bungalows and had the use of community halls, swimming pools etc. Through Charlie I inherited a stepson, Don, his wife Carolyne, and their three sons, Stephen, David and Jason. Donald and I had lost a son at birth and were not able to have another child so the boys are very special to me.

Charlie's family welcomed me with open arms and are also very special. There is his sister Gladys, her daughter Edith and her children, Donna, Jacqueline and Robert. Donna and husband Norman have three children – Normie, Kevin and Tara. Jacquie and her husband, Gord, have two boys, Ryan and Kyle. Robert is a bachelor. There are various other nieces and nephews all of whom I am very fond. Mary was the only one of my family to meet Charlie – this was on a return trip to Britain after visiting her son, Graham, in Australia.

Charlie and I had a very short time together – in less than two years he died of cancer. Shortly afterwards Nellie and Bessie visited me in Canada when Nellie and I decided to set up house together in England. Barbara and Steve and family have all visited us here as have many other friends.

Christmas is such an interesting time for me when old friends exchange once-a-year notes. Occasionally we meet up but not so frequently now as I grow older. The beautiful memories remain – they are mine to cherish. Yes, very special memories of a well spread out family – in Australia, Canada, United States, as well as here in Britain.

MARY

Young Graham surprised us all in 1984 by visiting England from Australia. It was my seventieth birthday, a very special occasion as I was the first member of our family to reach such a venerable age.

There were several parties planned, but Graham had a special treat in store. He organised a canal boat trip on the 'Blenheim', one of the longest narrow boats plying the Oxford canal, and invited Ivy and Nellie, both having returned to live in England in 1984, and Bessie, resident in Scotland, to join in on a reunion trip from Aynho to Napton Junction and back. It was a first for all, a dream holiday come true so different from the Panama and Suez canal and Nellie's 'barge journey' along the Nile (no Mark Anthony)!

We assembled at the wharf with a week's provisions and the usual baggage – the five of us plus some of Nellie's grandchildren who, it was hoped, knew something about canal boats – or so they led us to believe. We took one look at the canal and tried to imagine how we were going to get this long boat away from the wharf, between other boats berthed there, and into mid-stream. We just had to have a 'pilot' – there was no other way.

After a hectic start it was wonderful to be sailing along at three miles an hour, winding our way through villages but mostly across fields with only cows, sheep and the odd swan for company. Perfect peace. The children left the boat at Cropredy – the first village – as they were due back at school.

It was a time to reflect back over the years and say 'thank you' for being hale and hearty and within visiting distance of each other once again. As you can imagine we became very sentimental talking over old times. Suddenly Graham was very serious and said 'It has just occurred to me Mum, that I know very little about your early life. Living in Australia I miss being able to chat to you – how about filling me in on some of the details'.

'OK, I'll start at the beginning – its a long story.'

Mary – As An Army Wife

My story starts after Graham and I were married in 1940 and when we left Shanghai. For the rest of the story I shall use my pet name 'Gray' for him.

After the last few days of preparing to leave Shanghai, and the excitement of the very emotional send off we shared with other lads on their way to join the forces in India, it took us a little while to realise we were at last on our way. It was an uneventful journey and was soon over. We felt very special being the only ones of our group to be met – Dad and Nellie were on the dock waving frantically as we tied up in Bombay. Unfortunately Gray had to leave almost right away for Bangalore to begin his training with the Indian Army while I spent a very happy few weeks in Bombay with Dad and Nellie before leaving to join him.

I found India a very exciting and interesting place, and felt I had much to learn about its many cultures and religions. Everything was so completely different from the Shanghai I had known and loved.

* * *

I travelled alone down to Bangalore by train and found it nice and tidy and scrupulously clean. I was having a lovely time relaxing and thinking of all that had happened since leaving Shanghai and was feeling very pleased with myself. Pride goes before a fall – in the tropics nightfall comes early and with the disappearance of light so my confidence was shattered. I learnt the hard way that to get some sleep I had to leave the light on as when the carriage was in darkness the cockroaches emerged and started a game of 'hide and seek'. It was 'now you see them' and 'now you don't' as I put the light on or off. Rather an unnerving experience to say the least. Little did I know that this trip was only a first and that I would be travelling the length and breadth of India on my own during the following years.

I enjoyed my stay in Bangalore and met several nice families. There were many Cadets on the same course so we had lots of company and it was rather fun learning the ways of army folk. As a gift, one family gave Gray a sweet little Dalmatian puppy – later named 'Pal'.

After their course at Bangalore the Cadets were sent to Poona for a few weeks, and from there on to Abbottabad. It was a lovely hill station on the North West Frontier, south of the Kyber Pass, which was reached after a hair-raising drive up from the plains. It was in sight of snow capped mountains and near to Kabul where the Cadets eventually completed their training for the Indian Army.

Having Pal with us on our train journey was quite a problem, especially as the women travelled in their own carriage and the men in theirs. We shared looking after the puppy, having to take him on to the many stations we luckily stopped at. During one such move Pal could not be found – I thought Gray had him, and he thought I had. We did not know until the next stop that Gray eventually found him curled up and fast asleep in one of his suitcases!

As I now had the railway compartment to myself Gray was able to join me for the last lap of our journey. As we were nearing our destination there was a small explosion and we found bits of glass in the carriage. We automatically thought a stone had been thrown at the window. Wondering about this, Gray suggested a cool drink and proceeded to open the press-down old fashioned glass marble-stopper which, in those days was used in drink bottles, and we were again showered with flying glass – the bottle had exploded. The heat of the train and the constant motion caused the bottle to explode. The mystery was solved.

We broke our journey up to Abbottabad to see the Taj Mahal at Agra, where we stayed at a most quaint hotel run by two elderly sisters. Though the surrounding countryside was arid and drab, the garden of their hotel was a pleasure to see – beautiful flowers and greenery and it seemed all seasons' flowers and bulbs growing at once. On our table would be a fresh bouquet of flowers each day. The food was delightful yet simple. A lovely experience altogether – it was like a bit of home to us.

Whilst in Agra we paid a visit to the Red Fort. Our guide introduced us to the dungeon area, and as it was getting darker and darker, the guide switched on a torch. To Gray's complete horror he discovered that his forehead was literally only inches away from a beam on which hundreds of bats were clinging. These little beings were Gray's phobia, and not being too happy with them myself, we left in a great hurry! Gray was in a state of shock for several minutes.

* * *

We liked the hotel at Abbottabad, but unfortunately, once Gray, along with the others, had reported to the training school at Kabul, they were told that there was no accommodation for wives. The husbands were pretty hard put to find alternative lodgings at such short notice.

What a problem. Gray and his friend Jim decided to look together and fortunately, before long, found a tiny house right by the golf course called Rose Cottage which they decided to take – they were obviously attracted by the name 'Rose'! On inspection it was found to be a purdah house and, therefore, did not possess an indoor kitchen. However, it did have a mud-floored room off the inner courtyard where food, cooked outside by men, would be brought in for the ladies to consume. Soon an Indian man appeared and asked if we needed a cook. When told 'Yes, but we have no kitchen' he shook his head and said, 'No belong worry – I can do'. He was engaged and that evening produced an excellent meal of roast chicken with all the trimmings. He had done all this on an improvised oven made out of an empty kerosene tin, in the mud-floored room. Gray and his friend then decided to build an army stove and lean-to kitchen and set to with bricks and things, turning the little room into a fairly reasonable, if kutcha, kitchen which served us well during our stay.

Gray and Jim also bought an old car with a soft hood which helped them to get to and fro from the camp. Living near the golf course and it's Club we often spent an evening there on their dance nights. I was intrigued by the excellent Gurkha Army Band they had playing. They knew all the very latest tunes and songs and played them with much feeling and gusto, and gave the evenings a very happy atmosphere – they looked great in their pill-box type hats with chin straps worn at very jaunty angles.

Many a time whilst sitting out in the garden of Rose Cottage we saw these agile Gurkha men running down the rocky hill at the back of the cottage – this was all in an effort to keep fit. Their sure-footedness and skilful jumping from boulder to boulder was quite amazing, and they still gave the impression of being happy, carefree – not one bit exhausted.

* * *

Gray decided to buy Jim's share of the car to travel down to Rawalpindi as Jim would have to travel through tiger country to his new posting, and he and his wife Fay, thought that it would be risky with their small baby to travel in a car with a very shabby soft roof.

The evening before our departure our puppy became very ill and we had to leave him with the vet as rabies was suspected. On arrival at 'Pindi' a telegram was waiting for us confirming this. Of course, we were devastated, and as Pal was such a favourite at Camp and had been in contact with so many of Gray's colleagues we thought that it was only fair to warn them in case they also needed a course of anti-rabies injections. Pal had to be put down. It was thought that he had got rabies through the jackals that roamed around at night coming into our garden and chewing on one of his bones.

Because we had to send so many warning telegrams about Pal's rabies all over India, as by now all Gray's fellow officers were at their new postings, this made life very difficult for us. As we were young and joined up hurriedly from Shanghai without any financial backing, the telegrams were a costly business! However, we survived despite the dreadful tonga rides out to the British Military Hospital (BMH) for our injections – all in the tummy! The heat was exhausting and being four months pregnant didn't help matters. Once or twice it was so hot all I could do was lie on my bed under the fan and drape a wet hanky over my mouth and nose to cool the air I was breathing (creating my own 'Heath Robinson' humidifier). By the end of the course of injections into the stomach the doctor had difficulty in finding a new spot in Gray's middle into which to inject, but no difficulty was had with my expanding midriff!

Once again we were posted, this time to Ferozapore where our daughter, Wendy Rosemary, was born in early January 1942, in a American Mission Hospital. Gray was on parade the morning the doctor decided to induce labour, which involved me in drinking a small phial of castor oil. When I pleaded for an orange juice to help it down I was given another phial of water! *Ugh!* Thankfully all went well in spite of no help from gas or whatever. I didn't know that Gray had sent our Bearer to sit on the verandah outside my room and that he was detailed to hasten back with any news he could get. So not long afterwards, Gray came rushing in unexpectedly asking to see his baby and was taken to the nursery, where what he described as a row of meatsafes was pointed out to him – sort of take your pick! He lifted the lid of the first and saw a tiny Indian baby boy, 'No, that's not Wendy'! However, he soon found the right meatsafe! After about a week he took us home to a nice army quarter, and we were a happy family of three.

I have pleasing memories of the Mission Hospital. My room was newly whitewashed with a nice fire glowing in the grate and one of the sweet young nurses handed me a little bunch of narcissi which I held tightly all through the ordeal, and which I still have pressed and kept in a safe place in my memory folder.

We managed to engage an elderly Gurkha ayah to help me to look after Wendy. She was very amusing, as she would lull Wendy to sleep by singing 'I'm forever blowing bubbles' over and over again as she didn't know the rest.

When Wendy started to teethe she would cry and it always seemed to happen when the teacher called to give Gray his Urdu lessons. One day, feeling rather embarrassed about it, I asked him what the Indian ladies did when their babies cried. 'Oh', he said shaking his head from side to side, 'it is quite simple, all you do is put a little opium on your finger and let the baby suck it, and you will soon have peace'.

* * *

Another move, this time for a holiday to Ambala hill station for a few days prior to Gray leaving for Imphal, and so into action. It was so hot when we boarded the train that we placed Wendy's crib on top of a block of ice the size of two trunks on which the fan was blowing. She was covered with prickly heat and could not sleep but the improvised air conditioning kept her cool. On arrival at Ambala we heard that an Indian baby had died from heat exhaustion only the week before. How thankful we were to have the presence of mind to use the ice. Also fresh clean water was difficult to come by so Gray managed to persuade the engine driver to give us boiled water from the engine for Wendy's feeds. Fresh water was carried in bottles and was used only for washing Wendy.

* * *

Now that Gray was posted, I travelled to Kovilpatti, South India, to stay with Dad. He had a lovely home on top of a hill, and I think he was glad to have the company of his daughter and first grandchild. The train journey took nearly four days and Gray had arranged for his Punjabi bearer to escort me down as no nanny would travel such a long distance to a 'foreign land'. He was a north Indian and looked majestic in his white starched tunic, pantaloons, finely pleated puggaree, and with a broad gilt sash around his waist. The journey would have been impossible without his help as he collected my food at stations along the way and also water from the engine driver to make Wendy's bottles. All this was passed through the window of the carriage as I could not get on or off the train without losing my space. After only a week or so in Kovilpatti, the bearer decided to return north as the Indians in the south were not too friendly as they did not like north Indians to come and do their work for them.

* * *

During the very hot weather most women and children living on the plains went to stay at a Hill Station for a few weeks holiday. Poor Dad remained at Kovilpatti. It was so hot that even his evening bath, which was run for him each morning, needed blocks of ice to be added to cool it down before he could get in. We lived mostly on the large verandah where he kept his radio and gramophone. It was a very lonely life for both of us as the only other Europeans in the area were the missionary couple and Ada and Fred Ford from 'Tuti'.

I well remember standing at the verandah railings admiring the beautiful white turkey which Dad was fattening up for the house party that he expected from 'Tuti' to spend Christmas with us. The turkey suddenly seemed to jump up and fall backwards – literally dead to the world! It was discovered later that it had been bitten by a baby cobra. Needless to say Dad engaged a snake charmer who found that there was a nest of them in the roots of the Banyan tree. This horrified us, as Wendy had often played around this tree to keep in the shade.

Another time when I was leaning over the railings watching out for ayah and Wendy returning home from their morning walk visiting Grandpa in the office, I heard a dreadful commotion, and saw in the distance a lot of natives chasing a dog and trying to beat it with sticks. It came nearer and nearer to the house and then onto the road where Wendy and ayah were walking. The dog passed them, pursued by the beaters, then reversing it's tactics the dog ran off the road and attacked a local washerwoman and the donkey she was leading. By this time the villagers had caught up with the dog and they stoned and beat it to death. The dog had rabies – Dad offered to drive the bitten woman to the nearest hospital at Madura, but his offer was refused (the simple villagers were very suspicious of foreign doctors) and sadly she died, as did the donkey.

* * *

Joseph, Dad's 70 year old cook was really quite a character – he had his own herd of cows which provided fresh milk and cream every day. He also baked morning rolls for breakfast. This I discovered quite by accident. Being restless one night, I happened to look out of the window and noticed the light on down in the kitchen below – it was Joseph making the bread for Dad's breakfast.

The Doctor who cared for Dad and his staff was also an elderly man. When I first met him I thought what a lovely face he had – so gentle and kind looking and inwardly I imagined how Jesus looked.

Every evening at sundown an elderly man would walk over from the nearest village with a basket of jasmine flowers. The young brides in the area would pin a spray of these sweet smelling flowers in their hair. Noticing Wendy, the elderly gentleman took to presenting her with a garland of these flowers to wear around her neck. She loved the gesture and became quite attached to him and they chatted away to each other as though they had known each other for years and understood each other's language. At that stage she was a very lonely little girl not having any playmates.

* * *

When it became unbearably hot Dad persuaded me to take Wendy on a trip up the hill to Kodaikanal – Ada Ford was planning to go there for a few weeks so this was a wonderful opportunity not to be missed. No sooner had we made the arrangements when Gray surprised us by joining us on a well deserved leave of absence. Being pregnant, Nellie thought a holiday up in the hills a great idea and once Michael had left for Chittagong she travelled south to join us. It was lovely seeing the cousins – Wendy and Joy – play together.

Our holiday bungalow 'Mirabel' was up on a high hill. One day after lunch we decided to venture down into the bazaar to do some shopping, but had forgotten to take our daily dose of various vitamins necessary for expectant mums. On our way back, and not looking forward to the hard climb up the hill, we realised that we were being followed. The cook's son had been sent down to carry up our parcels for us, but first we HAD to take our vitamins. They were all neatly laid out on a tray with doily and glasses of water. There were nevertheless interested and amused stares from the bazaar crowds as we dutifully did as we were bidden – no doubt our audience was intrigued by our obedience – strange goings-on of the memsahibs in the tropics.

The year was 1944 and as you have gathered both Nellie and I were pregnant. Soon after her arrival she had a nasty experience – one night she rushed into my bedroom, white faced, saying 'There's a bandicoot (a rat the size of a full-grown cat) in my bedroom'. She had been disturbed by a scuffling noise and then a scratching across her head! She switched on the light and caught sight of this enormous rat jumping off Joy's cot – scampering into the bathroom. What to do? Here we were two women terrified and completely alone – how were we going to cope? We decided to try to keep the rat in the bathroom by stuffing Nellie's counterpane all along the bottom of the bathroom door to seal up the gap that was there.

No way would Nellie return to her room that night. Joy's cot was wheeled into my room and Nellie settled herself at the foot of my single bed (head to toe) – two very pregnant mums trying to sleep on a single iron 'indian cot', as they are called, with no room to manoeuvre to get comfortable. It was not the easiest way to get some sleep – each trying not to disturb the other! The next morning we discovered that the counterpane was full of holes where the rat had tried to eat its way into her bedroom again for more of Joy's nightly orange juice and biscuit. Nellie always kept these handy to keep Joy 'quiet' if she woke up in the middle of the night and disturbed Wendy and I in the room next door. The bandicoot was never caught and the counterpane looked very like a filigree table cloth, it had been so well chewed.

Another disturbing incident took place one day when Wendy was walking up the hill with ayah – they heard and noticed a loud buzzing sound and saw a swarm of bees circling the tops of the eucalyptus trees, heading nearer and nearer to them. Luckily ayah had the presence of mind to stand still, covering and sheltering Wendy under her sari until they had passed overhead and settled across the valley. Ayah usually brought a sprig of the eucalyptus tree back with her from these walks which she would put into Wendy's bath in the evening, saying, 'It is good for Wendy-babba's chest Ma'am and will make her legs nice and straight'!

*　*　*

Nellie was soon to have her baby and as it was such a difficult walk to and from the Nursing Home, there being no transport, not even a taxi service, Nellie used to go early each evening, before dark, to spend the night in the hospital – just in case. Of course, there came the time in early July when she didn't come back, having had Diana during the night. The next morning ayah came to me saying 'Where Missy Joy – me no can find her'. To my horror I spotted her way down the road, one little figure clad only in a short pink vest clutching a huge teddy bear. BUT, what a relief! We all seemed to be of one mind, to chase and catch up with her before she reached the main road. When we did catch her she announced, quite firmly, 'I'm going to get my mummy – she has gone to the bazaar'! Because she thought that was where Nellie went every evening, the hospital being just beyond the bazaar. It was an easy explanation to make to a tiny tot – rather than frighten her with the word 'hospital'.

All's well that ends well. We were delighted with the news that little Diana had arrived – another Stead grandchild to bring joy to us all.

During my pregnancy I developed very high blood pressure and, as the doctor wished me to go into hospital two months before the birth, it was decided to move into a bungalow nearer the nursing home. We were lucky enough to get the bungalow next to the nursing home. I had a spectacular view of the plains several thousand feet below, particularly when a forest fire swept through the trees, and got closer and closer to the top of our hill. It was frightening to watch especially the fire-fighters as they got so near the flames, but they knew what they were doing and soon had the fire under control. It was most alarming.

It was very pleasant living next to the nursing home. On Christmas Eve Nellie and the girls (young Wendy and Joy) arranged a special Christmas party for me – I was the only occupant in the hospital at the time – it was only a four roomed nursing home to start off with and being out of season, most holiday makers had returned to the plains. They arrived at the usual time armed with a small silver Christmas tree nicely decorated and surrounded it with presents 'sent' to me from their teddy bears and dolls and even some 'pretend' presents from aunties and uncles – plus Wendy and Joy (and Joy from Diana) made their own special presents. They even had a small chocolate cake (cup cake size) dolled up to look like a plum-pudding for us to share – small because they knew I was on a special diet and cake was a 'No No'. Nellie arranged a special bouquet of flowers for the doctor and nurses and my room was also decorated – with tinsel and baubles. The doctor's breath was almost taken away the next morning when she called to see me. She was so surprised and overcome and we shared a wee weep of happiness together.

With my blood pressure so high we were all so anxious for news of the baby's safe arrival and/or my survival. Graham Stead Shotter delighted us by putting in his appearance at midnight on 29 December, 1945 – weighing in at 8lb 4oz. What a lovely way to start off the New Year.

* * *

The War is Over

News had come through from Michael that he would be taking part of his demob leave at Kodai and would collect Nellie and the children and that the process of looking for a job was next on the list of priorities.

I was still in Kodai – Gray having been sent out to Malaya with the occupying forces. I was still plagued by high blood pressure and the doctor thought that living at such a high altitude was not helping me one bit and strongly suggested that I should return to the plains. I returned to Dad at Kovilpatti to await developments. I dearly wished to join Gray in Singapore (then a part of Malaya), but they were early days and the army was not ready to accommodate wives, having only recently regained Malaya. However, after a few months I eventually managed to get a passage there from Madras. When nearing Singapore we were told that we would be disembarking at Penang and not Singapore, but, ultimately, after a lot of confusion we were landed at Port Swettenham on the Malayan mainland. Luckily Gray heard of the change of plans, and after a lot of difficulty managed to pick us up and drove us all the way back in a jeep. It was a long drive, and at one stage very alarming, as we met a truck full of planters who warned us to be careful as there had been an ambush down the road. It was so dreadfully hot and, when passing through a little kampong, I was amazed and glad to find I was able to buy a bottle of Florida water – a cooling and refreshing cologne – which reminded me of my days in Shanghai. I never expected to find it in such a remote Malay village.

After a long hot drive we had a lovely meal with some friends of Gray's at Johore Bahru, and when we finally reached Singapore across the Causeway, Gray took us to an allocated Malay house in one of the suburbs which we were to call home until the army quarters were ready for wives. The house was very quaint.

After a couple of weeks Wendy became very ill with scarlet fever, and she had to be nursed at home, because all the hospitals were full of cholera patients at that time. We managed to find a good ayah for Graham and, by using Lysol impregnated sheets at his bedroom door, kept him pretty well isolated. After a very worrying start to our tour in Singapore, we were allocated a large airy quarter on the hill near the Alexander Hospital – at Pasir Panjang.

In the spring of 1947 we heard that Ivy and Donald were leaving England for a term of office in Hong Kong. The ship they were on would call at Singapore – how wonderful to see each other again and hear first hand news of the rest of the family.

We had already received the wedding presents Ivy had rescued from our apartment in the Embankment Building prior to her internment by the Japanese, and which she had packed and stored with a Swiss company for the duration of the war. It was exciting opening everything up – what happy memories they brought back. However, it was sad that over the years that followed, because of the many moves involved during our postings to different places, and indeed even moves made from different quarters within a town, a lot of them got stolen or broken. In spite of trying to pack them as well as the skilled packers of China, a couple of our lovely china and glassware pieces came to grief. When we eventually retired and had our own home for the first time, we only had a few of our presents left to enjoy.

After a few months we were moved to Kuala Lumpur (KL) and given a quarter out at Batu Caves. There was still considerable unrest and the tin-mine working near the Batu Caves was the main target of terrorists. We felt isolated, as the direct telephone line from the depot to our bungalow, strung along palm trees under the caves, was cut five times during one week, and our Malay ayah was warned and threatened not to visit our bungalow, or seek work with us. The mine was about a quarter of a mile away as the crow flies, but several miles away along a winding road. When it was under attack the gunfire sounded very close and our routine was to turn lights off and take the children out of their beds and place them on the floor under their beds, surrounding them with their mattresses. On one occasion a very sleepy little voice said, 'I like playing house like this'.

At one point the army decided, in conjunction with the police, on a 'show of arms' and our bungalow was used as a starting off point and, at one stage, about forty soldiers waited for the signal to 'go'. It was a success, but I was thankful when it was over.

One Sunday morning, when Gray went to the depot to check on a few matters, he took young Graham with him. Whilst walking over the ground to one of the bays, Graham in a childlike fashion was kicking at stones and things. Suddenly Gray noticed that one of the 'things' would not move when kicked, and after inspection he discovered that it was the tip of a bayonet. After further investigation and digging it was found that the whole area was an enormous arms burial dump, which must have been put there by the Japanese whilst they occupied Malaya.

We had many unpleasant incidents in KL, and I was glad when it came time for us to leave for England. Not long after our return to England from Malaya, I read in the paper that the Batu Caves was swarming with terrorists, no doubt they were able to look down on our bungalow and watch our every move.

* * *

During a religious festival Gray was introducing some friends to the Batu Caves, and one of the Sadhus there was slipping very tiny bangles onto the wrists of children. Intrigued by this Gray allowed him to slip one onto Wendy's wrist. It was amazing, the bangle was so small he obviously knew how to manipulate the hand so as to slip it on. When it was shown to me I became very anxious as the bangle was made of thin glass, and could not be taken off her wrist. Rather than let it break accidentally and perhaps cause a nasty cut, we managed to pad her wrist well and then break the bangle to get it off.

* * *

Return to England

Having been transferred to the British Army we spent a few days at Hastings before moving on to Blackdown near Aldershot. As mentioned earlier it was here that I made my first attempt at cooking with disastrous results. One Sunday, lunch was in the oven before we attended the Church service *en familie*. Young Graham was mesmerised – he hadn't been inside a Church before – and, after being seated, looked around and in a loud voice said 'Is this God's house?' It was a friendly Church! So much so that Gray got carried away – or maybe he was overly proud of my cooking – and invited the Colonel back for lunch! I said we were having roast beef with Yorkshire pudding, horse radish sauce – the complete 'works' in fact. The Colonel also knew it was my first attempt at cooking a complete meal on my own. I was more than a little surprised when I was complimented on the tasty 'roast pork'. A surreptitious hint for the future to spare me dropping another 'brick' perhaps? We had no vegetables as when I was straining the peas they disappeared down the sink. Feeling sorry for his hostess the Colonel thought perhaps he should help with the serving up of the apple pie: but by this time he must have been as nervous as I – the pie fell upside down on to the kitchen floor. I suppose one could have said 'Some upside down pudding ... ha!' Hoots of laughter and we have been pals ever since.

*   *   *

Nellie had contacted typhoid and when she was invalided 'home' to England naturally we welcomed her with opened arms. But, how to keep young Graham (aged 5) under control whilst Nellie was convalescing? BIG question and our main worry. Nellie was ordered to bed on arrival and there she stayed most of the time for quite a few weeks. The only time Graham saw her was when she was lying down on her bed – about two and a half feet off the floor! His contribution to 'The Get Well Plan' was to take up her mail each day, and her fruit juice. They struck up quite a friendship. He was very caring and good and Nellie was very impressed with him. She told me he was 'A perfect little gentleman'. I was proud of him until one day, when he took the mail in – he found Nellie standing up in front of her dressing table mirror brushing her hair. She looked of course – tall (five-feet five, not two and a half feet like before) – and in horror he said 'Oh Auntie Nellie, aren't you THUGHE!' – some gentleman – I felt so embarrassed for Nellie. We had a good chuckle and still do to this day as Graham has now grown up into an enormous 'thughe' man himself.

We were trying to train Graham not to be a nuisance to anyone. Nellie seemed a good person to practice on – how he hated not being a nuisance. In fact, he did not know what it meant – to be a nuisance that is. As Nellie was getting better she did little indoor baby sitting jobs for me, like minding the children when I had to nip out to the post etc. Nothing arduous. But always Graham was reminded 'not to be a nuisance' – particularly to Auntie Nellie.

Because she was unable to play with them out of doors, they were confined to barracks sort of thing and had to stay put, indoors in the sitting room, with her until I returned. (Poor Nellie really was not fit enough even for that small task.) The children both being extremely active were bored to tears on these occasions. On one such afternoon Graham had made a handful of paper aeroplanes which he flew across the room in a bored fashion – each time his aim was getting inadvertently nearer to Nellie. Finally when one at long last swished past Nellie's ear and hit her nose – she muttered something like 'Oh Graham, do stop it – do you have to be so rough?' Delighted, Graham said innocently … 'Am I being a nuisance?' 'Yes, you are' she replied. He was so happy – he at last knew the meaning of the warning and skipped off to find something else to do. His small vocabulary was increasing and he was satisfied. It amused Nellie to see his big blue innocent eyes widen with the excitement of knowing that, at long last, he had done something he never knew that he was supposed not to do. Lovely age – innocent five-year old!

Christmas Eve with 'Our Gracie'

Christmas Eve came around before we could say 'Jack Robinson'. Gray and I were invited to a dinner party at the house next door. Nellie was unable to attend – quite naturally – but she insisted that we went. Little did she know that we were preparing a super Christmas Eve supper for her. Just before Gray and I were about to leave the house for 'next door' Gray gave Nellie all the last minute instructions she might want to use in case needed. As it happened all she needed was a poker because all she had to do was bang the fire-grate as hard as she could – the hammering would vibrate in the sitting room in the next door house which was connected by the same chimney 'what-have-you' (flue I think it is called) to the one in our sitting room, directly below Nellie's bedroom. All had been tested in the afternoon so we were happy that the emergency alarm would operate if required.

It was a delight to see the utter surprise on Nellie's face as Gray and I, in full evening dress, together with the children – ready for bed – and Dad went in to wish her goodnight. The children were excitedly happy to get to bed early to await Santa's midnight visit – and Dad went on his way to visit some of his friends. Then I brought in, carrying as Nellie described ... 'A magnificently decorated tray conveying everything the festive season had to offer – including a glass of sherry'. I was followed by Wendy carrying a red Christmas candle which she placed on the mantelpiece. We had put a cracker on the tray, a little spray of flowers – poinsettias with a twig of mistletoe for good measure, a red napkin and ... oh, yes, a little red balloon which we knew would be special to her ... AND, of course, the Christmas meal. Nellie was overwhelmed! And as thoughtful as ever Gray dashed out and returned with a portable radio for 'company' (no TV in those days).

Well, by the time Nellie had had her sherry – eaten her meal ... 'Slowly savouring every mouthful ', she said, 'tears were streaming down my face as dear Gracie sang her heart out at the Variety Concert singing "Sally".' 'Sally' was one of Nellie's favourite tunes ... and sung by a person whom she has always greatly admired – a true Lancashire lass!

Nellie told me the next morning, she blew out her candle – forgot completely about the poker – placed the tray on a side-table which I had left for her then she snuggled down into bed. To quote Nellie, she said, .. ' I have had a delightfully nostalgic, happily tearful, Christmas Eve. My heart was full of gratitude for being given the solitary moments of enjoying Gracie at her best and', she continued' it made me feel good all through'.

The Zip in the Turkey

It was all go-go the next morning and so many happy Christmas wishes all round – including a telephone call from Michael and the children in Calcutta (how we wished they were with us). After Church service Gray and I tackled the Christmas lunch and prepared the turkey. By this time both of us had become fairly proficient cooks but, Gray had a surprise for the kids – and here, Nellie was included as one of them. Gray nearly drove me around the bend by insisting he was going to sew a zip in the turkey so that to have some stuffing – all he had to do was undo the zip and 'hey presto' – 'Your choice Madam?' – the stuffing appeared in true Stead tradition, a choice of two types!

* * *

As you know we moved from Blackdown to Aldershot from where Gray was later posted to Korea. Meanwhile the whole family seemed to be on their first 'UK leave' during our stay at Salamanca Lodge, Aldershot, and I became know as 'The Hostess'.

Miss Seed's School

While at Aldershot Graham, Wendy, Joy and Diana attended Miss Seed's School ... remember? They used to take their own little sandwich boxes and were all in the same class, although they were different ages and, learnt, I know not what! – but *manners* they certainly did. They were enjoyable days although the four children were real terrors with the antics they got up to. As mentioned earlier when describing Nellie and her 'gang' – the four, Shotter/Poole, kids were 'hell-bent on enjoying themselves with no destructive thought towards mankind'. (We grown-ups reminisced.)

* * *

Being the only boy with three girls Graham had to test everything first. No doubt they will never forget Tarzan. They were all standing on the top of a disused air raid shelter and the girls made Graham have a first-go – that was to 'fly' out to the branch of a tree, with the hope that he would, with the momentum follow on to the next branch and so on round the woods at the back of Salamanca – just like Tarzan, of course! No wonder Graham ended up in a crash-thud heap on the ground with a broken arm! Graham was brave and had a real hard innings with the girls. But, they loved him for his toughness.

I had a bit more patience with the children than Nellie did. She used to get upset when they wouldn't listen or 'see' danger ahead. So she resorted to nagging a bit. Joy, in her embarrassment with her mum's nagging would say 'You are just like a witch'! This did not help Nellie one bit. Poor Nellie it took her all her time to keep herself together in once piece without four rascals to cope with. One evening we were both so cross with them that we decided the only way to stop the harum-scarum four would be to put each one of them in a separate corner of the kitchen so that we could carry on making supper. More grumbles and 'mock' quarrels among the four! (Looking back now, I am sure they were just having us on, and were not really so wicked as we thought they were.) But they even managed to quarrel and complain because their 'corners' were not the same. Joy – was lucky because she had a water pipe running up hers ('not fair') – Diana ('not fair') had a window near her corner so she could see out! – Wendy's was near the heater. But, truly the most unfair corner was Graham's – all he had were two walls 'stuck' together with chipping paint and cracks. The complaints were worse than the punishment and we had no peace whatsoever so we let them out and told them to sit and 'be quiet' for 20 minutes, at least. They were reasonably good beneath stiffled giggles.

The most amusing story I can remember – but, here I go rambling on – but being a 'Rose'Mary I can't be blamed too much for that fault!

*   *   *

The girls and Graham managed to wrap up little stones in snow which they were aiming at each other (horrors!) but when Graham aimed at Wendy she ducked and Graham's 'snowball' crashed through the window of the Army Engineers' offices and hit the wall opposite. 'Heck.' They all came home with Graham twisting his peaked cap until the peak was nearly off! I insisted that Graham should go back and apologise to the officer. He said 'You come with me'. 'No way' said I. Just then, a uniformed messenger on a motorcycle turned up with a telegram for Nellie but Graham thought it was the Military Police to take him off to the station for an 'inquiry'! (Poor kid – he was quite white.) He hastily got ready and with his entourage of girls they returned to the Engineers' offices. Graham went in alone – still twisting his peaked cap and asked to see the Officer-in-Charge on some important matter. When the officer, who obviously knew why he was there, asked him. 'What can I do for you'. Graham said 'I'm sorry sir, but I threw a stone covered in snow at my sister and it crashed through your window by mistake. I have come to ask if I can have it mended, sir.' He continued, 'I'm very sorry sir, it won't happen again'. The officer (obviously taken by Graham's dilemma) said 'That's all right' – then, with a 'serious' smile said 'Just remember, next time lad, to aim straight!'

1952

It was lovely having Ivy and Donald stay with us as well before they had to return to Canada. Dad was with us too, but unhappily he suffered a severe stroke from which he did not recover, a very sad day for all of us and a tremendous loss which of course made our reunion a deeply sad time. Daddy was buried at Woking in Surrey. Bessie came down from Scotland and his sister Ada, from Newcastle, to attend the funeral.

Soon after Ivy and Donald had gone Bessie and Nellie were on their way back to India. Joy and Diana had started school at Crondall – and Bessie's three at the Dollar Academy. In fact by the end of the year all the family had departed in different directions and I was happily awaiting Gray's return from Korea.

* * *

Prior to Nellie's departure and while we were still alone at Salamanca Lodge I made up an evening dress for Nellie. She had been given a beautiful sari with a wide gold border which I promised to make into a ball gown for her. Finding myself alone one Sunday I decided to make a start, but unhappily I couldn't find any scissors. After searching frantically and not being able to go out and buy any (it being Sunday), and our neighbour was away in hospital, I had no choice but to make a start cutting out with a pair of tiny curved nail scissors. After several hours of nail biting frustration I found the deed done! Luckily the dress with the gold border cascading from the neckline to the hem turned out successfully and Nellie wore it for the first time to a dinner dance at the Savoy Hotel, London. Michael lost out on this party as he was on the high-seas on his way to India.

Our host thoughtfully sent a taxi to drive us to London, and we found it a little embarrassing dressed in our nicest dance dresses driving past people in a queue for buses after their day's work. We had a most pleasant time and met some interesting people at the dinner. We were bought corsages of orchids and roses to wear. They were beautiful. We were a couple of 'cinderellas' though, as we had to leave at midnight in order to be taken back by taxi so that our baby-sitters could go home.

* * *

We had the very unpleasant experience of being at the Farnborough Air Show when a prototype jet aircraft fell apart and plummeted into the crowd – twenty-six spectators died. The aircraft had just successfully broken the sound barrier. Many others were injured in this tragedy. The disaster claimed the lives of the pilot and his observer.

* * *

When Gray returned from Korea we were posted to Glencorse near Edinburgh where we spent a very happy two years, in nearby Penicuik, in a newly built army quarter.

It was at Glencorse where Gray first met Ted Blessington and not long afterwards Isobella – (Ted's wife) – better known to all as 'Scottie' and we became an inseparable foursome. Like ourselves, they had two children – Christopher and Peter – roughly the same ages as Wendy and Graham. We used to visit each other often and our stay at Penicuik was, to us, our most happiest 'army days'. Little did we know then that the Blessingtons and ourselves would spend most of our army and civilian lives in each others company.

We enjoyed starting the garden from scratch, even though we were by no means experts in this field. I had difficulty convincing Gray that bulbs, were not attractive when planted out in straight rows like soldiers on parade, but would look charming planted out in clumps of varying sizes. Our neighbours knew of this difference of opinion, but they were particularly amused when they could see, by my actions, that I was asking Gray to turn round a rose bush because he had put it in the wrong way round.

We fell in love with Scotland and, before we left for Germany, had a mini family reunion.

It was a great day taking out Ivy May, Alasdair and Craig, our nephews and niece, whilst they were at school at the Dollar Academy. Especially, as at that time the Poole gang were spending a few days of their leave with us. As the cousins had not met up for such a long time, it was decided to have a grand picnic, and we invited Granny Moodie to join us. Unfortunately, when the day came it was teaming with rain and, having so many young people who had been looking forward to this special day for so long, we decided in spite of the weather to carry on with our plans. Michael kept saying, 'Look, there is a patch of blue sky over there', so we

would drive trying to catch up with it. These patches were so
elusive, and in the end after many tries we had to admit defeat of
ever finding a dry place in which to have our picnic. In the end we
lunched in our cars. The Moodie clan started off on the outing so
neat and clean in their school uniforms, and Ivy May even had a
little pair of white cotton gloves. I'm afraid, when we returned
them to the Academy, they were very muddy and wet little people!
Granny Moodie really enjoyed herself – she was a very happy-go-
lucky sort of person, and all her grandchildren, nephews and nieces
plied her with the nicest goodies, and I believe in the end she'd had
most of the cakes!

Germany

When we began our tour of Germany we lived in a house seconded
by the army. We had a German girl, Freda, to help with the house-
work – she was keen to learn English and asked young Graham to
teach her. They enjoyed playing rounders as well as other games but
if Graham was busy she would climb the big willow tree at the
bottom of the garden and relax reading.

Not being army property we were not allowed to prune trees or
shrubs, though we were expected to mow the lawn and keep the
garden looking tidy. When we left, the house went back to the
owners and we heard later that several incendiary bombs were
found in the Willow tree.

Ted and Scottie Blessington, last seen at Penicuik, Scotland, had
also been posted to Bielefeld. We were two happy families and
what made life easier for us 'overseas' was the fact that we found
ourselves being posted to areas not too far from each other – so we
could still visit easily.

Bessie, Alastair, Ivy and Donald came over for a visit. We hadn't
seen each other for a long spell so it was lovely to be together.

I wondered why Ivy and Donald disappeared two or three times
during the day to their room, and only when they had left to
return to Canada did I learn that poor Ivy was having a miserable
time with boils on her back, and that they slipped away so that
Donald could attend to the dressing of them without causing any
anxiety to us.

There were many laughs during their stay. Ivy tried to buy a
marzipan pig as a gift for me. The pig was in the shop window and

once she was in the shop the only way she could make herself understood was by pointing and grunting like the pig she was trying to buy. The shop-keeper must have been enjoying her antics as she kept her grunting a long time before the pfennig dropped, so to speak! We all enjoyed the marzipan – a gentle reminder of Dad and his safe at Pingliang Road.

Bielefeld was only the starting off point for us in Germany – we were posted to several different places during our tour of office and so were able to keep in touch with friends as well as make several new ones.

Gray and I first met John and Lillian Davies in Paderborn. John (Colonel John B Davies OBE) was Gray's CO at that time and their friendship was cemented there and then. They remained the closest of friends for the rest of their service life and in retirement days found themselves always 'there' when most needed. And, it was so very nice for me because Lillian and I were very close too – although we did not have an awful lot in common, we were very compatible. I loved my painting, gardening and pottering round in the kitchen, Lillian didn't – but she was most interested in everything I got myself involved in and most encouraging. She took the place of Ivy, Bessie and Nellie in some small way when they were not there and I grew very fond of her.

Wendy and Graham attended the British Army school, Prince Rupert, at Wilhelmshaven, which was built near the submarine pen. The evening before they were due to return after the holidays, Gray and I were having dinner with friends, and Wendy was in her room busily writing. As I left, I suggested she get to sleep soon as it would be an early start the next day. On our return I found the following on my pillow. Of course, I didn't know whether to laugh or cry when reading it, and consoled myself that it was a new craze going around among her age group.

WILL OF WENDY, R. SHOTTER

Now that I am gone from mankind, as it is known on the earth; I shall have made out this heritage document with the views that it shall be obeyed.

Signed — W.R. Shotter.

Mummy and Daddy may have any thing they wish of mine, even overlooked the following list. The same applies to my younger brother - Graham. S. Shotter.

List I

Diana J. Poole. — all dolls and their clothing.
mummy — A small terrier by the name of R. Pal XVIII (if living)
Graham — Skates and all books wanted.
Peter Brunton — Watch received on x'mas of 1955.
H.L. Joy Poole — Writing Case and all writing instruments (to help her write more letters)
Joy. M. Moodie — All bags (2) received on X'mas of 1955
Moodie Brothers - Nothing but my blessings. xxxx ✝ xx
Granny & Grandpa, All Aunties and Uncles — Anything which is not mentioned on this list.
Roberta Oliver — All Broaches, hair slids, Necklaces, bangles.
Sheena McNeil - All braclets and other Jewellry.
Janet Burnet - All scents and perphums.

List 2 — All others following will get a lock of hair which is curly (not straight)

P.T.O.

Olive Walson P.R.S

Glen Wagstaff P.R.S (left now)

mum-dad - Grey. (Junior)

Pal Teldi kim (R.Olivers dog)

Roberta Oliver (Scotland)

Eleneor Scott Lasswade

Irene Timning   "

Mrs Beresford   "

Mrs Miss Guld   "

Elizabeth Taylor "

Jean Stoddart "

athy Neil   "

+ Dickson Scotland

intie Kally gaunt and co.

          And if any hair over give to all persons
     mentioned on list N° 2. 1

              Signed - Wendy Rosemary Shotter

         Daughter of Graham Brean Shotter
         Daughter of Rosemary Stead (maiden name)
         Sister of Graham Stead Shotter.
         Mistress of Royel Pal XVII.

    I wish to thank you all for your love and understanding
       of me, who was a terrible nuisance. amen.

New Year Resolutions. 1956

① Write home and to Peter regularly. (every week)
②. Work hard in class and always do your best.
3. Consider your health. (have walks on the dyke.)
4. Wash in warm than cold water alternitly every morning
5. Keep your diary up to date.
6 Wash socks and hankies every two days. (at night)
⑦ Don't mope! (be cheerful and don't pity yourself.)
8. Appreciate smale gestures and return them.
9. Plan pocket money before using for tuck.
10. Follow D. Watson's examples.
11. Say prayers every night.
　　Signed —— Wendy Rosemary Shotter

Occupation   School-girl
             follower of Chri

PRIVATE.

PERSONELL.

Unhappily Graham broke his other arm during one of their holidays and left for school in plaster. He had only been gone two days when we received a telegram urging us to go up to the RAF hospital near the school as Graham was on the Dangerously Ill (DI) list and in intensive care – suffering complications caused by Asian flu. We found him in an oxygen tent, but thankfully he got well again as quickly as he had become ill. Gray often teased me saying the only time in his life I had ever asked him to drive faster was when on our four hour journey to the hospital.

For a short time Christopher and Peter Blessington were also at school in Wilhelmshaven. Later, of course, they grew up and naturally went their different ways – Christopher to Sandhurst, Peter and Graham following later. Christopher and Peter stayed in the army but for his career Graham emigrated to Australia where he became Director of the Melbourne Zoo – a position which he thoroughly enjoyed. Like Wendy, Christopher is an artist and they shared many hours painting and getting tips from each other, and at times sharing fair – and sometimes to them seemingly unfair criticism of their art work! They were great pals.

While Joy and Diana were in school at Crondall they spent many of their summer holidays with us in Germany. On one of their visits our little dog Pal (all Gray's dogs were called Pal) must have been bitten by another dog, but we didn't know about it until he began to smell. At that time Gray was very busy handing over our quarter to the quartermaster, and the girls decided to bathe Pal gently with a solution of Dettol. After a while they pointed out to me a ghastly wound hidden away in the long hair of his neck. When Gray saw it he took Pal to the vet immediately, accompanied by the two girls. I continued handing over the quarter as we were due to leave for Dusseldorf that afternoon. The vet had to operate on Pal, and, by wrapping him very carefully in a blanket, he was able to accompany us on our journey. The vet mentioned that if Pal managed to eat a little on arrival, that he would pull through. I think the loving care he received from his self-appointed nurses when Gray was attending to the dressing of the wound helped him to a quick recovery. They were wonderful and didn't turn a hair at the sight of the ghastly wound.

In Paderborn we met Prim and Cecil Moretti – they had a daughter, Caroline, and so our circle of close friends grew and grew.

Michael and Nellie, accompanied by Joy and Diana, visited us at Paderborn on their '57 leave from Singapore. The girls had visited us several times, and had fun explaining things to their parents. They were most impressed with the country and loved our friends. Nellie thought that at long last she had become a linguist when she found she could say in German 'what cost-a dis-a'. We spent many happy hours together with friends and there were numerous parties. On one occasion Nellie and Michael forgot to take the door key with them and failing to make any of us hear them ringing the doorbell they had to spend the night in the car. Needless to say they had a rude awakening the next morning when early risers were off to work while they were creeping back home in full evening dress.

The Blessingtons were transferred to Celle and we moved on to Hannover. It was at Celle that Christopher, Wendy and Joy were taken to their first ever nightclub. The junior teenagers (Graham, Peter and Diana were entertained elsewhere). It was a very special party – a most romantic evening and the girls had their first taste of champagne! Joy kept the empty bottle for years and eventually, I gather, Nellie made it into a lamp with an orchid flower, made out of broken shells stuck on to it. This was her 'masterpiece' when she started her little boutique in the Seychelles.

On reflection, we had a wonderful time in Germany with many happy memories – and although at that time we were 'occupying' Germany it was so hard to think we had, not so long before, been at war with such delightful people and had had such fun with them. We were sad to leave Germany.

England

On our return from Germany we rented a holiday flat at Brean Downs and later motored over to Wales to attend the wedding of Nellie and Michael's daughter Joy. Nellie has told you all about that great event.

After the wedding all the Steads left for our holiday flat and continued with the celebrations. Gradually they departed leaving only the Shotters and the Pooles. The latter had rented a house at Havant, Hants, for their leave so as soon as it became available they moved down there.

* * *

Gray soon received his new posting, back to Singapore again, and I left to stay with Nellie at Havant, as Wendy and David were planning a spring wedding and I wished to remain behind and help with the arrangements. I spent the next few months there – the winter of dreadful snow storms and bitterly cold weather.

On many an occasion we were unable to go out and not having a TV were hard put to entertain ourselves and not get bored. Nellie came up with a grand suggestion, as only Nellie could, of holding a fancy-dress party. She gave us an hour to dress up in anything we could find – nothing in the house was considered 'private' – it was a question of first come first served. The results were amazing – Santa Claus, Mrs Mop, a Carrot and even an Egyptian Mummy. A good time was had by all.

When Nellie and family were due to leave, also for Singapore, I moved into the flat Wendy had rented at Corsham, Wiltshire. There I stayed until after Wendy and David's marriage from where I left to join Gray in Singapore. Ted Blessington gave Wendy away, Joy was her matron-of-honour, Ivy May, Bessie's daughter, came down from Edinburgh to be a bridesmaid and Wendy's student friend, Rosemary, was also a bridesmaid. Gray being stationed in Singapore was unable to be present, but he sent very beautiful orchids for the bridal party.

Singapore

I left by ship soon after the wedding – what a delight it was to get away from the cold weather of England. I couldn't get enough of the lovely sunshine but when I reached my destination and Gray drove me to our home, I said to myself 'Singapore is hotter than I thought. How on earth am I going to survive the year or so before leaving again.' Of course, I didn't know then that this car of Grays had a heater which could not be turned off. In the end, and after much effort, the whole of the heating system had to be ripped out.

One Sunday morning whilst having coffee on the verandah, a policeman came up the drive pushing before him, and by the scruff of his neck, a Malay youth. It turned out that the youth had been arrested for burglary, and he had asked for our case to be taken into account. It seems that a few nights previously he had put his hand through the wire screening of the window by my bedside, and stretching his hand over my head lifted Gray's wallet out and taken a bill for ten dollars, and then replaced the wallet. Actually that morning Gray had missed the ten dollars and could not remember spending it. The mystery was now solved.

A friend of ours had a similar experience when on awakening she found an arm stretched over her whilst in bed. She grabbed the arm and hung on for dear life. Being a very strong and large person, she was able to hold on until help came. This poor burglar was pulled hard by his colleague outside the barrier and between them they broke his arm.

There was a very popular Chinese hairdresser in the village and when there was a big dinner at the mess, most of the ladies called for a hairdo. It was a first visit for one or two wives just out from England, and they were all accepted and their hair washed, and then they were politely asked to wait awhile. After a time the overflow was invited to sit and wait out in the yard where chickens were scampering about. When a chappy appeared with a hose, one wife thought he was going to dampen down her hair as it was already drying out in the heat, and then she thought, 'I wonder what Mother would think if she saw me now.' Time passed and soon the husbands called to collect their wives, only to find that they were still waiting to have their hair done. The Chinese are known for being industrious, and rather than send customers away they frantically tried to 'do' everyone. Many irate husbands left and attended the dinner alone.

Return to England

When we left Malaya for the last time Gray was posted to Chepstow, Wales. We lived in a lovely white cottage at Tintern, which was previously a forge. A trout stream ran at the bottom of the garden, and it was set in a beautiful valley near the river Wye.

It was wonderful being able to have the family and our first grandchild spend weekends with us, after having been separated for so many years. Abingdon, near Oxford, was our next station and it was here that I was again 'hostess'. The family, Ivy, Bessie and Nellie, came and went but the highlight was Uncle Miller and his daughter, Joan Gandy (Dad's Goddaughter), coming to stay for a few days. It was a big surprise. They had made their home in Australia after the war and we never thought we would meet again.

When Gray moved towards retirement he became a Retired Officer (RO) and then three years later he fully retired. For the first time we found our very own home – a pretty little bungalow surrounded by fields in the village of Preston in Wiltshire, and very close to Wendy and David's lovely thatched cottage at Catcombe. A happy ending to a satisfying and fulfilling career.

Gray Becomes Ill

We were not there very long before Gray became desperately ill so we sold our home and moved into Wendy's as I found it difficult to look after him by myself. John and Lillian were very supportive and after Gray died they were the mainstay of my life visiting me ever so often to give me a few hours of fellowship. We would have coffee and share a piece of John's favourite chocolate cake and chat about the good old days and things new.

Like John and Lillian, the Blessingtons and the Morettis kept in close touch. Although Prim and Cecil are no longer with us and Gray has left us too, the Davies' and Blessingtons are still in touch – such dear dear friends.

* * *

After the reunion on the boat with Graham we repaired to Nellie and Ivy's home in Kings Sutton to get ourselves ready for the next party – this time held by Wendy and David at their home in the country in Wiltshire. This was a different type of celebration at which all the family, daughters, sons, nieces, nephews and their children were also invited. All descendants of Emily and Walter Stead – two beautiful people who set sail more than sixty years ago for a 'new world' with very little knowledge of what lay ahead.

* * *

There you are Graham, that should bring you up-to-date with the various happenings as well as funny incidents which have occurred in my life. As Mother sometimes said to Dad, when teasing us as children, 'careful now, there will be tears yet!' To coin her phrase, we now know 'There will be reunions yet!'

* * *

Sadly Mary left us on 21 April 1991, and one of the loveliest cards was received from one of Nellie's granddaughters which read: 'Please remember ... there are many people thinking of you ... and caring about you ... I just happen to be one of them.' In the card Joanna wrote 'Dear Granny, Aunty Ivy and Aunty Bessie. I am very sad to hear about Aunty Mary – she was such a sweet and *trendy* Aunty! I'll miss her and her *stories* very much.'

So we just end by lovingly saying 'au revoir'.

Glossary

ayah (Indian) child's nurse or lady's maid.

amah (Chinese) child's nurse or lady's maid.

aquacade display of synchronized swimming.

bearer Indian equivalent to an officer's servant.

bandicoot rat as large as a cat.

BMH British military hospital.

banyan tree Indian fig-tree whose branches take root in the ground.

bazaar Oriental market.

cheong sam a long or short gown with a split up both sides – having short or long sleeves and a 'Mandarin' collar, worn by either man or woman.

ghat (Indian) steps leading to river; two mountain chains along east and west sides of southern Hindustan.

kutcha makeshift, rough.

maskee (Chinese) never mind; it does not matter.

memsahib European married lady.

puggaree Indian's light turban; thin scarf of muslin worn around a hat and sometimes falling down behind to keep off sun.

purdah a curtain screening women from sight of strangers; Indian system of secluding women of rank.

sadhu Indian holy man.

sari (Indian) length of cotton or silk wrapped around body, worn as main garment by Indian women.

tiffen break light meal; lunch.

tonga (Indian) a small light two-wheeled carriage or cart.